"WHATEVER IT IS,
I'M AGAINST IT"

"WHATEVER IT IS, I'M AGAINST IT"

Resistance to Change in Higher Education

BRIAN ROSENBERG

Harvard Education Press

Cambridge, MA

Third Printing, 2023

Paperback ISBN 978-1-68253-828-9

Library of Congress Cataloging-in-Publication Data is on file.

Published by Harvard Education Press,
an imprint of the Harvard Education Publishing Group

Harvard Education Press
8 Story Street
Cambridge, MA 02138

Cover Design: Endpaper Studio
Cover Image: MicroStockHub via iStockphoto.com

The typefaces in this book are Minion Pro and Myriad Pro.

For Carol

I don't know what they have to say
It makes no difference anyway
Whatever it is, I'm against it!
No matter what it is
Or who commenced it
I'm against it!

Your proposition may be good
But let's have one thing understood
Whatever it is, I'm against it!
And even when you've changed it
Or condensed it
I'm against it!

I'm opposed to it
On general principles
I'm opposed to it!
(He's opposed to it)
(In fact, he says he's opposed to it!)

For months before my son was born
I used to yell from night to morn
"Whatever it is, I'm against it!"
And I've kept yelling
Since I first commenced it
"I'm against it!"

—Harry Ruby and Bert Kalmar, sung by Groucho Marx
as Professor Quincy Adams Wagstaff, *Horsefeathers*

This is true.

—Tim O'Brien, "How to Tell a True War Story"

Contents

Preface

When you look in the mirror
What do you see?
Is it who you think you are
Or who you want to be?

—Jimmy Cliff

NHLANHLA THWALA IS THE PROVOST of the African Leadership University, an institution about which I write at length in the closing chapter of this book. I would describe him as a master of metaphors, some invented and some borrowed, and one of his favorites has stuck in my mind as I first conceived of and then composed the narrative that follows: you can't see the label from the inside of the bottle.

I have for nearly five decades been living inside the bottle of what might be described as classic and privileged forms of American higher education: through undergraduate and graduate school at research universities; through work as a faculty member, dean, and president at three residential liberal arts colleges; and finally—sort of—as a "president in residence" and part-time visiting professor at the Harvard Graduate School of Education. There is an ironic twist to my postpresidential landing spot. The first job for which I was an unsuccessful finalist, though far from the last, was assistant professor of English, specialization in Victorian literature, at Harvard. That rejection set me on a different, non-Ivied path that was, for me, much more fulfilling, though there is something peculiar about returning so much older and I hope a little wiser to the place where I first interviewed as a terrified graduate student.

While I have not completely vacated the "bottle" of American higher education, I am certainly less enclosed within it than I have been since

I traded my home on Long Island for U Hall 3 on the Cornell University campus in Ithaca, New York, in 1973. My position as at least quasi-external observer has allowed me to see and process things about which I didn't think too much—about which I didn't *allow myself* to think too much—when I was in the classroom or an administrative office. During my fifteen years as a faculty member, I would push back, hard, against anyone who questioned the practices and assumptions of the faculty. During my time as a chief academic officer, I tried my best to advocate both for the faculty and for the administration and worried more about that balancing act than about higher education as a whole. And during my time as president of Macalester College, my job was to make the case before both internal and external audiences for the value and effectiveness of that particular institution and the liberal arts more broadly. During all those years, there were aspects of higher education about which I was troubled, and as a president especially I spoke and wrote about some of these, but for the most part those concerns were secondary to my focus on simply doing my job.

Since I left Macalester in June 2020—three months after the unwelcome arrival in the United States of COVID-19—several factors have combined to direct my attention to the imperfections in the system within which I have spent my professional life. To begin with, I have simply had an opportunity for the first time in many years to reflect on my own work and career. I have also had a chance to teach about higher education, which has meant taking an honest and critical look at the subject of my classes; anything less would have been a disservice to my students. And finally, and maybe most important, I have worked for the past two years on helping to build a university in Africa, where many of the practices and assumptions of American higher education are at least contested and at times wholly unsuitable. There is nothing quite like a dramatic change in environment to make you question the things you took for granted.

I still believe in the transformative power of higher education and in the value of college. I still believe that there are hundreds of thousands of people, faculty and staff, who work every day to enrich the lives of students. But there is so much about the current state of higher education that could be strengthened and so much that is unfair and unsustainable. The areas that need improvement are clear, and the forms that improvement might take are not entirely a mystery. Yet this industry that ostensibly fosters growth and transformation in its students just cannot seem to change or transform itself in ways beyond the incremental. Allude in any room filled with college employees to the resistance to change and you'll get lots of head nods and smiles of recognition. Still, that resistance persists, as if it is a condition that is forever unalterable.

So I set out in this book to try to understand and explain why this is the case. To be honest, the diagnosis of the illness was far easier than finding a prescription for the cure. But any solution has to begin with an acknowledgment of the problem, and I hope that this book will at the very least serve that purpose. One of the ironies of academic culture is that, at institutions built around a commitment to critical inquiry and the open exchange of ideas, there are some orthodoxies that one simply does not question. My goal here is to question them. A president or dean who does not pay obeisance to the model of the scholar-teacher, the necessity of majors, or the wonders of shared governance will not be a president or dean for very long. Within almost any college or university, there are important things that, like Lord Voldemort, simply Must Not Be Named. For me the days of college administration are done, along with the need to self-censor—within reason. If my arguments seem at times to be deliberately or even overly provocative, it is because I believe that at this point a gentle nudge will have about as much impact on the thinking of many in higher education as—to use another metaphor—a fly on the hide of an elephant.

I have tried throughout the narrative that follows to weave together evidence-based arguments and recollections of my own journey as a student, teacher, and, especially, college president. To describe this as anything like a memoir would be to go too far, but I can say that nearly every aspect of academic life about which I write I have also experienced firsthand. There is a difference between being a theorist or external observer and being a practitioner. Far too many of higher education's fiercest critics have never or rarely worked within higher education, which does not render their views invalid but often renders both their criticisms and their proposed remedies imperfectly informed or unrealistic. The consulting firm Bain and Company spent who knows how much money on a recent report detailing the precarious financial state of colleges and universities in the United States. It ends with "five steps to retool for the future," noting with the assurance of a weight-loss book that "universities can follow these principles to improve their financial outlook." Among the recommended steps are the following: innovate, transform the economics, simplify the mission, and optimize operations. Sure. I could have saved them that money and pointed out that while the steps are obvious, the impediments to taking them are enormous and deeply baked into the system. The challenge is not in figuring out what higher education should do but in figuring out how in the world it can do it: the irresistible force of economics and demographics is running straight into the immovable object of college governance and culture.[1]

The other reason I draw on personal experience is that this book is as much confession as criticism. There is hardly an error in judgment, an act of self-interest, or a stubborn refusal to change discussed here of which I have not, at some point, been guilty myself. I was trained in graduate school to put discipline and department above all; I believed that tenure was the only just reward for my work; I criticized the college administration with only the haziest idea of what I was talking about; I led inclusive but ineffectual strategic planning processes; I backed away from challenging the faculty too directly even when I believed that they were wrong. I was a fairly typical product of the system of incentives that we in higher education have created. It is because I have lived it that I feel some level of comfort in writing about it. I am neither fundamentally different from nor better than the faculty members and administrators about whom I write: I *am* them, only gifted with the time and late-career vantage point to be able to see more clearly what for decades I have been acculturated to ignore.

I hope my observations prove to be of some use. I am certain that they will spark much disagreement. That's okay. Unchallenged consensus can too easily lead to complacency. If the least I accomplish is to provoke a thoughtful defense of the status quo, that will be something. If I inspire even a few people to try to improve the status quo, that will be even better.

Chapter 1

The Case for Change

Why can't I change after all these years?
Why can't I change my ways?
I find it so strange after all these years,
I'm still more or less the same.

—Passenger

ABOUT FOUR YEARS into my seventeen-year term as president of Macalester College, I met in my office with the director of our Center for Scholarship and Teaching. The woman who directed the center was almost certainly the most widely respected faculty member on campus, good at pretty much everything and relentlessly devoted to the improvement of the institution. She had that hard-earned and surprisingly rare quality within any college community: near-universal credibility with her colleagues.

The topic of our conversation was the relationship between the two focal points of her work, scholarship and teaching. She'd been digging into the subject with some energy and, after careful examination of both internal evidence like teaching evaluations and external studies with larger data sets, had concluded that in fact there was no positive correlation between traditional measures of research productivity and effectiveness in the classroom. This conclusion has been confirmed many times since, very recently by David Figlio and Morton Shapiro, who note that "regardless of which measure [is] used, top teachers are no more or less likely to be especially productive scholars than their less accomplished teaching peers."[1]

This is of course a big deal, given the firmly held belief, particularly at research-intensive liberal arts colleges like Macalester, that excellence in scholarship and excellence in teaching are mutually reinforcing. That belief informs everything from hiring practices to tenure decisions to

1

salary increases. It lies at the heart of the way the college describes and thinks about itself. The *Macalester College Faculty Handbook* includes, for instance, the following statement: "It is generally believed that the best teaching is informed with current knowledge of the discipline and conducted with the enthusiasm of discovery and of dialogue with others whose knowledge is firsthand. The dissemination of knowledge follows its creation."[2] This reads very much like handbook language—only partly comprehensible—though the phrase "it is generally believed" hints at the absence of actual evidence. Generally believed by whom, and on the basis of what?

We decided that this was a subject of enough interest and importance to be worthy of a broader discussion within the faculty. Neither of us expected rapid or dramatic change, but the first step toward improvement of any kind seemed to be consideration of the evidence. We scheduled a voluntary town hall meeting at which the director would present some of her findings and lead a discussion, and ahead of that meeting I sent a letter to the faculty that included the following passage, over whose wording I labored for some time:

> [One important] point . . . seems overdue for consideration: that is, the particular role that we expect scholarship to play in the lives, and eventually the evaluation, of faculty. Let me venture this guess: many faculty members are reluctant to raise this topic out of fear of being considered insufficiently rigorous or productive as scholars. So I will raise it, and by asking the question in this form: have the expectations for scholarly productivity at Macalester grown to the point where they are distorting the professional development of our untenured and some of our tenured faculty and are working against other interests—such as teaching, advising, and course development—that we recognize as critically important? Have we moved closer to a university model and further from a liberal arts college model of the teaching/scholarship/service balance than is healthy? I am prepared to listen carefully to the argument that the answer to these questions is "no," and I embrace without reservation the notion that teaching at the highest level must be informed by serious and ongoing scholarly work in one's field. But the question of whether we are currently over-emphasizing

traditional forms of scholarship, behind which lies an interesting and powerful institutional history, should not be one that we shy away from discussing, even if it touches upon—indeed, perhaps because it does touch upon—our most firmly held beliefs about academic excellence.

No surprise: things did not go well.

The response at the town hall meeting was mostly hostile, though not so hostile as the subsequent comments over email or in hallways. I was accused by one faculty member of trying to "turn Macalester into a kindergarten." Even those less hostile to the findings simply ignored or dismissed them. Not only was there resistance to change: there was resistance to *talking about* change. Simply raising this subject was seen by many faculty members as an assault on the values of the college.

After a couple of weeks of intense pushback, the director and I independently reached the same conclusion: it wasn't worth it. Given all the day-to-day pressures of running the college and serving our students, we simply did not have the energy to engage in a debate that was likely to inflame the faculty and ultimately lead nowhere. During the remainder of my presidency, I never revisited the subject in any serious way—though I was periodically reminded by a faculty member or two of my audacity in visiting it at all.

I dwell on this story not merely because the irony of defending the role of research by ignoring the research on the topic is exquisite, but because it is emblematic of a widespread problem within higher education in the United States. The resistance to anything like serious change is profound. By "change" I don't mean the addition of yet another program or the alteration of a graduation requirement, but something that is truly transformational and affects the way we do our work on a deep level. This remains a realm in which the decision by the Cornell University Department of English to change its name to the Department of Literatures in English merits a news story.[3] Among the top ten "most innovative" universities on the 2022 list in *U.S. News and World Report* are such radical actors as MIT, Stanford, Purdue, and the University of Michigan, which says a good deal about how narrowly innovation is imagined in this space. (Macalester is number sixteen among the most innovative liberal arts colleges. I have no idea why, but neither do I understand why Grinnell,

Pomona, or Connecticut College is on such a list.) Virtually any administrator or faculty member who begins with an idea for transformational change will eventually reach the same conclusion about the battle: it's not worth it.

Writing about nonprofits, Jim Collins notes that change "feels like turning a giant, heavy flywheel. Pushing with great effort—days, weeks, and months of work, with almost imperceptible progress—you finally get the flywheel to inch forward." That feels right. But with enough determination and persistence, he suggests, will come "breakthrough! . . . The flywheel flies forward with almost unstoppable momentum." That feels not so right in the world of higher education, where there are precious few moments of "breakthrough!" but lots of inching forward.[4]

For years I have pondered the question of why an industry so widely populated by people who consider themselves politically liberal is so deeply conservative when it comes to its own work; why scholars whose disciplines are constantly evolving are so resistant to institutional evolution; why colleges and universities that almost always speak in their mission statements about the transformative power of education find it so difficult to transform themselves; why virtually no fundamental practice within higher education—calendar, tenure processes, pedagogy, grading—has changed in meaningful ways for decades, if not centuries.

These questions are regularly asked, but I am not persuaded that the most common answers are accurate, or at least sufficient. Faculty tend to blame bureaucratic administrators; administrators tend to blame stubbornly entrenched faculty; many outside higher education tend to blame pretty much everyone having to do with the enterprise. Yet I do not believe that higher education attracts more than the usual share of bad actors or is populated by people who don't want to be good at their jobs.

The answer, as is so often the case, lies in the structures, practices, and cultures that have developed within higher education. That is, there are reasons for the inability to change that go well beyond the temperament or competence of particular individuals. "What's weird," observes one nonprofit leader, "is that higher ed is different from any other industry, in that there's a bias toward never changing anything."[5] Frustrating, to be sure, but "weird" only if one fails to understand the way this particular industry functions. If maintenance of the status quo is the goal, higher education has managed to create the ideal system.

And thus the questions at the heart of this book: What is it about the structures, practices, and culture within higher education that has for so long prevented transformational change in an industry that, by most measures, is under enormous pressure and failing to deliver fully on its promise? Why do even institutions on life support fail to go in radically new directions? And is there anything that can be done about this?

Change is hard. With rare exception, and for understandable reasons, most people are not fond of it: even for the most daring of us, it can lead to feelings of helplessness and anxiety and, of course, to lots of extra work.[6] Change to long-established, carefully protected structures and assumptions is harder still and carries with it the serious risk of disruption and failure. This is why transformational change rarely happens from within complex organizations, why disruption tends more often to come from external than from internal actors, and why it is essential to make the case that such change is not merely interesting or recommended or rich with potential, but necessary.[7]

I understand that terms like *transformational change* and *disruptive innovation* are used loosely and ad nauseum these days and are often associated with those whose motives and methods are, at best, questionable. Kevin Gannon complains that "the avatars of innovation always seem to be people like Bill Gates, Steve Jobs, Elon Musk, Jeff Bezos—you know: the lone, courageous mavericks who boldly fight the entrenched and stodgy forces of inertia. Except of course that the faces of innovation tend to be mostly white, almost always male, and often strengthen, rather than undermine, the most inequitable features of the status quo." This observation is only true if one doesn't know where to look. As I hope to show, the most interesting innovators bear little resemblance to Gannon's examples, and his later call for innovation to come "from inside the house" faces a formidable set of obstacles.[8]

Whatever one calls it, real change—major change—to higher education in the United States is *necessary*.

This argument is neither new nor, at this point, especially controversial, though it is only fair to acknowledge that there remain some who believe that warnings about the need for change are "a farce" and whose response to evidence of colleges at risk is, literally, "Ugh."[9] The argument is also not equally applicable across the board to a higher education sector that comprises thousands of institutions widely varied in size, wealth, prestige, and funding model. Nineteen percent of institutions hold 84 percent of the endowment wealth in the country; remarkably, ten universities hold nearly 40 percent of the total endowment wealth.[10] Admission rates at the country's most selective schools would at this point be laughable, were it not for the disappointment of the thousands of students who are turned away. Change at these colleges and universities is not essential to their survival (which is not the same as saying it would not be beneficial to students). Change beyond the cosmetic within the next decade or two is, frankly, unlikely.

But of the nearly four thousand two- and four-year postsecondary institutions listed by the National Center for Education Statistics, perhaps one hundred might be described as largely immune to the current and future pressures of the marketplace—and that might be a generous estimate.[11] The rest—private colleges and universities, regional public institutions, community colleges—are faced with challenges to both their financial and their educational models that might be different in kind but are dauntingly similar in seriousness.

The economic challenge facing nearly all of higher education in the United States can be explained in terms that are complicated or simple. Since I am by training an English professor, and since others have already done an excellent job of providing the complicated explanation, I will opt for simple.[12]

1. The cost of providing the services at a traditional college or university is very high and has risen for decades more rapidly than inflation or the cost-of-living index.
2. At all but a handful of institutions with enormous endowments, revenue from students funds the majority of that cost.
3. There are not enough students who are both willing and able to pay the full cost of higher education.
4. There are not enough students, period.

Cut through all the graphs and economic data and the problem is straightforward enough for even an English professor to understand: when the service you provide costs more than people are willing and able to pay for it, when you are unable to lower the cost of that service, and when the number of your potential customers is shrinking, you have what one might describe as an unsustainable financial model. To be fair, the cost of higher education has been called "unsustainable" for so long that one is reminded of Inigo Montoya's observation in *The Princess Bride*: "You keep using that word. I do not think it means what you think it means." Perhaps. But there are reasons to believe that this time it *does* mean what we think it means.

There is no single explanation for the rapidly rising cost of traditional higher education. Analysts have pointed with some accuracy to everything from the volatility of state funding, which has the greatest effect on public institutions, to a more expensive regulatory environment, to increased consumer expectations, to an amenities arms race.[13] But by far the most convincing explanation is a phenomenon with the appropriately off-putting name of "cost disease," sometimes called "Baumol's cost disease," sometimes called the "Baumol effect"—which sounds a little less depressing. Initially defined by William Baumol and William Bowen in the 1960s in studies of the performing arts, cost disease describes a condition that is particularly prevalent in service professions: rising wages in parts of the economy where there is accompanying productivity growth— typically but not exclusively manufacturing—will drive up wages in parts of the economy where there is little or no productivity growth.[14] Rising cost absent rising productivity is a sustainable situation only when that cost can be passed along to the consumer in the form of rising price.[15]

And so we have our current dilemma: productivity growth in some parts of the economy has driven up the cost of hiring educated workers more rapidly than inflation; a very high percentage of workers—faculty and staff—in higher education have postgraduate degrees and have thus become more expensive to employ; labor costs are easily the largest percentage of any college or university budget; "productivity"—by virtually any measure—has not increased along with costs in higher education; college, therefore, costs more than it used to. During my time at Macalester, employee compensation consistently accounted for about two-thirds of our operating expenses, and our ability to increase compensation tracked consistently with our ability to generate increased revenue from students.

One common explanation for rising college costs is unsupported by the evidence. In a now famous (or infamous) 1987 op-ed in the *New York Times*, provocatively entitled "Our Greedy Colleges," then–secretary of education William Bennett argued that "increases in [federal] financial aid in recent years have enabled colleges and universities blithely to raise their tuitions."[16] "Blithely" is, I admit, a nice flourish. What has become known as the "Bennett Hypothesis" has ever since been among the clearest litmus tests for the political affiliation of higher education pundits and (quasi-)researchers. Put simply, if it comes from the American Enterprise Institute or the American Council of Trustees and Alumni, the research will confirm the Bennett Hypothesis; if it comes from almost anywhere else, it will not. The most comprehensive review of the evidence and research on whether things like increases to the Pell Grant or increases in federal loan limits lead to increases in tuition was done for the nonpartisan American Council on Education by Donald Heller, then dean of the College of Education at Michigan State. His conclusion is clear: "While the Bennett Hypothesis may be intriguing, there is little compelling evidence that it holds true with respect to the price-setting behavior of colleges and universities in the United States. . . . While any change in federal financial aid may be a very small piece of the puzzle that leads to year-to-year tuition increases, there is scant evidence that it is a major contributing factor."[17]

Bennett's argument about "greedy" colleges is typical of a tendency by critics of higher education on both the right and the left to turn what is fundamentally an economic problem into an ethical problem. We have created a system in the United States in which we expect colleges and universities, especially those that are private but increasingly those that are public as well, to come up with their own sources of funding: in essence, to act like businesses, even if they are nonprofit businesses. Then we blame them for acting like businesses and call them greedy or duplicitous. Leaving aside the tiny, atypical group of extremely wealthy institutions, colleges and universities do not develop market-based strategies and hire expensive consultants because they are "greedy" or seduced by a neoliberal ideology: they do these things because they are trying to stay alive in an environment and within a system that threatens their continued existence. Even as astute an observer as Kevin Carey, who gets many things right about higher education, is quick to move from a description of current practices to judgmental words like *scam* and *sham*—words that generate clicks but that attribute nefarious motives to practices that are typical of any business that relies on revenue from consumers to survive.[18] We speak of higher education as a public good, fund it as if it is a private good, and then blame it for developing strategies for maximizing revenue in an increasingly competitive environment.

Two important external factors continue to worsen the financial picture for colleges. Beginning around 1980—when government became the "problem"—more and more wealth in the United States has become concentrated among fewer and fewer people. According to the Pew Research Center, "In 1980, the 90/10 ratio in the U.S. stood at 9.1, meaning that households at the top had incomes about nine times the incomes of households at the bottom. The ratio has increased in every decade since 1980, reaching 12.6 in 2018, an increase of 39%." The rich, Pew notes, "are getting richer faster," while the middle class is shrinking.[19] For a very small group of Americans, college has actually become *easier* to afford, due to rapid increases in wealth and aggressive discounting by institutions seeking to enroll their children. For everyone else it has become harder to afford.

Then there is the "demographic cliff," which combined with cost disease seems to situate higher education in some sort of zombie/disaster film starring the Rock. (Jon Boeckenstedt takes us further into disaster film territory by calling it a "demographic perfect storm.")[20] An exhaustive analysis of demographic trends by Nathan Grawe, an economist at Carleton College, suggests that the traditional college-going population will drop by about 15 percent between 2025 and 2029 and will not recover anytime soon.[21] The percentage of white public high school graduates, who for many reasons make up a disproportionate percentage of college students, is already below 50 percent and, according to Boeckenstedt, "will drop to about 42 percent of all graduates in 2036, the farthest year out we can predict."[22] The decline is steepest in the Northeast and Midwest, where many of the most endangered institutions happen to be located, and is likely to have the greatest impact on those that are least selective. Throw in the "baby bust" that seems to have been caused by the first year of the pandemic, along with the aging population in the United States, and it seems reasonable to forecast an extended future of diminished demand.[23]

Even before we go over the cliff, we have seen a steady decline in the number of students enrolled in postsecondary education that has been accelerated but not initiated by the pandemic. Figures released by the National Center for Education Statistics in the spring of 2022 are sobering. From the fall of 2011, when the decline began, to the fall of 2020, undergraduate enrollment dropped by 12.3 percent. Community college enrollment decreased by 2.6 million students between 2009 and 2020. From 2009 to 2019 the decline was 26 percent, and then in the ensuing, pandemic-shadowed year enrollment dropped another 12 percent. Men are disappearing with particular rapidity: a drop of 2.2 million students from 2010 to 2020. The long period of decline suggests that it is independent of any particular, short-term set of economic conditions but has deeper causes rooted in the cost and perceived value of college. Perhaps the most worrisome trend is that fewer high school graduates are choosing to go directly to college, a shift that is being described as "unprecedented." In some states the numbers are genuinely shocking: in Arizona in 2020, only 46.3 percent of high school graduates enrolled in college, a drop of more than 6 percentage points from the prior year; in Tennessee the number was 52.8 percent in 2021, a decline of 9 percentage points from 2019; in Indiana the college-going rate declined 6 percentage points from 2019 to 2020. The elite institutions that make all the news are overflowing with applicants, but the effect of these trends on most other colleges and universities has been "devasting"—and, again, we have not yet gone over the demographic cliff. Precisely how much of this can be attributed chiefly to the pandemic and to a strong labor market is difficult to gauge, but Doug Shapiro, director of the National Student Clearinghouse Research Center, has remarked, "I thought we would start to see some of the declines begin to shrink.... I am surprised that it seems to be getting worse." Nothing on the horizon suggests that these trends will be reversed anytime soon.[24]

Forecasts of demographic gloom are nothing new to higher education, and consistently those forecasts have been wrong. But as Karin Fisher notes, "this time looks different," and "higher ed may have reached the limits of Houdini-ing its way out of decline." In the past, Fisher explains, there was always a strategy or an economic or societal change that helped colleges dodge the predicted falloff: the creation of the Pell Grant, an increase in the enrollment rate of women, more international students, the shift to a knowledge economy, and the rising economic benefits of the bachelor's degree. None of those developments is likely to be repeated, and in fact some appear to be reversing, yet for the most part, according to historian John Thelin, "colleges are mining strategies of earlier generations, and they're running out." Most observers agree that higher education will shrink over the coming decades and that the extent of that shrinkage might be limited by attracting more students from two important groups:

currently underserved high school students of color and adult, or "nontraditional," learners. To attract more of those students, however, colleges and universities that rely on the current high-cost, campus-based model would have to do the one thing at which they are least adept: change rapidly and dramatically. It is the height of fantasy to expect more underrepresented students to flock to a service that costs more than a luxury car to provide or to expect working adults to live in a residence hall and attend in-person classes every Monday morning.[25]

I could dwell on other causes of financial stress, including the growth of low-cost (and often low-quality) online education, the entry into the marketplace of well-funded for-profit players (how long before we are tormented by the specter of Musk University?), the yet to be fully determined impact of a global pandemic, and the declining public confidence in higher education, but I have a personal limit on how much bad news I will include in a single chapter. I will leave the final word to higher education CFOs: in one 2022 survey, 28 percent (35 percent in private institutions, 19 percent in public) did not believe that their institutions would be financially stable for the next five years; in another survey from the same year, 35 percent did not anticipate financial stability over the next decade.[26] CFOs tend to be fairly gloomy, but if even half of them are right, that represents a very large group of financially unstable colleges and universities.

Colleges have typically responded to financial pressures in two ways: by cutting things and by discounting the price.

The narrative around cuts generally follows the same template: "The economic and demographic headwinds are strong; we are moving proactively to make our college/university more financially sustainable; even though we will be offering fewer things with fewer people, this is all about improving the student experience; we are *not*—really and truly—in a state of financial exigency." I understand the need to put forth such narratives, but sometimes they result in contortions in reasoning that are truly remarkable. Saint Mary's University of Minnesota—a typical example of an at-risk institution—announced in 2022 the elimination of eleven majors and thirteen full-time faculty with the following statement: "How [we asked ourselves] can we best prepare our students for work, for a life of ethical service, to pursue the greater good and the truth in all things while answering their questions about meaning and purpose?"[27] Among the programs to be closed are English, history, music, and (yes) theology. The emphasis going forward will be on business, technology, and the natural sciences. This is, to say the least, a novel way of preparing students for lives of meaning and service, though it sounds more palatable than the truth: we hope to survive by shifting resources away from the arts and humanities, which students are abandoning in droves, and into business, tech, and the sciences, where we might find a place in a highly competitive market. In 2014, Hiram College in Ohio, deeply in debt, "dropped majors including art history, music, philosophy and religion and added sports management and international studies in an approach it calls 'the new liberal arts.'"[28] Or, I should say, The New Liberal Arts". Reader, they trademarked it.

The campus and alumni response to these cuts follows a pattern as formulaic as the announcements: shock; grief; outrage; protests. Sometimes a vote of no-confidence, sometimes a threat to withhold all giving. Not infrequently, when met with this wholly predictable reaction, the cuts are reduced or entirely reversed, leaving one to wonder what sort of response these administrators and board members expected. The University of Wisconsin at Stevens Point made national news in 2018 when it announced a plan to eliminate thirteen majors. Drama ensued. After reducing the number of proposed eliminations to six, Stevens Point ended by eliminating . . . none—which neither addressed the long-term budgetary challenges nor entirely placated the community, which remained angry that the plan had been proposed in the first place.[29]

The announced cuts at Saint Mary's and Stevens Point would be a very big deal, but even small cuts can generate an outsized response. When I arrived at Macalester in the fall of 2003, the college was one of a handful in the Midwest to have a varsity Nordic ski team, though the team had very few members (nine, I believe) and was very expensive to maintain. Based on the recommendation of an athletic director concerned about his budget, I announced that Nordic skiing would be converted to a "club sport," a more appropriate status given its size and outsize cost. This was, in other words, not even a cut, but something more like a downgrade.

This announcement managed to inflame not just the Macalester campus but, as far as I could tell, the entire Nordic skiing community in the United States. Three hundred emails later, I had been accused of everything from undermining Nordic skiing in America to threatening Macalester's standing as a liberal arts college. (Imagine if Twitter, Facebook, and Change.org had existed in 2003. My presidency would have been very brief.) I did stand firm, but I also received an early lesson on the difficulty of taking anything away from a college community.

The practice of discounting the price is far more widespread than that of cutting programs. The number to which college CFOs pay the most attention, after net tuition revenue, is probably what is known as the discount rate—that is, the percentage of tuition that is not collected as a result of awarding financial aid. That number has been steadily rising for years, most dramatically at private colleges and universities and especially sharply during the past decade. According to a study by the National Association of College and University Business Officers, the discount rate for incoming students at private, nonprofit institutions rose from 42 percent in 2010–11 to 52.6 percent in 2019–20.[30] By 2021–22, in the midst of the pandemic, that number had risen to 54.5 percent, and nine in ten incoming undergraduates were receiving some sort of discount—that is, were not paying the posted tuition price, which in this context has become almost meaningless. For those more focused on net tuition revenue, that number for incoming students declined by 3.2 percent, inflation adjusted, between 2020–21 and 2021–22.[31] This is entirely consistent with my experience at Macalester: when I arrived, we were concerned about discount rates in the low forties; by the time I left, we were relieved if the discount rate for incoming students was reasonably close to 50 percent.

Private higher education in the United States, in other words, has become more or less the equivalent of Nordstrom Rack, selling name-brand goods at a discounted price, though, unlike at Nordstrom Rack, the discount keeps getting larger and larger. Or, as Gordon Winston wrote a quarter century ago, "If [a] Ford dealer were acting like the typical college or university, he'd be selling the Taurus that costs him $20,000 to put on the showroom floor for a price of $6,000. Not on a year-end clearance, but all the time. Year after year."[32] This is, in effect, the inverse of what happened to home and automobile prices during the first years of the pandemic: in those cases, demand drove the actual price above the listed price; in this case, the absence of demand is driving the actual price well below the listed price. And virtually no private institution is immune to this phenomenon, though some are particularly adept at attracting affluent students, and a tiny group of ultra-wealthy institutions discount not because of any lack of demand but because they can easily afford to do so and because it is necessary to diversify their student bodies.

If the average discount rate is well north of 50 percent, and if the high sticker price is scaring away a large number of prospective students, it seems reasonable to ask why less selective private colleges do not simply lower that sticker price and reduce or eliminate the discounting. A handful have in fact done so: Rider, Fairleigh Dickinson, and Drew Universities in New Jersey and Concordia University and Concordia College in Minnesota have all cut tuition by 20 to 35 percent; Southern New Hampshire University cut tuition by 50 percent, though its high-volume, blended instructional model is unusual.[33] Typically schools that adopt this strategy are struggling in highly competitive markets and have excess capacity.

There are two reasons why more colleges, particularly those with stronger admissions profiles, do not adopt this strategy. The first is what is widely known as the "Chivas Regal effect," which "works on the premise that some consumers use price as a cue to quality. All things being equal, a consumer may assume that a high price equals high quality even if there is no objective reason to believe this."[34] A whiskey that costs $100 must be better than one that costs $50; a car that costs $50,000 must be better than one that costs $25,000; a college whose listed price is $70,000 must be better than one whose price is $35,000. If the brand is strong enough, differences in price might not matter: Princeton's tuition is lower than Franklin & Marshall's, but no one is likely to make judgments about quality on that basis. For most private institutions, however, price and perceived quality are closely correlated.

The University of the South, also known as Sewanee, tested this hypothesis in 2011 by cutting tuition by about 10 percent. Two years later, tuition was increased by 10 percent when the cut did little to alter Sewanee's strength in the marketplace.[35] By the fall of 2022, Sewanee's tuition had climbed to about $52,000, almost exactly the same as the tuition at its competitor Rhodes College, which had never attempted the cut. Two recent studies of private, nonprofit colleges that pursued the strategy of deep tuition cuts concluded that the results were "negative or mixed."[36] And consider this: another study, published in 2016, found that "schools set tuition *higher* [my emphasis] after a sharp decline in rank, particularly those that appeal widely to college applicants and whose rivals are relatively more expensive."[37] This is not unlike a winery that raises the price of its products to get them placed on a higher shelf in the shop, even when the juice in the bottle has not changed.

The second reason has to do with the question of who would benefit most, and who would suffer most, from a tuition reset and the elimination of discounting. The simple answer in this case, as in so many others, is that the wealthiest families would be the winners and the least wealthy families the losers. Let's imagine that College X has a sticker price of $50,000 and a discount rate of 50 percent, meaning that students on average pay the college $25,000. The college, like most, offers a mix of need-based aid and what is euphemistically called "merit aid," meaning that the cost of attendance will vary widely within the student body. Typically, the most affluent students would pay the most—even with a discount—and the least affluent students would pay the least, since they would be receiving some sort of need-based aid. Changing the price to $25,000 for all might seem to yield the same net revenue, but it would also mean that the affluent family paying $40,000 would get a larger discount and the high-need family paying $10,000 would have to produce another $15,000 in tuition—or, more likely, be unable to attend at all. This is not unlike the regressive impact of the call to make public college "free for all": "A national free-tuition plan would provide disproportionate benefits to the relatively affluent while leaving many low- and moderate-income students struggling to complete the college degrees that many jobs now demand. Ironically, free-tuition programs would exacerbate inequality even as they promise to level the playing field."[38] In a society marked by profound inequities in opportunity, sometimes the solution does not lie in creating uniformity in price.

Perhaps the most visible sign of these many financial challenges is the steady crumbling of the physical plant on most of the nation's campuses. Colleges and universities have been building at a rapid pace for more than seventy years, and now many are saddled with more infrastructure than they need or can maintain. The deferred maintenance backlog on just a single large campus—the University of Minnesota Twin Cities—is estimated to be $4.2 billion, or roughly half the cost of rebuilding LaGuardia Airport. For the California State University system it is $5.8 billion.[39] At many smaller, struggling colleges, the backlog as a percentage of the annual budget is much worse. Unlike other businesses faced with a declining need for physical space, most colleges can neither sell off their buildings, which might sit in the center of a campus, nor pick up and move to a new location. The costs associated with maintaining a campus for decades or even centuries are enormous: at Macalester, the price tag for a new heating system alone was about $6 million, an amount so large and so frustrating that I suggested (without success) that one of the new steam boilers be named after me. Millions more were spent annually on windows and roofs, air-conditioning units and athletic fields, and every year new items were added to the to-do list. Gordian, a facilities consulting firm, notes in a recent report that "the scale of deferred capital renewal at schools has reached a level that cannot be tolerated"—but which no one has a feasible plan to reduce.[40]

If the financial challenges facing higher education were magically to disappear—if costs declined, the middle class were reborn, and demographers discovered that the number of high school graduates was actually going to increase—there would still be good reasons to consider transformational change. Indeed, the most compelling reasons that the sector needs to change are not economic but pedagogical. Higher education continues to rely without serious reflection on too many practices that we know to be relatively ineffective. Health care in the United States, like higher education, rests on a shaky economic model that might be (that word again) unsustainable, but while the *cost of care* is a major problem, the *standard of care* has changed and improved dramatically over time. What might be described as the standard of care in higher education, by contrast, has remained surprisingly static: it continues to rely heavily on practices that were widespread when phrenology and bloodletting were in vogue. As Jonathan Zimmerman writes in his excellent history, "College teaching has probably seen *less* change than almost any other American institutional practice since the days of Henry Adams." This would be reasonable if longstanding pedagogical approaches had been tested and proved to be worth preserving; instead they have been continued without serious questioning and despite growing evidence that there are better ways to do things. Of course there are exceptions, and it remains to be seen whether temporary changes demanded by the pandemic will become permanent changes to long-standing habits, but for now the contemporary classroom is not dramatically different from the ones I inhabited as a student in the 1970s or, for that matter, from the ones in 1920 or 1850: Henry Adams, who wrote about college teaching in 1907, "would feel right at home" today.[41] Erasable markers have replaced chalk and technology has advanced beyond the overhead projector, but at its heart the pedagogy has not evolved.

Consider, for example, the lecture, "the style of teaching that has ruled universities for 600 years."[42] Six hundred years ago barbers were still performing surgery. Scott Freeman, a biologist at the University of Washington, traces the history of the lecture back even further to 1050, when universities were founded in western Europe and when barbers were just *starting* to perform surgery.[43] The evidence that lectures are an ineffective way of teaching is both voluminous and incontrovertible— Eric Mazur, one of the pioneers of the "flipped classroom," notes that "it's almost unethical to be lecturing if you have [the] data" about its weaknesses—yet lectures in classrooms large and small, in person and over Zoom, remain not just common but very, very common. The danger of even the best lectures, Mazur warns, is that "they create the illusion of teaching for teachers, and the illusion of learning for learners."[44] An analysis of more than two hundred studies of undergraduate STEM teaching methods led to the conclusion that "approaches that turned students into active participants rather than passive listeners reduced failure rates and boosted scores on exams by almost one-half a standard deviation."[45] In other words, learning by doing is more effective than learning by listening. I would not go so far as to say that the lecture should suddenly vanish altogether—what would we do with all those lecture halls?—but given its centrality to higher education and the evidence that it does not work very well as a teaching method, shouldn't this be something about which faculty are thinking and debating pretty regularly? Isn't the topic worth at least a faculty meeting or two?

The article in *Harvard Magazine* from which one of the Mazur quotes is taken was published in 2012 and is entitled, rather optimistically, "Twilight of the Lecture." More than a decade later, the sun is little closer to setting. Or as Steven Mintz, who predicted in 2013 that there would be fewer large lecture classes a decade later, wrote in 2022, "Whew, was I mistaken."[46]

Molly Worthen is among the many passionate defenders of the lecture as a mode of instruction. In an essay that is rather dismissive of the "active learning craze"—would that it were a craze—she argues that "those who want to abolish the lecture course do not understand what a lecture is": not a dry "declamation of an encyclopedia article" but the construction of a "long, complex argument." In abandoning the lecture "because students find it difficult . . . we capitulate to the worst features of the customer-satisfaction mentality that has seeped into the university from the business world." Leaving aside the fact that Worthen fortunately missed some of the encyclopedic declamations through which I sat as a student, she is partly correct—a good lecture can be a work of intellectual art—but, in the end, she misses the point: the question is not about the brilliance of the lecture itself or even about the enjoyment of listening to it, but about how much the student typically learns and retains. Here, the evidence is clear: less than the student would learn through a more active and engaged form of teaching. Lectures, which do not need to be "abolished" but whose prominence needs to be sharply reduced, are not a problem because students find them hard; they are a problem because the information they convey doesn't stick.[47]

The lecture is in some sense a representation in an individual classroom of the way the university positions itself in relation to its students: as a keeper and dispenser of information and knowledge that would otherwise be unavailable. Yet is this as accurate today as in decades past? Mazur again: "Information comes from everywhere now: the University is no longer the gatekeeper of information, as it has been since the Renaissance."[48] Today's students have access to more information on their phones than students could access in the Harvard library half a century ago. Has higher education adapted its methods to reflect this new reality? In 2012, the Pew Research Center surveyed more than a thousand experts in education and technology in an attempt to gauge their expectations for higher education by the year 2020. Sixty percent agreed with the following statement:

> By 2020, higher education will be quite different from the way it is today. There will be mass adoption of teleconferencing and distance learning to leverage expert resources. Significant numbers of learning activities will move to individualized, just-in-time learning approaches. There will be a transition to "hybrid" classes that combine online learning components with less-frequent on-campus, in-person class meetings. Most universities' assessment of learning will take into account more individually-oriented outcomes and capacities that are relevant to subject mastery. Requirements for graduation will be significantly shifted to customized outcomes.[49]

So: no. In February 2020, before the start of the pandemic, there had not been "mass adoption" of distance learning; there had not been a widespread transition to hybrid classes; assessment had not shifted to a greater emphasis on individually oriented outcomes and capacities. While these things were occurring at the margins, for the most part the 39 percent of respondents in 2012 who predicted that "in 2020, higher education will not be much different from the way it is today" were proved correct.[50] Most surprising to me is that a majority believed otherwise.

Another feature of higher education that could do with an update is the academic calendar. During my decades as a student, teacher, and administrator, I've been associated with six colleges and universities, and at every one the central work—teaching students—happened at full bore for two-thirds of the year. (To be fair, this is not the case at many two-year and some four-year institutions.) Of what other essential industry is this true? Imagine if hospitals or supermarkets or the postal service took a pause in January and another from June through August. I never did get over the strangeness of walking into Macalester's $50 million arts complex in the middle of July and finding the lights off, the air conditioning on, and, sometimes, not a single other person in the building. Occasionally I would cross paths with a solitary faculty member working in an office or a small group of middle school students participating in a summer arts program. Our $40 million recreation center was used in the summer for activities like cheerleading camps and sports academies, which never involved Macalester students and brought in very little revenue. I cannot think of another industry that makes such inefficient use of an expensive physical plant.

The evolution of the "summer break" in both colleges and K–12 schools is often, but erroneously, linked to the country's agrarian roots. In fact "kids in rural, agricultural areas were most needed in the spring, when crops had to be planted, and in the fall, when crops had to be harvested and sold." The creation of the summer break had more to do with the absence of air conditioning and the desire to escape from the city than with the demands of the farm and had nothing whatsoever to do with student achievement. It has stuck around, in both K–12 and higher education, because we like it, even though most experts agree that it does more to harm than to help student learning.[51]

Because shutting down for three months in the summer is not sufficient for most colleges, many also take a long winter break, whose creation
has been linked to everything from the Christian calendar to the oil crisis
of the 1970s.[52] At Macalester students are off for about five weeks, from
mid-December to late January. Once upon a time the break was used for
J-term courses, but in the early 1990s the faculty voted to eliminate those
courses but elected then—and has elected ever since—not to alter the calendar, which falls under their control. The result is that classes are taught
for fewer than thirty weeks a year, just enough to meet the minimum
requirement for accreditation.

The strongest arguments in favor of the eight-month academic calendar at colleges and universities are the following: it allows students, faculty,
and staff to decompress after the intensity of a term (though try making
that case to someone who does almost any other job); it provides time for
students to help fund their education through working; and it allows faculty both to prepare their classes and to engage in scholarship. At research
universities and many liberal arts colleges, this last argument in particular
is the one most commonly voiced.

The interruption of teaching in the service of research is regularly
justified on two bases. Research universities in particular are essential
drivers of innovation, and faculty are therefore fulfilling two roles: teaching students and advancing society through the creation of knowledge.
This argument is powerful when it comes to the STEM disciplines, but it
moves onto shakier ground when applied to most fields in the humanities.
Try as I might, I cannot convince myself that the world is a better place
because I published a book on Dickens's *Little Dorrit*—though it did help
me get promoted—nor can I convince myself that writing that book was
more valuable to society than teaching my students to write and to read
carefully and to appreciate the power of literature. I suspect that most
academic administrators agree, since this view of the faculty member as
researcher has surely contributed to the increasingly central role played by
the sciences at the university and the increasingly peripheral role played
by the arts and humanities.

The second justification is that productive scholars make better
teachers, an argument whose lack of basis I have already noted. Still,
it is worth repeating: the most influential segment of higher education
bases everything from its calendar to its reward system on a model of the

teacher-scholar *for which there is no evidence.* There are great and not-great teachers; there are great and not-great scholars. Those categories do not overlap in any easily predictable way, yet at the most elite colleges and universities, and even at many that are not so elite, we simply pretend that they do.

The strongest arguments against the typical calendar are both financial and educational. The simplest way to reduce the cost of a four-year college degree would be to make it a three-year college degree, and this could be accomplished rather easily by expanding the length of the school year. There is nothing magical about either the four-year degree or the requirement of 120 credits, neither of which is the norm in places like the United Kingdom, Germany, and parts of the continent of Africa and both of which are based more on tradition than on any particular evidence of efficacy. One can argue that the credit requirement is tied to the expectation of breadth as well as depth, at least in liberal arts education, but it is more difficult to argue that these credits must be spread out over four years interrupted by extended breaks. Previous attempts to offer a three-year degree have been met both with resistance from faculty, who were concerned about academic rigor, and with a lack of enthusiasm from students, who seemed to want the full, four-year college experience.[53] A recent project led by Robert Zemsky and Lori Carrell called "College in 3" is working with thirteen public and private institutions to pilot a three-year degree, though it is too soon to determine whether the rising cost of tuition will increase the appeal of the shorter time to completion or whether the effort will gain broad traction with faculty, students, or CFOs.[54]

Pedagogically these long breaks make little sense. While the evidence for a "summer slide"—that is, a decline in achievement levels after a long break—is not incontrovertible, it is strong, and it suggests that the decline is worse among students of lower socioeconomic status.[55] There is little research about the effect of long breaks on the educational attainment of college students in particular, but what holds true for younger students would seem to hold true for older students as well: "Over the summer . . . the flow of resources slows for students from disadvantaged backgrounds but not for students from advantaged backgrounds. Higher-income students tend to continue to have access to financial and human capital resources (such as parental education) over the summer, thereby facilitating learning."[56]

As long as I am challenging orthodoxies, let me go a step further and ask another question: Why do we assume that it is effective and efficient to try to prioritize teaching and research in the same institutions? The largest and most influential universities in the United States combine undergraduate and graduate teaching with research institutes, hospital systems, professional schools, semiprofessional sports teams, major real estate holdings, and who knows what else. In some sense Harvard is like Pfizer with a football team, bringing together under the same brand multiple activities that have little or nothing to do with one another.

Andrew Delbanco has traced the various forces that led early American colleges to evolve after the Civil War into the first versions of modern universities, "modeled to one degree or another on the renowned German universities of the day."[57] Research gained ascendency over teaching, and professional schools were added to the traditional education core. At around the same time, in 1869, the University of Michigan began operating the first, very small version of a university medical center.[58] Big-time intercollegiate athletics were a later development, signaled by the creation of the Intercollegiate Athletic Association of the United States, now known as the National Collegiate Athletic Association, in 1906. The net result is unsurprising. "Despite a good deal of academic propaganda to the contrary," Delbanco notes, "the fact is that when modern university leaders determine how to deploy resources, which 'fields' to invest in, and so on, undergraduates tend to be of marginal consequence."[59]

This situation would be bad enough if the devaluation of teaching were limited only to major research universities, but the well-established hierarchy of prestige within higher education has led very different kinds of institutions—liberal arts colleges and what are known as "comprehensive" public and private universities—to emulate many of the practices of their more highly regarded brethren. At the most well-resourced private colleges, teaching loads have generally shrunk over time and research expectations have increased; even at many less selective colleges and universities, research has become more important and teaching less so. As with program cuts, the verbal gymnastics around these changes can be remarkable: when ultra-wealthy Swarthmore College dropped its teaching load from five to four courses, the ostensible aim was to "improve faculty-student engagement" (does anyone believe these things?)—as well as to "increase opportunities for faculty to conduct research, and increase the college's competitiveness in the job-market for professors."[60] Community colleges might be the last set of institutions in the country at which teaching is without question the single, central priority, and of course faculty members at those colleges are the least well-compensated and the least respected within the academy.

If neither the fragile economic model nor the pedagogical weaknesses are sufficiently convincing arguments for change, consider the stark reality of completion rates, the single greatest inefficiency in the higher education system in the United States. The data collected by the National Center for Education Statistics make for an alarming read. Highlights include the following: at nonprofit, "four-year" institutions, 56.8 percent of the cohort that began in 2014 graduated within four years; the number for students who identify as Black is 34.3 percent. The number for all students who identify as male is 51.3 percent.[61] For a variety of typically unsavory political reasons, Congress passed a law in 1990 permitting four-year colleges to publish six-year graduation rates and two-year colleges to publish three-year rates, and while this does make the numbers look better, it is, as Jon Marcus writes, "like judging the performance of an airline by the percentage of its flights that take up to twice as long as scheduled to reach their destinations."[62] All of these numbers are much lower for those two-year colleges, though given the students they serve and the varied paths of those students, it seems almost unfair to lay these failures at the feet of those colleges.

More broadly, we need to be very cautious about equating completion rates with quality. The fact that, on average, highly selective institutions graduate students at three times the rate of open-enrollment institutions does not mean that they are doing a better job; it means that they are doing a different job with different students.[63] The outputs tell us a lot about inputs but very little about what happens along the way. Still, no matter how one parses or analyzes or explains the numbers, it seems hard to argue that a system with this level of incompletion is not ripe for transformational change, especially considering that the economic benefits of college increase dramatically when one actually obtains a degree.[64] We should not be content with a future in which nearly half of male students and nearly two-thirds of Black students start but do not finish college on time.

The combination of high cost, questionable pedagogy, and low graduation rates, mixed together with a large dollop of intense political partisanship, has led to one final challenge for higher education: a rapid erosion of public trust. The Boston Consulting Group has used artificial intelligence to analyze both the economic value of trust to large, publicly traded companies and the foundations on which trust is built: competence, fairness, transparency, and resilience. Unsurprisingly, they found that trust is both extremely valuable and extremely dynamic. It matters, and it is easily lost.[65]

The news here for higher education is not good. Survey after survey shows that public trust in the value and fairness of higher education— once among the most trusted industries in the country—has sharply declined. A 2019 Pew survey "finds that only half of American adults think colleges and universities are having a positive effect on the way things are going in the country these days. About four-in-ten (38%) say they are having a negative impact—up from 26% in 2012." A Gallup survey in 2018 found that "between 2015 and 2018, the share of Americans saying they had a great deal or quite a lot of confidence in higher education dropped from 57% to 48%." Similar results were obtained in a 2022 survey conducted by New America, in which only 55 percent of respondents agreed that higher education was having a positive effect on "the way things are going in this country today," a sharp decline from 68 percent only two years earlier.[66] Most of this decline, it is true, comes from self-identified Republicans for reasons that may or may not be fair, but colleges rely in many states on support from Republican legislators and in all states on enrollment of the children of Republican parents, and in the New America survey, nearly a quarter of Democrats had a negative view of the impact of higher education.[67] And while it is tempting to blame all of this on politics, it is hard to escape the conclusion that factors identified by the Boston Consulting Group like competence, fairness, and transparency are also playing a role and contributing to the steady drop in respect for and enrollment in college. Consider this: in yet another recent poll, by Morning Consult, the age group with the least trust in higher education was Gen Z—that is, adults aged eighteen to twenty-five. When your target demographic is the one that views you least favorably, you've got a problem.[68]

If you want to get a sense of just how far college has fallen in public esteem, polls are less revealing than a recent book by left-leaning journalist

Will Bunch, who believes (or at least the provocative subtitle of his book asserts) that "college broke the American dream and blew up our politics." That's a lot to lay at the feet of higher education. "We are refusing to admit," Bunch argues,

> that somewhere in the middle of a long and stormy postindustrial night, the [American] dream has morphed into a nightmare. That a ladder greased with a snake oil called meritocracy has changed from joyous kids climbing higher than their parents to a panicked desperation to hang on to the slippery middle rungs. And that even at the polluted top, neither bewildered parents nor stressed-out graduates are quite sure what they've just bought for all that cash (or, increasingly, a mountain of debt).[69]

Nightmares, snake oil, and pollution: now we've moved from disaster film to horror film. While there is some reality buried beneath Bunch's hyperbole, he idealizes a past that was far more inequitable than the present, overstates (like many) the problem of student debt, and makes the common mistake of equating "college" with a small group of highly selective schools. But the point here is not accuracy; it is to pile blame on an industry that seems to have become everyone's favorite target. These attacks from every direction are frustrating, but—let's be honest—they are in part a result of the unwillingness or inability of colleges and universities to address their most pressing problems from within.

The response of higher education to the pandemic would seem to offer a counterargument to my claims about the entrenched resistance to change. Confronted with a potentially existential challenge, the industry pivoted to online instruction with surprising agility and managed both to avoid the most dire economic outcomes and to serve students more effectively than might have been expected. We should be careful, however, not to overstate the lessons to be learned so far from the adaptation of colleges to the pandemic. We know now that they can move quickly when forced to do so and that much more can be accomplished online than many assumed. What we do not know is how lasting or how truly transformational the pandemic-related changes will turn out to be. As impressive as what has been termed the "Great Pivot" has been, it has centered mostly on the mode of delivery of teaching and other services like mental health counseling and advising: absent changes in pedagogy or pricing, movement from the classroom to Zoom is merely the same stuff, different medium.

To date, the evidence suggests that colleges and universities strongly prefer the "old normal" to the "new" and are doing everything they can to return to it. The prevailing attitude at many of the more secure institutions seems to resemble that of Dick Startz from the University of California, Santa Barbara: "In the longer run, nothing much will change about desire for higher education—so demand will return to normal. Nothing much will change about the cost of delivering higher education—so supply will return to normal. Online instruction might grow as a niche product, but for most purposes human contact is superior. In a few years, college finances should be back to their usual state of at least getting by."[70]

"At least getting by": less than inspiring and, for more and more colleges, an iffy proposition in the medium and long term. Startz seems wrong about demand, unless increased demand for elite colleges and decreased demand for everyone else is considered "normal," but he seems closer to right when it comes to the financial model (little changed) and the mode of instruction. The pandemic years are more likely to be viewed by traditional colleges as an interruption than as a permanent shift in direction. Stanford's John C. Mitchell worries about what he sees:

Two years after the burst of energetic innovation and unexpected discovery, my biggest frustration is that most colleges and universities, including my own, are turning their backs on all we learned. Remote work is strictly regulated. Online teaching is out. Innovations like active or mastery-based learning, long known to experts in education, are falling by the wayside as old habits return all too easily. Transformation is nowhere in the vocabulary. Most importantly, there are no broad efforts by college leaders to codify what we learned or leverage the resourcefulness, ingenuity, empathy and understanding we gained by powering through the pandemic. It's as if we spent two years building the foundation for a new future, only to abandon it for the familiar discomfort of a system widely in need of reinvention.[71]

In Mitchell's own department at Stanford, Computer Science, final exams were eliminated during the remote pandemic year, then came back, in-person, the following year; small, regular quizzes, or "concept checks," were added during the remote year, then discontinued; a revise and resubmit policy was instituted during the remote year, then discontinued.[72] And these are the people who are the most comfortable with and adept at using technology—imagine what is happening in history departments.

Unlike Startz, I think that the most lasting effect of the pandemic on higher education is likely to be a heavier reliance on online instruction, which is already more than a niche product and which has the potential to reduce costs, to reach a larger and more diverse group of students, and, as Mitchell notes, "to address traditional problems like student preparation, degree completion, and transition to jobs."[73] But this will only be the case if colleges are willing to rethink measures like student-to-faculty ratios and to reimagine their target markets. Having about the same number of faculty teaching about the same number and type of students via Zoom instead of in a classroom will not alter the fundamental economic model of higher education, nor will it change the pedagogical paradigms. It will not alter the academic calendar or recalibrate the relationship between teaching and research. In other words, it will not bring about anything like disruptive change on its own.

Another pandemic-driven development appears to be a surge in interest in what are sometimes called "microcredentials" or "stackable" credentials—that is, weeks- or monthslong certificate programs, usually in vocational fields, that can stand alone or be combined or "stacked" into associate's or bachelor's degrees. These programs have for years been central to the work of technical and community colleges, but the growth of online education and the economic disruption created by the pandemic gave them "a huge burst of momentum." Online providers of stackable credentials like Western Governors University and edX, now owned by 2U, saw dramatic growth during the spring of 2020.[74] Whether that growth was a temporary response to an extraordinary economic disruption or a more persistent pattern is still unclear—2U laid off 20 percent of its workforce in the summer of 2022 as a result of declining enrollments—but it does seem likely that both the high cost of college and the growing number of adult learners will keep the stackable credentials option alive.[75] It is wholly predictable that

> the institutions furthest along with stackable credentials are non-conventional ones. Some traditional universities say they want to add them, too, but longstanding practices are hard to alter. . . . Conventional institutions that are working to come up with stackable credentials . . . have been slowed down by accreditation requirements, occasional faculty resistance, the need for certification bodies and academic departments to collaborate and the difficulty of explaining to consumers how the process works.[76]

The only part of this summary with which I might quarrel is the characterization of faculty resistance as "occasional."

The authors of an article in the *Harvard Business Review* argued in the summer of 2021 that "universities and educators must resist a complete reversion to their pre-pandemic practices." The pandemic provided "a unique opportunity to conduct experiments and innovate" and it "lowered resistance to change and thus helped higher education institutions get rid of deeply entrenched, dysfunctional practices that would be difficult to shed under normal circumstances." Among the deeply entrenched practices that purportedly have changed are the requirement that students come together at the same time, long-standing modes of student evaluation, and reliance on a massive physical infrastructure. Perhaps higher education will "get rid of" these things at some future date, but for now, they are still very much around. One would be very hard-pressed to find a traditional, in-person college that has announced a permanent shift to more online or asynchronous instruction or one with a physical campus that has decided to rely less on its buildings. Most of the revisions to the academic calendar that were made during the pandemic—summer sessions or divided semesters—are being reversed. Students are back to taking graded examinations. Meet the new boss, same as the old boss.[77]

Here is the closing advice from the authors of the *Harvard Business Review* article: "Universities must embrace this unique opportunity to retain at least some beneficial practices adopted during the crisis. To do so effectively, university leaders must conduct thoughtful investigation and discussion to identify which practices have been successful, clear any obstacles to those practices becoming routine, and be deliberate in ensuring that the changes stick."

It sounds good, and I anxiously await the follow-up article, "A Guide for University Leaders on Clearing All Obstacles to Change and Ensuring That Changes Stick."[78] That will be helpful.

I have been very hard in this chapter—though not Will Bunch hard—on a sector in whose importance and potential I deeply believe and to which I have devoted my career, perhaps because we tend to be hardest on the people and institutions we most value. Even with all its flaws, higher education does far more good than harm, engages in many effective practices, and changes countless lives for the better. But if it were willing to think seriously about transformational change, let alone to initiate it, if it were willing to examine its own ways of working as carefully as it examines many of the disciplines within its curricula, it could provide more benefits to more people more consistently and avoid what looks increasingly like a bleak future for many institutions. The industry seems at the same time both to acknowledge and to ignore this reality. In a recent, comprehensive survey of chief academic officers at institutions of all kinds—private and public, nonprofit and for profit, large and small, two-year and four-year—99 percent reported that "their institutions are somewhat or very effective at providing a quality undergraduate education" and 98 percent reported that they were similarly effective at "preparing students for the world of work." That suggests a remarkably successful collective enterprise. Yet in the same survey, 13 percent described the academic health of their institutions as failing or poor—so maybe not quite so successful. Only 55 percent believe that "students emerge from general education courses with sufficient writing skills"—raising the question of how they are defining effective education in the earlier question. Ninety-three percent believe that the liberal arts are central to an undergraduate education, though 73 percent expect to see the number of liberal arts institutions decline over the ensuing five years. Sixty-nine percent believe that any new funds for academic programs will need to come from reallocation rather than new revenues, yet only 24 percent believe that their institutions are likely to cut any programs, meaning little opportunity for reallocation and, presumably, for the creation of those new programs. In one of the surveys of CFOs to which I alluded earlier, only 26 percent indicated that their institution would finish 2021–22 with a positive operating margin absent federal relief funds, yet an even smaller percentage—one in six—reported that their institution had "made 'difficult but transformative changes' in its operations to 'better position itself for long-term sustainability.'" This all seems a peculiar combination of wishful thinking, worry, and denial.[79]

Inside Higher Education's 2023 survey of college and university presidents is equally head-spinning. Almost 80 percent believe that "their institution will be financially stable over the next decade," at the same time as 70 percent believe that their "institution needs to make fundamental changes in its business models, programming and other operations." Three-quarters agree that the "perception of colleges as places that are intolerant of conservative views is having a major negative impact on attitudes about higher education," and almost 60 percent agree that "public doubts about the affordability of higher education are justified."[80] The threats seem to exist everywhere but on their own campuses. Kevin R. McClure, who studies and teaches about higher education, notes somewhat gently that these presidents are "perhaps operating more on hope than on strategy." Rick Staisloff, whose firm consults with dozens of colleges and universities, views the survey results with concern: "If the opinions expressed here were true, higher education could continue doing what it is doing, the way it is doing it. . . . I would not advise any president in the United States today to carry their current model forward as is."[81] And Paul Friga, who also consults with many of these colleges, notes with some bewilderment that "there still seems to be this feeling that 'we'll just get by somehow.'"[82] For some of these institutions, that might end up as a sad but appropriate epitaph.

Robert Zemsky describes higher education as "an industry that believes in marginal change. Anything that smacks of changing anything all at once has got to be crazy."[83] Stig Leschly, CEO of the think tank College101, characterizes what passes for innovation in higher education as marginal, "a lot like when Britannica Encyclopedia went on to the CD-ROM."[84] They are not wrong, but they are describing a condition and not a cause. My goal in what follows is to attempt to understand the cause and to explore what, if anything, can be done about it. I begin by examining the role of broad factors including reputation and incentive structures in the process of change in this most immutable of industries and then consider the incompatibility of some of higher education's most deeply embedded practices, such as departmental autonomy, shared governance, and tenure, with the need for transformation. I conclude with at least a gesture toward a possible path forward. While I make no claim to having all or even most of the answers, the beginning of any solution must be an honest and thorough understanding of the problem.

Chapter 2

Reputation

Your reputation follows you wherever you go
Don't get a bad reputation.
Your reputation can't be bought, it can't be sold
Don't get a bad reputation.

—Donna Summer

SOME YEARS, Macalester College is a twenty-six.
Other years it is a twenty-five or twenty-four or twenty-seven. Once during my tenure as president it was a twenty-three (trustee congratulations), once a twenty-nine (trustee concern). Never in seventeen years did it stray outside that range.

The colleges with which Macalester has the largest admissions overlap are Carleton and Grinnell: unsurprising, since a student interested in a selective liberal arts college in the Midwest would be likely to look at all three. Carleton is a six, sometimes a five and sometimes an eight. Grinnell bounces around a bit more but is typically an eleven or a fourteen.

If reducing a complex institution to a number seems ridiculous, well, welcome to the world of *U.S. News and World Report* rankings, which may, as Education Secretary Michael Cardona suggests, be "a joke," but if so, the joke is on all of us.[1] These rankings have no meaningful relationship to quality but, like it or not, are a reasonably good proxy for reputation: to some degree they establish it, but more often they simply reflect and confirm it. When the rankings diverge dramatically from what the market believes—as in the notorious case from 1999 when Cal Tech was ranked as the top national university, ahead of Harvard and Princeton and Yale—the response of *U.S. News* is to change its methodology so that the universe reverts to its proper alignment.[2]

Year in and year out, students who are admitted to both Macalester and Carleton or Macalester and Grinnell more often choose Carleton or Grinnell. The imbalance with Carleton (top ten) is particularly noteworthy. This could of course be because Carleton and Grinnell are simply better colleges, or do a more skillful job of recruiting, or offer better financial aid (though all three colleges meet the full financial need of admitted students). Or it could be because they are more highly ranked—that is, have more reputational strength. There is no way to know for certain, but what we do know is that rankings and selectivity are very closely related, even though, in its most recent tweak to its methodology and in response to another wave of criticism, *U.S. News* has eliminated acceptance rate from its rankings criteria. This move, like all the other tweaks by the publication, is essentially meaningless, since acceptance rate correlates so closely with most of the other criteria that are still used to rank colleges.[3]

The relationship of most within higher education and even many consumers of higher education to *U.S. News* is strangely voyeuristic: no one likes to admit that they look, but everyone does. Presidents and trustees who say that they don't care when their ranking drops are generally not telling the truth, nor are those who claim to feel no schadenfreude when the ranking of a competitor drops. Very few students will admit to selecting a college on the basis of a ranking, but admissions data and research tell a different story.[4] The relationship to rankings is also, often, profoundly hypocritical: many of the same institutions that rightly criticize the validity of a system that is both biased toward wealth and wildly random will be quick to advertise a rise within that same system.[5]

Those who believe that much will change as a result of the highly publicized "withdrawal" from the *U.S. News* rankings by some prominent law and medical schools and a couple of undergraduate colleges need to think again. To begin with, these institutions have no power to "withdraw" from anything: they can stop submitting information, most of which is publicly available, but *U.S. News* can and will continue to include them in their rankings. The 2023 rankings in law and medicine, the first released post-"withdrawal," look, according to the *New York Times*, "striking similar" to those of the year before.[6] And law schools at Yale and Harvard are in no danger of losing prestige, applicants, or access to judicial clerkships or top law firms: their symbolic gesture is not meaningless, but, like most gestures that are risk free, it will in the end have minimal impact.[7]

Here is the truly interesting thing: there is nothing that Macalester could do right or Carleton or Grinnell could do wrong to measurably alter those rankings and reputations. They are about as immutable as anything in this unstable world, particularly at the upper end. Perhaps in some other strand of the multiverse Macalester could leap ahead of Carleton in the rankings, but in this universe their relative positions are fixed. Colleges and universities have been caught up in scandals and have been the subject of awful publicity and have had dreadful leadership, but aside, occasionally, from a transitory hit, none has seen any real alteration in the perception of the brand. The University of Michigan and Michigan State University together paid out about $1 billion in settlements to the victims of serial sexual abuse, yet neither has seen any weakening of its strength in the marketplace. USC has employed an impressive roster of scoundrels yet continues to become more selective.[8] The quote attributed to Benjamin Franklin—"It takes many good deeds to build a good reputation, but only one bad deed to lose it"—might apply in most instances, but not when it comes to universities.[9]

About the only thing that might make a positive difference in the relative standing of Macalester would be a gift of say, $1 billion, since that would generate headlines and since *U.S. News* rankings are essentially a measure of institutional wealth—but even that would take time and would not be guaranteed to change anything. Macalester did in fact receive a similar gift, inflation adjusted, from the estate of DeWitt Wallace in 1990, and it took until 1997 for the college to break into the *U.S. News* top twenty-five for the first time.[10] About the only thing that might make a negative difference to the standing of Carleton or Grinnell would be a fiscal crisis severe enough to affect students, which is more than a little unlikely at schools with endowments of over $1 billion and $3 billion, respectively.

I have in my career been employed at three liberal arts colleges situated at different points in the higher education food chain: Allegheny College, Lawrence University, and Macalester College. At each I have listened to and participated in endless conversations about strengthening the brand of the college. At each I have read and helped develop strategic plans with that goal in mind. Every one of those attempts has essentially failed: four decades after I first entered the professoriate, the relative positions of the three institutions are unchanged.[11] Macalester is more selective and has more money and a stronger brand than Lawrence, which is more selective and has more money and a stronger brand than Allegheny, which is more selective and has more money and a stronger brand than, say, Monmouth College, and so it goes—this despite the fact that, to be completely honest, I noticed no real qualitative difference among the faculties at Allegheny, Lawrence, and Macalester (they were all very good) or the quality of the education provided. If there was a difference, it was in the level of preparation of the students, which has everything to do with inputs, which has everything to do with . . . reputation.

This reality raises an important question: If there is nothing that one can do to alter the perception of an institution for the better, how much does it diminish the incentive to actually *make* the institution better?

Brand strength in higher education is both the most important thing and the most unchangeable thing, which can make for a lot of frustrated boards of trustees and admissions offices. Despite the absence of evidence that anything really works, institutions keep trying. When in January 2022 the New York State Board of Regents loosened the requirements for being called a "university," a number of colleges rushed to change their names. With admirable honesty and unflagging optimism, a spokesperson for St. John Fisher College—now St. John Fisher University—acknowledged, "For us, university status conveys greater prestige [and] has stronger reputational value domestically and internationally."[12] This belief makes sense, since universities are higher than colleges in the pecking order both domestically and internationally, but I can find no evidence that such a name change actually improves things that matter, like admissions or financial stability. In 2009, the College of St. Catherine in Saint Paul, Minnesota, became St. Catherine University. Neither its fiscal health nor its admissions profile has improved as a consequence.

Building a brand in higher education is typically not the work of years or decades but of centuries. Harvard was founded in 1636, Yale in 1701, Princeton in 1746, Columbia (then King's College) in 1754. Williams College was founded in 1783, Bowdoin in 1794, Amherst in 1821. The only two universities ranked in the top twenty by *U.S. News* in 2022 founded later than the nineteenth century are Rice (1912) and UCLA (1919), and the majority began their lives before the Civil War. Newcomers—by which I mean institutions less than a century old—very rarely make their way onto such lists, and then only through an enormous infusion of cash or rapid changes in demography.

U.S. News and World Report began ranking universities and colleges in 1983, when the only input was a reputational survey completed by the presidents of those same universities and colleges: that is, opinion unsupported by evidence.[13] The top four universities in that first year were Stanford, Harvard, Yale, and Princeton. In 2022, after the addition of columns filled with ostensibly meaningful data, the top four universities were Princeton, Harvard, MIT (previously tenth), and Yale, with Stanford checking in at five.[14] Over nearly forty years the rankings (and reputations) of the top universities have remained almost eerily stable; the data, mostly related to inputs and wealth, have for the most part merely served to confirm the earlier, long-established opinions. What possible metric could persuade the public that the University of Minnesota was "better" than Yale? Probably the most noteworthy change since the first Reagan administration is the decline in the rankings of a number of public universities, almost certainly a consequence of the enormous wealth accumulated during that period by elite private universities and the lack of comparable growth in state funding.[15]

Reputational stickiness among liberal arts colleges is not very different: as of 2022, Williams College had been ranked number one for twenty years in a row. It is to *U.S. News* rankings what Alabama football is to the AP Coaches Poll, only more consistent and without a television contract. The top three in 1983 were Amherst, Swarthmore, and Williams; the top three in 2022 were Williams, Amherst, and Swarthmore. Public universities have seen a little more movement, mostly because of population growth in the West and South, though Berkeley and Michigan were one and two in 1983 and were two and three in 2022 (behind UCLA).

Some publications have attempted to rank colleges using metrics that differ from prevailing opinion.[16] Since 2005, *Washington Monthly* has been ranking institutions based on "their contributions to the public good" rather than on "wealth, exclusivity, and prestige." In 2021, the University of Wisconsin–Madison was ranked above Harvard and the University of California San Diego was ranked above Princeton and Yale.[17] More recently, a nonprofit called Heartland Forward ranked universities on the basis of "technology transfer," or the process by which innovations improve the economy of local communities. North Carolina State was ranked above MIT.[18] However meaningful and reliable the criteria, no one takes such rankings seriously other than the schools that happen to be ranked surprisingly high: UC San Diego features its *Washington Monthly* ranking on its homepage, as does North Carolina State with its Heartland Forward ranking. Princeton and Harvard are about as likely to mention *U.S. News* on their homepage as Le Bernardin is to erect a billboard on the Long Island Expressway.[19]

Coincidentally, *Fortune* also began ranking the "World's Most Admired Companies" in 1983, when the top five were Exxon, General Motors, Mobil, Texaco, and Ford. Eleven out of the top twenty were oil companies. The only "tech" companies in the top one hundred were IBM (6), Texas Instruments (79), Control Data (80), Hewlett-Packard (81), Unisys (85), and Digital Equipment (95). Control Data and Digital Equipment no longer exist as independent companies, nor does American Can (89) or Whitman Chocolates (95), and most of the oil companies have merged with or been acquired by other companies. The only two media companies mentioned were CBS (31) and Warner Communications (92). Manufacturing companies dominate the list.

The top five in 2022 were Apple, Amazon, Microsoft, Pfizer, and Disney—none of which made the top one hundred in 1983 and one of which had not even been founded. None of the top five from 1983 made the top one hundred thirty-nine years later, and in fact the majority of names from 1983 are nowhere to be found. Seventeen names on the 2022 list are categorized as internet or technology companies. Two entertainment companies (Disney and Netflix) are in the top ten. The list is now dominated by retail, financial services, airlines, and pharmaceuticals (the last clearly having a direct connection to the pandemic). The number of oil companies in the top one hundred: zero. The number of oil companies in the top three hundred: zero. These changes tell a revealing story about both the altered nature of the national and global economy and the altered perception of various industries. From a reputational perspective, Exxon and General Motors were the Princeton and Harvard of 1983. In 2022, Princeton and Harvard were still Princeton and Harvard; Exxon and GM still existed, and at least Exxon was still making lots of money, but their brand strength had been obliterated.

A look at market capitalization tells the same story of change. As I write, the largest companies in the United States as measured by market cap are, in order, Apple, Microsoft, Alphabet (Google), Amazon, Tesla, Berkshire Hathaway, and Meta (Facebook). Five of the seven did not exist in 1983; Microsoft did not go public until 1986; and the original version of Berkshire Hathaway, a textile business, shut down in 1985, when Warren Buffett and Charlie Munger began diversifying into other industries.[20] Of course, there is no precise equivalent to market capitalization for nonprofit colleges and universities, but if one measures wealth by the size of an institution's endowment, the richest have remained the richest: Harvard had the largest endowment in the country in fiscal year 1983 ($2.4 billion) and in fiscal year 2022 ($53.2 billion).[21]

I would not go so far as to suggest that there is no reputational movement whatsoever within higher education, only that such movement is rare and happens within a fairly narrow range. *U.S. News* rankings are an imperfect proxy for these changes since small shifts up or down in those rankings are arbitrary and meaningless, but it is noteworthy that Northeastern University moved from being number ninety-eight among national universities in 2007 to number forty-two in 2014. A combination of a highly desirable location and a genuinely innovative experiential model made a difference. (Boston University also jumped up during the same period without any of the curricular changes, so location does seem to matter.) But by 2022 Northeastern had dropped back to number forty-nine, so the odds of it eclipsing the reputation of Tufts or Boston College seem small; the odds of it becoming a reputational peer of one of the national elites seem nonexistent. It is actually easier to move metrics like admissions numbers and fund-raising totals than it is to move the perception of the brand.

My favorite example of brand strength in higher education and of the desire of some institutions to improve it comes not from *U.S. News* or the *Times Higher Education* World University Rankings but from Monopoly. The board game. There are now hundreds of different themed versions of the game, including ones tied to Pokémon, *Star Wars*, and various cities and countries around the world. Schools including the University of Texas at San Antonio and Holy Cross have paid tens of thousands of dollars to make their way onto a Monopoly board to create a "brand experience."

For the Cambridge, Massachusetts, version, however, Harvard and MIT are included free of charge, and in fact a "Harvard spokesperson clarified that *the university* elected not to charge Top Trumps [the maker of Monopoly] any royalties or fees for the company's use of the university's name and brand." Harvard does not need Monopoly; Monopoly needs Harvard.[22]

Reputation is both so important and so fixed in higher education because the industry is perhaps the best example—and among the most expensive examples—of what economists and marketers call a "credence good," in contrast to a "search good" or an "experience good." A search good is a product or service that "has attributes and quality that are easily verified before purchase."[23] Frequently cited examples of search goods are furniture, consumer electronics, gasoline, and paper towels—all products whose characteristics and value are relatively easy to determine in advance. An experience good is one "whose price, quality, or some other attribute remains unknown until purchase." Typical examples are a restaurant meal or a bottle of wine: "Once a person has consumed the food or wine they can readily evaluate their satisfaction with it." (And, I suppose, once you have consumed a particular wine or eaten in a particular restaurant several times, it might move into the category of a search good.) Credence goods "may be the most interesting to marketers, because even after their purchase and use, customers may still be unable to assess their quality."[24] Markets for credence goods, moreover, are often ones "in which the information asymmetries are of the form that sellers are also experts who determine customers' needs."[25] Or as Gordon Winston puts it more simply, "To a remarkable extent, people *don't really know what they're buying*" (his emphasis).[26] Many forms of medical care fall into this category, as do some forms of consulting services, as does higher education. You pay the physician or consultant or professor without knowing precisely what you need, they provide what they decide you need, and you have in the end no sure way of knowing that you needed it.

As one moves from search goods to experience goods to credence goods, the importance of prestige increases: in the absence of verifiable evidence of quality, reputation becomes supremely powerful. "Prestige," Dave Wieneke observes, "is the currency of credence goods." Also important are "rankings by expert judges," which accounts for the outsize influence of *U.S. News* and the proliferation of other, less widely read rankings of colleges and universities: if we cannot judge quality on our own, we turn to those who claim (or pretend) that they can.[27] And if there is no way for the consumer to determine the actual quality of a service, there is also no way to determine whether that quality is improving or declining and little opportunity for a provider—in this case a college or university—to alter its reputation.

Unfortunately, credence goods can create a set of bad incentives. When customers cannot judge the quality of a service even after purchase, "providers may have limited incentives to increase quality . . . and the resulting quality may be inefficiently low."[28] Even worse, "with a credence good," according to Winand Emons, "the information asymmetry between buyers and sellers obviously creates strong incentives for sellers to cheat on services."[29] While it might not be entirely fair to call the lack of emphasis on undergraduate teaching at research universities a form of "cheating," it is certainly an example of reputation obscuring reality. More blatant forms of cheating have been found in the data reported by some colleges and universities to *U.S. News*: Temple, Villanova, Tulane, Bucknell, and Claremont McKenna are among the schools that have acknowledged submitting false data to the rankings king, and Columbia, ranked number two at the time, was pulled from the 2022 rankings due to serious questions about its data. Not all these schools have admitted to deliberate falsification, but the erroneous data seem never to make the institutions look worse.[30]

Health care is often likened to higher education as a credence good, and the reputational stickiness of hospitals has something in common with that of universities, but the relevant factors for most consumers tend to be different. The Mayo Clinic, the Cleveland Clinic, and Massachusetts General are the Ivy League of health care, and their brands do attract patients with the means to travel and the opportunity to research things like surgical outcomes. But most people do not. In a 2005 Gallup poll, consumers said that quality of care is most important to them when choosing a hospital, but

> when focus group participants are asked how healthcare quality is judged, the room tends to get silent. Quality measures are given top priority, but the public has only a vague idea of where to find reliable measures or how to use them. . . . Without access to objective, accessible information, [consumers] tend to fall back on information they can assess that has meaning for them. Are

the people who work at the hospital nice? Is it close to home? Many people have the feeling they should be using criteria related to medical outcomes to make their choices, but, in reality, default to these lesser concerns because they're easier to evaluate.[31]

Many people also have primary care physicians whose views they will trust more fully than the *U.S. News* rankings of hospitals, which are not nearly as influential as its rankings of colleges. Given the choice, few people will opt for Hofstra University over Harvard because the faculty are nice or because it is closer to home or because their high school biology teacher went there. But when it comes to their health, and in the absence of clear qualitative information, people will tend to prioritize a sense of comfort, trust, and familiarity even over the lure of a luxury brand. The point of going to an Ivy League school is to go to an Ivy League school; the point of going to a hospital is to get well.

Though higher education has a more important social function than most other experience and credence goods, the market dynamics are not fundamentally different. The auction price in 2022 for a single bottle of the 2018 vintage of Domaine de la Romanée-Conti Romanée-Conti Grand Cru, a red Burgundy that is annually among the most coveted and expensive wines in the world, was about $30,000. This price bears little relation to the cost of production but is driven by a combination of reputation, expert opinion, ego, and scarcity (only about five thousand bottles are produced each year).[32] Wines in this ultra-luxury category are also widely considered a good investment, since their value often (though not always) increases over time. Twenty years ago, Pappy Van Winkle bourbon could be purchased in a local liquor store for under $100; today, after a series of articles and reviews extolling its virtues, the same product is nearly impossible to find and can fetch over $10,000 at auction. It became, in a wonderful phrase, "famous for being famous."[33]

Demand for elite higher education is also created by reputation and scarcity, though, because of the social mission and nonprofit status of these colleges and universities, that demand is reflected less in price than in selectivity. Between 1992 and 2012, the acceptance rate at the University of Pennsylvania dropped from 38.9 percent to 12.3 percent; by 2022 it had dropped to 8.4 percent. Yale went from 21.9 percent to 6.8 percent to 4.5 percent. The same pattern can be seen at every Ivy League university, at peers like Stanford and the University of Chicago, and at the most selective liberal arts colleges.[34] This increase in demand is not being driven by fundamental changes in these institutions or by demographics; it is not being driven by new evidence of their effectiveness in educating students or even of their links to earning potential, since the evidence there is, at best, mixed.[35] It is being driven by the fact that it seems more important than ever for a college or university to be "famous for being famous."

The stability of academic reputation and its disconnection from evidence of quality affect different institutions in different ways. For the small group of colleges and universities at the very top, these factors render anything beyond slow, incremental change virtually impossible. Transformational change is difficult and risky, and organizations take on that difficulty and risk either because they are forced to do so or because they are prompted by a powerful desire to be better. An institution for which demand far outstrips supply and whose reputation is more or less untouchable has no need to change, and individuals within such an institution who nevertheless push for change are likely to confronted by a wall of intransigence. If you are perceived by influential "experts" as the best and treated by the market as the best, it seems pretty safe to assume that you are, in fact, the best, and what could be better than that? If Apple could have run back the iPhone 7 year after year, increased the price, and seen a rise in demand, why would it have messed around with an iPhone 8? Now imagine if Apple were in a position to say no to 90 or even 96 percent of those who wanted to purchase its product and you have the situation of the most selective universities and liberal arts colleges.

Experts in organizational change regularly note that "complacency is not an option for 21st century organizations striving for longevity and sustainable profitability."[36] But what if it is an option? Elite colleges and universities have proved quite convincingly that complacency is not an impediment to either longevity or economic sustainability and so have every reason to feel, as it were, complacent about complacency. As hesitant as I am to agree with Scott Galloway, he is right when he says that "the strongest brand in the world is not Apple or Mercedes-Benz or Coca-Cola. The strongest brands are MIT, Oxford, and Stanford."[37] With apologies to MIT, Oxford, and Stanford, a good case can actually be made that Harvard's is the strongest brand in the world. Not the strongest educational brand: the strongest brand, period. No other has been so universally associated with the pinnacle of quality so visibly for so long.

One unfortunate side effect of this remarkable brand strength is its contribution to public misperception of the state of American higher education. During the first six months of 2022, Harvard, Yale, Stanford, and Princeton were collectively mentioned in the *New York Times* about twice as often as the term *community college.* Together those four universities enroll about sixty thousand students; community colleges enroll between seven and eight million. The imbalance during the same period in the *Washington Post* is even greater. Frank Bruni and others have written dozens of columns on what the *Times* has called college admissions "madness" and "mania," and the stock "higher education" photo in the paper appears to be of Harvard Yard. The only madness about all this is the perception that the main problem with higher education in the United States is the number of students being rejected by the Ivy League and other hyperselective colleges and universities. Clearly the audience for these publications is not representative of the overall population and is especially likely to be focused on elite institutions. But it is also an audience with outsized influence on policy, and if that group fails to grasp the actual state of the country's higher education system, there is little chance that people will work to improve it.[38]

Institutions below the top tier—that is, the vast majority of them—face a different motivational problem. It was possible within twenty years for Apple's brand strength, financial position, and market share go from being negligible to surpassing those of IBM. History suggests that it would not be possible for the brand strength, financial position, and market share of a mid-tier college or university to surpass those of Brown or Bowdoin within twenty years—or, for that matter, forty or sixty. It is not even clear that a mid-tier institution could measurably close the gap. This often leads not to complacency but to something close to a sense of resignation: Why do the hard work of change if there is little chance that it will make any difference? If transformational change is unlikely to make our situation dramatically better, why take the risk that it will make it dramatically worse?

My career has been bookended by stays at Ivy League institutions as a student and as whatever one calls a former college president, but in between I spent nearly forty years at colleges that were secure enough to avoid confronting existential threats but not secure enough to avoid acknowledging the importance of change altogether. As I noted earlier, at all three there were aspirations to "move up," yet at none, at any point, was there serious discussion of change beyond the incremental. At each there were somewhat more radical ideas that always seemed to stand just beyond the boundaries of polite conversation. Allegheny College is situated in rural Pennsylvania and has a strong history of a serious commitment to sustainability. Why not go all in on being an environment-focused liberal arts college? Lawrence University is distinctive in being a small college with a highly regarded music conservatory. Why not build a curriculum around creativity? Macalester is a small liberal arts college located in the heart of a three-million-person metropolitan area. Why not place urban engagement at the heart of programming? The answers in each case were more or less the same: too much risk of alienating some group of prospective students; too much inevitable resistance—closer to rebellion, actually—from faculty, students, and alumni; too little potential benefit. In other words, "It's not worth it."

It is also unhappily the case that colleges tend both to exaggerate their own distinctiveness and to overestimate the visibility of distinctiveness to the consumer, part of a broader pattern of making strategic decisions by looking inward rather than outward. Read websites and admissions materials and you might become convinced that the United States is blessed with thousands of institutions whose cultures and programs are impossible to find elsewhere. Ask most inhabitants of a liberal arts college campus and they will tell you that the one thing that cannot be lost is the "X College culture" or the "Y College way of doing things." Ask most prospective students and they will complain that these colleges are difficult to tell apart. Wesleyan's Michael Roth has noted, with regret, that "the market punishes distinctiveness."[39] It might be more accurate to say that the market is indifferent to what higher education calls distinctiveness and what most external observers would call minor differences and that it cares much less about minor differences than it does about reputation. Rarely—very, very rarely—will a student choose Illinois Wesleyan University (number eighty-nine in *U.S. News* in 2022) over Roth's Wesleyan University (number seventeen) because they find the programs in Illinois more "distinctive." Illinois Wesleyan identifies as a distinction its focus on experiential learning. As does Illinois's Knox College. As does Illinois's

Monmouth College. As do hundreds of colleges and universities across the country.

The other reality about distinctiveness at colleges is that it tends not to remain distinctive for very long. Colleges and universities watch each other, or at least those they consider peers and competitors, very closely. An original idea that seems appealing to the market will quickly find its way to other institutions. Macalester was among the first colleges in the United States to make internationalism central to its mission and programming—the United Nations flag was raised in the heart of campus in 1950—and for years it remained a genuine distinction, though not one that necessarily elevated the stature or financial stability of the college. (It took DeWitt Wallace's millions to do that.) Once colleges caught on to the fact that international students could be an important source of revenue, however, we began to see one version or another of internationalism featured at hundreds of institutions. By the time Macalester did market research in the past decade, it had become clear that the college's international focus had ceased being a powerful distinguishing feature for prospective students. This is why the most valuable distinctive features are those that are difficult to copy: Macalester's situation as a highly selective liberal arts college in a city is not something that can be replicated at more than a small handful of its peers.

The colleges that would seem to have the most incentive to innovate are those that have nothing to lose—that is, those that are reputationally weak and looking at declining enrollments and growing budget deficits. This is not a small group. A study in the spring of 2022 identified seventy-four public and private nonprofit institutions that had closed, merged, or been acquired since 2016, an impressive number considering just how difficult it is to end the life of a college.[40] Various studies and measurements—some no doubt overly bleak—identify as many as five hundred institutions that are flashing warning signs.[41] Based on an admittedly limited set of financial metrics, a recent report by Bain argues that a staggering 49 percent of public universities and 26 percent of private institutions are currently on an unsustainable financial path.[42] Yet the colleges that need to innovate most are the ones with the fewest resources—in time, money, and energy—to do so. Brian Mitchell, former president of Bucknell, observes that "those colleges and universities that survive are likely to be not the ones with the biggest endowments but the ones that are the most creative and . . . the most entrepreneurial." I agree with half of this prediction: colleges with the biggest endowments have a much better chance of survival than even the most creative colleges with the smallest. But creativity and an entrepreneurial mind-set do matter and are rarer than one might expect. The pattern followed by struggling colleges is generally the same: cut underenrolled programs (typically in the humanities), add something more vocational, and hope for the best. This is not innovation; it is stalling. Mitchell rightly calls it incrementalism and notes that "if in fact you're practicing incrementalism, then you're in real danger now and could be in grave danger shortly."[43]

Boldness rather than incrementalism sounds good in theory, but in practice it is extraordinarily difficult. Even when a college is on its deathbed, important constituencies will push back, hard, against changing the very things that landed it there. Mills College in California is both an illustrative example and a cautionary tale. Between 2015 and 2020, enrollment at the all-women's, progressive college—two-thirds of whose students were students of color and more than half of whose students were Pell eligible—declined by a staggering 50 percent. When initial plans to close were altered to a plan to merge with Northeastern University, the college was sued by its own alumni association, which delayed the agreement, and then by its own students.[44] Typically colleges that are on the edge of extinction make increasingly draconian cuts to stave off closure, float ideas for more dramatic change that are rejected by the community, announce that they are closing, and get sued by their own alumni, students, or employees: see Sweet Briar, Antioch, Hampshire, Mount Ida, and many others. Presidents of the college are often blamed and resign; members of the board of trustees are often blamed and resign. About the only thing that is not usually blamed is the inability of the institution to be creative and entrepreneurial. The focus is more often on what the school has been than on what it should become. Carmen Ambar Twilley, president of Oberlin College, has offered a warning to higher education at what she calls "an inflection point": "We need to stop asking 'Does this feel like us?' . . . and ask 'What's the right thing to do?'"[45] We need, in other words, to acknowledge that what the college was like twenty years ago will mean little to its students twenty years from now—or two years from now. What will matter is how we are meeting the needs of the students who have yet to enroll.

The bottom line? There might not be a single obvious right answer to Twilley's question about the "right thing," but there are some obvious wrong answers: chasing rankings to alter reputation is one, clinging to the past at the expense of the present and future is another. Macalester—or Carleton or Grinnell or Lawrence or Monmouth or even Columbia—might forever be consigned to a place in the pecking order of *U.S. News*, but all have a chance to become more effective and accessible versions of themselves. That would most certainly be a right thing.

Chapter 3

Incentives

So why get wet? Why break a sweat?
Why waste your precious breath?
Why beat your handsome brow?
Nothing changes
Nothing changes
Nothing changes anyhow.

—Anaïs Mitchell

THE QUESTION I WAS ASKED most often during the last of my seventeen years as president of Macalester College, and a question I get asked from time to time still, is the following: What do you consider your most important accomplishment as president? Typically I either politely decline to speculate or offer some generality about institutional culture, alumni engagement, or diversity. If I were to be completely honest with the questioner—and completely honest with myself, which is the more difficult thing—I would say the following:

Nothing much.

This is neither false modesty nor self-pity, but a clear-eyed assessment of the actual difference that a president can make at a well-resourced, highly selective, deeply traditional college or university. I actually feel pretty good about my time at Macalester, since I managed to avoid the most damaging mistakes that a college president can make. I do not believe that I ever brought embarrassment to the institution; I did not run from my responsibilities; I did not mangle the budget; I did not make things worse. Fund-raising improved, the student body grew more diverse, and I like to think that I played some role in those developments. Those who believed me to be villainous were, I think, in the minority. And, of course,

I persisted for roughly three times the average tenure of a contemporary president, which brings to the college a certain reassuring sense of stability and allows medium-term plans to be carried out. If you are the president of a college gifted with financial health and a strong brand, your prime directive is similar to the line often but erroneously attributed to the Hippocratic Oath: "First, do no harm."[1] Such presidents are "like the chief executives of Chanel or Rolex, burnishing brands that operate at the highest end of the higher ed market."[2] To paraphrase comments made to me by two different presidents of very elite colleges, if my job was "not to screw things up," well, mission accomplished.

I have become something of a student of the encomia that are published when long-serving presidents retire, and mine might look familiar enough. During those seventeen years, we ran capital campaigns that met their goals—the goals are always designed so that they can be met, however long it takes—we built and renovated several buildings, we added new programs (though eliminated none) and enrolled class after class of terrific students. But these things happened before my arrival and will continue to happen now that I have departed. Parting tributes often mention the growth of the endowment, which almost never has much to do with the president and everything to do with asset allocation and investment returns, helped perhaps by the occasional very large gift. The one thing for which I deserve the most credit (or, in the opinion of some, blame) is leading a process that ended with the alteration of the college's policy of need-blind admissions, a step that was both financially prudent and hard to swallow. That was difficult, important, and professionally risky. As a result of that change, Macalester is on much firmer financial footing than it would otherwise have been, though it remains a shift that I wish had not been necessary.

What I did not manage to do was inspire any of the changes to the financial model, pedagogy, or tradition-bound processes about which I write in this book. As my opening story about teaching and research demonstrates, I did not even have much success in sparking discussion about such changes. Early on I was somewhat more willing to make my opinions known about curricular matters in particular, but—like someone who has touched an electrified fence—I came to realize that such actions brought pain but little progress. Because I sat at the top of "the administration," my interventions were as likely to harden opposition to change as they were to bring it about.

My history is a history of the problem and not the cure. I don't beat myself up about this because I fail to see how I could have done much more, stayed within the confines of college governance, managed the college effectively, and kept my job. There was no incentive whatsoever for me to attempt to be disruptive or transformational because the odds of success were so low and the price of trying was so high. Regardless of the fact that nearly every presidential job description and nearly every presidential search committee speaks to the desire for a "change agent," the truth is that an actual change agent is something that only the most desperate college communities want—and even the desperate ones are not sure about it.

In addition to being a student of presidential tributes, I am also a student of Macalester history, and so I have read much about the work of my most revered predecessors. James Wallace, president from 1894 to 1906, traveled the country raising money from Presbyterian donors for this new Presbyterian college: at that point Macalester was, in effect, a start-up, and absent his success in finding start-up funding it probably would not have survived. Charles Turck, president from 1939 to 1958 (making me number two in length of service), shifted the focus of the college in the years after World War II to the education of what he called "citizens of the world," a move that was not without attendant controversy but that shaped the institution in fundamental ways. That came at a point in the postwar era when higher education more broadly in the United States was rapidly expanding and seemed more open to change than usual. John B. Davis, president from 1975 to 1984, is often referred to as "the man who saved Macalester": when DeWitt Wallace, son of James, founder of *Reader's Digest*, and for decades the college's largest donor, withdrew his support in the early 1970s, Macalester came within a hair of shutting its doors. Davis brought Wallace back into the fold and kept morale up during a period of deep fiscal stress. Macalester then had more in common with today's struggling private colleges than with Carleton or Grinnell. When *Reader's Digest* went public in 1990, the college's endowment ballooned suddenly to over $300 million due to stock gifts from Wallace and its fortunes changed dramatically.[3]

During all of these periods, Macalester seems to have been, by choice or necessity, a reasonably malleable institution. By the time I arrived in the fall of 2003, it was a college with an endowment of a half-billion dollars and a place in the top twenty-five-ish of *U.S. News and World Report*. Different time, different place, very different challenges and opportunities for its president.

One of the distinctive, and distinctively complicating, features of higher education is the number and variety of the constituencies that believe they have some right to "ownership" of the institution. Boards of trustees, administrators, faculty members, students, parents, and alumni all in some sense consider a college or university to be "theirs." For public institutions, legislatures, governors, and even taxpayers can be added to the list. Each of these groups has little power to create change on its own but considerable power to impede it. Each itself comprises individuals with a wide variety of opinions. Finding common cause within any group, let alone across a spectrum of these groups, can seem like an impossible task. Though the legal answer to the question of who owns a nonprofit is "no one," the reality sometimes feels closer to "everyone."[4]

For change beyond the incremental to occur in higher education, some, most, or all of these constituencies must want it to happen—that is, must have the proper incentive structure. Psychologists and economists in particular have devoted years of research and reams of paper to examining the role of incentives in human behavior, but at bottom the role of incentives is not hard to fathom: people usually try to do things that they believe will lead to positive consequences, however defined, and to avoid things that they believe will lead to negative consequences. Sometimes incentives are divided into the intrinsic and extrinsic. Intrinsic incentives are those that come from within and stem from one's belief in the value or simple pleasure of a task; extrinsic incentives are things such as money, promotions, recognition, not getting burned by touching a hot stove—or not getting fired. Since profound change is so difficult, few people will be inspired to undertake it purely on the basis of intrinsic incentives, which means that it must be encouraged by extrinsic incentives as well.[5]

Given the competing goals and multiple constituencies within higher education, and the status of most institutions as not-for-profit, the extrinsic motivations are much more varied and complex than for, say, a publicly traded, for-profit company. For the majority of such companies, the main incentive is to make as much money as possible, not simply because most people like to make money (though there's that), but because the boards of such companies are legally required to make the interests of their shareholders (that is, money) their top priority: they are bound by what are known as the "duty of care" and the "duty of loyalty" to focus on profitability.[6] Some companies, public and private, are trying to expand their range of incentives by becoming what are known as B Corps—that is, corporations whose responsibilities also include commitment to things like environmental sustainability, the social good, and the welfare of their employees.[7] Even for such corporations, however, the range of incentives remains relatively narrow and clearly defined.

Higher education, by contrast, is marked by varied and competing incentives. Leadership guru Jim Collins notes that "for a social sector organization, . . . performance must be assessed relative to mission, not financial returns."[8] Fair enough. But compared with most "social sector" organizations, colleges and universities are marked by less agreement about precisely what that mission is and how it should be carried out, which often leads to competing definitions of success and to competing priorities. The extrinsic incentives of a tenured faculty member and an incoming student or of a college president and an alumnus are often not aligned and are sometimes incompatible. About the only consistency across all of these groups is that none is motivated by obvious incentives to push for transformational change.

Many discussions of change in higher education focus on the role of the president, despite the fact that the majority of college and university presidents have little opportunity and less incentive to act aggressively as change agents. Most presidential job descriptions read like calls for a messiah: the 2022 search prospectus for the presidency of Drew University proclaimed that the university "seeks a bold visionary who is innovative, entrepreneurial, inspiring, and financially astute." Don't we all.[9] In reality most presidents are far from messianic, and it is not even clear if a messiah could be transformational within most college and university settings. Presidents of nonprofit colleges are less like CEOs of for-profit companies than like mayors of small to midsized cities—though mayors who are subject to recall at any moment. Mayors have city councils and taxpayers and unions and school boards and zoning commissions and a whole host of other groups that limit their ability to act either unilaterally or ambitiously; college presidents have faculty senates and boards of trustees and students and (sometimes) unions and other groups that similarly limit their power and influence. Mayors at least have the advantage of having been popularly elected; presidents are selected by small search committees and are sometimes considered illegitimate even before they arrive on campus. Nearly all mayors, moreover, belong to a particular political party and can therefore take clear positions on a range of divisive issues. College presidents are increasingly hesitant to take any positions on anything. In a recent survey of more than 150 presidents conducted by the *Chronicle of Higher Education*, 93 percent anticipated that speaking publicly about national politics would be very or somewhat controversial. Even on issues that related more directly to campus life such as gender and sexual identity, racial justice, free speech, and COVID-19 policies, a majority expected any remarks they made to be controversial. "Now," one president observed, "you have to make sure you don't ruffle feathers no matter what you feel or what your conscience is dictating."[10] This caution might seem, and sometimes is, self-serving, and it has in my view served neither higher education nor civil society well, but controversy can bring risk to the institution by threatening important things like state appropriations and alumni donations.[11]

The college presidency is becoming an increasingly tenuous job. According to a survey done by the American Council on Education, the average presidential tenure declined from 8.5 years in 2006 to 6.5 years in 2017. It is hard to imagine that the average tenure has not declined further in ensuing years.[12] The survey showed that nearly 45 percent of presidencies lasted four years or less—that is, no longer than the stay of the (slight) majority of undergraduates. Presidents of public institutions are the most transient, lasting on average about five years. A 2018 study by the Community College League of California revealed that the tenure of presidents and chancellors within that system declined from 7.2 years between 1998 and 2008 to 5.2 years between 2008 and 2018. While the data for earlier decades are sketchy, it does seem as if it was much more common in the years before 1980 for presidents to serve considerably longer terms. For every Leon Botstein (nearly a half century and counting at Bard College), there used to be multiple Frederic Boatwrights (fifty-one years at the University of Richmond), Nicholas Murray Butlers (forty-three years at Columbia), and Charles William Eliots (forty years at Harvard).[13] While some presidents of better-resourced institutions are awarded tenure and can slide into faculty positions, the majority are simply let go—admittedly, at times, with healthy severance packages.

Faculty votes of no-confidence in presidents are also on the rise. In 2021, "at least 24 institutions saw votes of no-confidence in their leaders," the highest number on record. "Seven years out of the last eight have seen the highest number of no-confidence votes recorded." And while it might appear that such votes are losing their impact, since 1989 the presidents who were the subject of such votes were out within a year over 50 percent of the time.[14]

Either presidents are getting steadily worse or, more likely, it is getting steadily more difficult to succeed at the job. While there are examples of presidents behaving unethically, inappropriately, or incompetently, these instances are, in the greater scheme of things, relatively rare, or at least no less rare than faculty members behaving in this way. The much greater visibility of presidents, however, draws disproportionate attention to these examples and colors the perception, both inside and outside higher education, of the people who take on the challenges of the presidency. I've met many. The vast majority are thoughtful and principled people trying their best to do a nearly undoable job. The vast majority are also under enormous pressure on a daily basis and spend far less time thinking about transformational change than about dealing with the current crisis or fending off waves of criticism. As is often the case in critiques of higher education, there is a tendency to blame individuals for problems or failures that are in fact structural and systemic. My answer to a question posed in the *Boston Globe*—"College presidents are leaders, but why not innovators?"—is simple: because in reality, job descriptions notwithstanding, they are not actually hired to be innovators and are not provided with the conditions within which to innovate.[15]

Given the precariousness and difficulty of the position, there are virtually no incentives for most college presidents to try to be true change agents. If being a president is like walking a tightrope, being one who tries to change things in a major way is like walking a tightrope blindfolded while hopping on one foot. Without a net. The risk might be worth taking if the president actually had the ability to change things, but given the nature of shared governance (which I shall explore in a later chapter) and the entrenched resistance to change, that ability for most presidents exists only on the margins. What Richard Chait says about tenure reform can be applied, to one degree or another, to any push for institutional change that is more than incremental: it "consumes too much political capital at too fast a pace with too uncertain a payoff to justify the effort."[16]

The easiest way to survive for extended time in a presidency is to stay in your lane: raise money, give speeches, show up at sporting events, and balance the budget. But do not try to interfere with the actual, core academic work of the institution. There be dragons.

Sometimes circumstances will give presidents the opportunity to act with boldness or courage and to make a difference on a particular issue. I can think of many presidents who responded to tragedies or protests on campus or to external events in ways that truly mattered. Presidents can improve relations with alumni, lift up the importance of issues like diversity and sexual violence prevention, build stronger bridges to the local community. These accomplishments are not unimportant, but they are essentially doing the same things more effectively, not doing things that are disruptive or transformational. They are examples of steering the boat skillfully but not of rocking it.

Presidents who enter determined against all odds to be change agents usually have a very short half-life. Often they come from the worlds of business, politics, law, health care, or the military and end up like Admiral William McRaven, who managed to lead Navy Seal teams and the United States Special Operations Command but was defeated by the University of Texas system after three years.[17] Chait, reflecting on the challenges faced by these leaders, notes that "in order to be successful, those presidents need to adapt to the culture of the institution they're running rather than expect the institution to adapt to them"—which is exactly right but is hardly a recipe for anything resembling change agency.[18] These business leaders "are often hired to shake up the status quo," learn that the status quo is not having any part of being shaken up, and either adapt or depart.[19]

What about the exceptions? There are in fact a handful of recent and current presidents who have done more than steer the ship and have more dramatically transformed their institutions: extraordinary individuals like Freeman Hrabowski, who, through three decades of leadership, grew the University of Maryland, Baltimore County, from "a small school in the suburbs of Baltimore, into one of the nation's top producers of engineers and scientists of color."[20] But systemic change cannot be dependent on the work of extraordinary individuals, who are, by definition, rare. Michael Crow of Arizona State represents a different and more divisive kind of transformational leader, one who pretty much ignores processes like shared governance, imports a corporate model into an academic context, and imposes his will on an institution. He has in two decades grown Arizona State from a well-known "party school" to the largest and least traditional public university in the country. Both his style and his vision are polarizing but clearly have impact.[21] During Leon Botstein's half-century tenure at Bard, the college has served as "a kind of petri dish for his many pedagogical hypotheses" and has ignored most rules about everything from fund-raising to the admissions process.[22] He is a force of nature, but nature has only so many forces.

Without dismissing the abilities of these presidents, I remain skeptical of the claim that they are simply more inspirational or visionary than others, and believe the truth to be more complicated. One thing that these unusual presidents clearly have in common is placement at an institution that is at least somewhat ripe for change. The University of Maryland, Baltimore County, was a fairly new, struggling campus when Hrabowski arrived; Arizona State was not highly regarded; and Bard was severely underresourced relative to most of its peers. Place Hrabowski at Dartmouth, Crow at the University of Michigan, or Botstein at Bowdoin and their impact, I suspect, would be very different. Another factor is a tenure that is measured in decades rather than years: changing a college takes time that most leaders are not permitted. My own experience might or might not be typical, but as a relatively young, first-time college president, I felt during my initial years as if I were doing two jobs at once: being a president and proving to people that I *could be* a president. There is a trial period in these jobs during which the most pressing questions within the community are very basic: What kind of person is this? Does he know what he's doing? Can he be trusted (or as trusted as a president ever manages to be)? Is he committed to this place, or is this a stepping-stone to something else? People who ignore the importance of these questions tend not to remain in their position for very long. Only after this period had passed—maybe three or four years—did I feel as if I could devote myself fully to the actual work of the presidency.

Boards of trustees are the ones responsible for hiring (and firing) the president and for safeguarding the mission of the institution. The composition of these boards makes it unlikely that they will push for dramatic change in anything other than the most extreme set of circumstances. The boards of regents of public universities in the majority of states are appointed by the governor or the governor in concert with the legislature and tend to be guided more by the priorities of electoral politics than by a deep knowledge of higher education.[23] Since most states are under Republican control, this means a lot of drama about critical race theory, transgender athletes, and the radical "wokeness" of college campuses but not a lot of concern about what any particular college is actually doing. Free speech is championed, unless it's the kind of speech they don't like, in which case bills are introduced to prohibit it. In states controlled by Democrats, the focus is largely on price, in the form of various "free tuition" programs, and not on either cost or quality. New Mexico recently signed into law, with great fanfare, a generous free tuition plan for state residents, without emphasizing that it was funded for one year only, largely with pandemic relief dollars, or explaining how the graduation rate of roughly 50 percent at its flagship university would be improved.[24]

This is not the case at private institutions, whose boards tend to be more sizable and composed chiefly of alumni, parents, and others with a close connection to the college or university. In my experience, they generally care deeply about the institutions they oversee, but they are part of a large group—according to the Association of Governing Boards, the average size is twenty-nine—whose engagement with the college is episodic and whose role is split between governance and providing philanthropic support. R. Owen Williams, former president of Transylvania University, whose board at one point numbered an impressive fifty-five people, rightly observed that "to govern effectively, you have to know as much as you can about the underlying enterprise" and that many board members "tended not to know as much as they needed to know."[25] The Association of Governing Boards, moreover, includes among the jobs of a college board selecting the president, assuming fiduciary responsibility, and overseeing the work of faculty and students—but not driving change.[26] Boards that have strayed too far from these responsibilities and that have pushed for substantial institutional change have tended to get battered by other campus constituencies. The rare trustee is willing to take on that burden, but most would prefer to attend the periodic meeting and then return to the main business of their lives.

Alumni might seem like a group well positioned to push for change, since they far outnumber current students and faculty and are relied on for philanthropic support. But while alumni will often lobby for change on matters related to large social issues—racial justice and divestment from fossil fuels are at the top of the list—they tend to be relatively silent and even reactionary on matters related to basic operations or the curriculum. If they are engaged enough to care about the college, it is likely that they feel wedded to some program or activity that positively affected their lives; to no new initiative or alteration in practice do they feel a comparable bond. They also have much closer ties to faculty, who often stick around for a very long time, than to the latest people to pass through the revolving administrative door, and therefore to be more aligned with faculty resistance to change than with a call for change from the top. Who are you going to trust: your beloved history professor or a president you've never met? In all my time at Macalester, I can think of no instance in which an alumnus or group of alumni advocated strongly for the elimination of or dramatic change to anything, aside from a few politically conservative alumni who, like their legislative cousins, felt that subjects like gender studies and the study of racism should go away. But even a hint that a program might be eliminated, no matter how underenrolled or ineffective it might be in its current form, drew howls of protest and threats to withhold gifts that had often never been made in the first place. Expecting alumni to endorse a radical change in direction of their alma mater is like expecting the fans of a baseball team to cheer the trade of a beloved player who is well past his prime: emotion will trump rational judgment almost every time.

Colleges also shy away from telling alumni that change is necessary. In one of countless "how-to" articles about alumni engagement, Sara Jackson writes that "every alum wants to hear how their alma mater is sprinting and advancing. . . . No alum wants to hear that enrollment is down, staff/faculty are unhappy, and the university is hurting for money."[27] Since at most colleges enrollment is down, staff and faculty are unhappy, and everyone is hurting for money, this makes for something of a communications challenge. Alumni magazines are resolutely upbeat, with just enough mild self-criticism—maybe a letter from a disgruntled alumnus—to seem admirably frank. But unless the institution is very obviously on the brink of shutting down, "sprinting and advancing" will not be replaced by "limping and hanging by a thread."

Given the ubiquity of protests, sit-ins, and building occupations on college campuses, it might appear that students are arguing for transformational change. To the extent that this is true, it applies to a very specific and circumscribed set of issues. These tend to fall into one of two categories: those that relate to social justice and those that would benefit current students. The vast majority of student protests are aimed at social and political issues that affect but neither are limited to nor originate on college campuses: racism, climate change, sexual violence, Israel and Palestine, living wages, unionization. Understandably, they want their institutions to become more diverse and inclusive, more committed to sustainable practices; more controversially, they often want their institutions to take positions on issues that might be divisive and that stand at a distance from the educational mission or to prohibit the appearance of speakers whose views are unpopular. They are angry about matters as important as student debt and mental health and as quotidian as campus food and funding for clubs. They want names removed from buildings and faculty added to overenrolled departments. Like virtually everyone else in our anxious and fractured country, they want things to be *better*. Absent other places to be heard, they raise their voices and take out their frustrations on the campuses they call home.

But these actions are quite different from pushing for change to the fundamental structures and practices of higher education. It would be unreasonable and unrealistic to expect this from students, who tend to view the academic programs and approaches that existed when they matriculated as stable and whose lives would mostly be complicated by the disruption of those programs and approaches. How does a current student benefit from the elimination of a department, changes to the calendar, or alterations in the financial model? I have no doubt that, if asked to vote, the overwhelming majority of students at every college and university in the country would choose to increase the current endowment draw to enhance operations at the expense of future generations: not because they are selfish but because they are human and because something as distant and unclear as an endowment seems like an easy and obvious source of funding. I can say the same of students as I said of alumni, but more emphatically: not once in seventeen years did any lobby me to eliminate anything, while hardly a day went by when one or more did not lobby me to add something new or expand something beyond its current size. Even the most politically radical students are, when it comes to the preservation of the academic programs they know, conservative.

Also like alumni, students are deeply reluctant to criticize faculty on programmatic matters (as opposed to issues like inclusivity in the classroom and sexual harassment), even when those matters are almost entirely under faculty control. Typically, when they are angry about the absence of a particular major or about hiring in a particular department, they train their ire on "the administration"; more often than not, "the administration" has far less decision-making authority on these issues than does the faculty. Students at Macalester frustrated at their inability to get into computer science or biology courses did not complain to the faculty members who voted not to discontinue underenrolled departments: they complained to the provost or the president, despite our very limited power to do very much about it. This is wholly understandable. On a college campus, faculty hold power over students: both tangibly in the form of grading and less tangibly on the basis of classroom dynamics. They are the experts and, with the occasional exception, command respect and even adulation. Administrators, by contrast, despite their lofty titles, actually hold little power over students except when those students do things like violate codes of conduct. Presidents and deans represent the forms of institutional authority against which students are inclined to chafe. Year after year, in our survey of incoming Macalester students, the majority indicated that they planned to participate in protests while in college without yet knowing against what or whom they would be protesting. If pressed to be more precise, my guess is that they would specify "the administration." When was the last time students occupied the office of a philosophy professor?

From time to time, students will push for change to course content, generally because they consider it to be insufficiently inclusive or excessively disturbing. This is especially true of required core courses. Students at Reed College protested against the "white supremacy" embedded in the school's hallmark Humanities 110 course.[28] Yale students demanded that the English Department "decolonise" the reading list in a required class.[29] But these arguments for change to a syllabus are very far from arguments for disruptive change to the business of education itself.

Of all the important constituencies within higher education, the one with the least incentive to change in ways beyond the incremental comprises full-time permanent faculty: those on the tenure track and—especially—those who are tenured. This is not because they are temperamentally or constitutionally or politically opposed to change or because they are stubborn; it is because there is little for them to gain and much for them to lose from transformation of the institution. It comes back to the question of extrinsic incentives. Unless the college is facing closure or dramatic cuts in compensation, a slow pace of change brings job security, the ability to repeat well-understood tasks, less power ceded to the administration, and all the basic comforts of the familiar. Professional life might not be ideal, but if you are tenured, it is more stable than that of the overwhelming majority of workers, including the staff and non-tenure-track (NTT) faculty at one's own institution. The pandemic has brought to higher education a host of additional sources of stress, but compared with the plight of a frontline worker in health care or the hospitality industry or retail, the situation of a tenured faculty member looks pretty good. And despite a steady stream of angry opinion pieces in the education press, most faculty members do seem to recognize this. A large-scale study of more than thirty thousand faculty conducted by the TIAA Institute in 2018 found that the majority were generally satisfied with their jobs—a surprise, perhaps, to those who, like me, have spent their adult lives attending faculty meetings.[30]

Transformational change, by contrast, brings increased risk of departmental closures, the introduction of new pedagogies and technologies, the promise of additional work, and all the disruption that comes with the unfamiliar. Even leaving aside the health risks, the pandemic has brought a taste of just how challenging and disorienting wholesale change can be. In this instance faculty had no choice; given a choice, how many people would elect to turn their worlds upside-down? This is perhaps the chief reason that disruptive change almost always comes from without: it is easier to train new employees in a new way of doing things than it is to convince existing employees to replace the old with the new. And when it comes to tenured faculty, replacing existing employees with new ones is simply not an option.

Other, more subtle roadblocks to pedagogical change in particular exist among faculty. Joel Smith and Lauren Herckis at Carnegie Mellon University attempted to understand why even faculty at one of the most technologically innovative institutions in the world were slow to adopt new teaching strategies. What they discovered, using anthropological research

methods, was that the impediments were far more cultural than intellectual. "Faculty typically form a very strong mental model of what consti-
tutes quality instruction in their discipline, *based on their own personal
educational experiences.*" This model is "difficult to displace, *even with
evidence-based alternatives*" (emphases theirs). Faculty, in other words,
were themselves taught in a particular way, had achieved a level of success on the basis of those teaching methods, and were strongly inclined to
reproduce those methods in their own work.[31] "Asking faculty to do something that conflicted with that model in any way," Smith subsequently
observed, "is a mistake."[32] Scott Freeman, who has for a decade been pushing for change in STEM pedagogy, makes a similar point:

> Although faculty are evidence-based people in their fields, we're
> still human beings. And often, people demanding levels of rigor
> and evidence in their field switch to teaching, and all of a sudden
> they go back to intuition. So commonly you'll hear from people
> that, well, it worked for me. Which means that something's wrong
> with my students, because it was fine for me and look where I am
> now. And that's just a human thing: personal empiricism.[33]

As Ray Schroeder concludes, "Emulating those who taught us is the default
approach to new faculty teaching. Whatever felt good to us as students is
the selected method."[34] This is why evidence-based arguments against
lecturing, such as those voiced by Eric Mazur, have for many faculty been
unpersuasive. Such a pattern is not unique to higher education but can be
found in other fields—such as the law—marked by long-standing ways of
working and by powerful resistance to the unfamiliar.

At this point it is only fair to acknowledge that there are many faculty
members at colleges and universities of every kind who are intrinsically
motivated to be pedagogically innovative. I have been privileged to learn
from and work with many of them. They would probably be the first to
admit, however, that their individual transformation has not led to more
wholesale institutional transformation and that the effort they've put into
being better teachers brings far more internal than external rewards at
most institutions. "The system," Freeman explains, "doesn't reward change,
especially in teaching. If you're an average faculty person and you read
these papers and talk to colleagues who are getting really excited about

teaching and innovating and seeing their students do better, you could say, well, that would be great, but that's going to cost a lot of time and energy."[35] And if you're at a highly selective institution, it's not going to bring a better chance of receiving tenure or a promotion. Derek Bok, too, writes that "the incentives for professors to improve their teaching are . . . remarkably weak." "In most four-year colleges, surveys of professors repeatedly find that the number of pages of published research is the single most important factor in making tenure and promotion decisions. Other studies covering a wide variety of four-year colleges have shown that research is routinely rewarded when salaries are set, while the number of hours spent on teaching is *negatively* [my emphasis] correlated with compensation."[36]

It takes a lot of intrinsic motivation to be innovative in the absence of extrinsic incentives and the presence of extrinsic impediments. Steven Mintz, an evangelist for change in higher education for more than a decade, acknowledges that "these gradual, piecemeal innovations may well have a cumulative impact" but suggests that "we should remain skeptical until evidence of large-scale change is apparent."[37]

There are three sizable groups within higher education that have plenty of extrinsic incentive to push for more than incremental change: NTT faculty, graduate students, and the many employees who are grouped together under the label "staff." Unfortunately these are the groups with the least power to effect change. When colleges speak of "shared governance," most members of these groups at most institutions are not included in the sharing. "If we want our institutions to change," Joshua Kim observes, "we should listen to those with the least status."[38] For the most part, in an industry as attuned to status as higher education, we do not.

It is by now widely known that the number of college faculty members who fall into the NTT category has been steadily increasing and today makes up a large majority of the whole. A report released by the American Association of University Professors, drawing on data from 2016, concludes that 73 percent of instructional positions at that time were off the tenure track. Full- and part-time NTT faculty occupy a majority of the teaching positions at institutions of every type.[39] They receive lower pay, fewer benefits, and far less recognition than their tenured and tenure-track colleagues: for this group, the status quo would surely seem ripe for disruption. Yet at many colleges NTT faculty have little role in decision-making at the departmental or institutional level and little leverage through which to increase that role, given the abundance of labor and shortage of jobs in most disciplines. For an increasing number of NTT faculty, the response to this problem has been to unionize. From 2013 to 2022, more than 120 new faculty union chapters have won recognition; during that period, "the number of faculty union chapters at private, nonprofit colleges has shot up by more than 80 percent."[40] But while unions might be an effective vehicle through which to improve wages, benefits, and job security, they are unlikely to be nearly as effective at or interested in transforming higher education. Many of the unions currently representing NTT faculty—such as the Service Employees International and the United Auto Workers— know a lot about negotiating labor contracts but very little about the particular enterprise in which NTT faculty are engaged.

Many PhD and master's degree students are in the same vulnerable, discontented position as NTT faculty—indeed, many serve as NTT faculty—and this group too has been engaged in some highly visible battles to unionize. Students studying for an MBA at Wharton or a PhD in computational science at MIT should be feeling quite optimistic, but for most students at less highly regarded institutions or in less employable fields, the graduate degree in its current form is risky and sometimes exploitative. Kevin Carey overgeneralizes when he argues that "universities see master's degree programs as largely unregulated cash cows that help shore up their bottom line"—but only slightly.[41] And PhD programs, especially in the humanities, continue to admit far too many students and produce far too many graduates for the job market: in one recent year, 1,150 new PhDs in history for 340 tenure-track openings, and that fails to account for all the historians with a recently granted PhD who are still looking for work.[42] The beneficiaries of these graduate programs are obvious: the universities who receive tuition dollars and low-cost instruction and the tenured and tenure-track faculty who get graduate assistants and the opportunity to teach graduate courses. The ones with the most power to effect change are the ones with the least incentive to do so.

The term *staff* at a college or university can refer to anyone from an instructional technology specialist to an admissions officer to a custodian. It is difficult to generalize about the motivations of this group to change, since a disruption of the current system would have a highly variable impact: some jobs would go away, some new ones would be added, and some would probably stay the same. What we can say is that this group has little to no ability to participate in decision-making at the highest levels. I suspect that the bylaws of Macalester College are typical in specifying a governance role for the board of trustees, the president, the CFO, and the faculty, but none for other staff. The faculty handbook is quite specific in describing the responsibilities and authority of the faculty; the staff handbook mostly describes employment expectations and codes of conduct. Absent from the many forms of equity championed on college campuses is equity between these two groups of essential employees. "Faculty and staff," Jeffrey Selingo notes, "occupy two very different worlds—a chasm like few others in the American economy."[43] Paula Krebs, executive director of the Modern Language Association, acknowledges that colleges have a "class system": "If faculty members occupy a position analogous to the upper class, staff members seem to be, if not exactly working class, then let's say second class."[44] When faculty members write that "the authority of academic administrators is only solid to the extent that they themselves are credible practitioners of the scholarly life" or that "participating meaningfully in a university community means being seen as a scholar," it doesn't take, well, a scholar to infer that the work of nonfaculty is seen as lacking authority and meaning.[45] Particularly striking is the fact that the op-eds from which these passages were taken were both published during the pandemic, when many of those whose work is seen as being of lesser importance did not have the luxury of working over Zoom.

Though there are no guarantees, one is most likely to find the incentives for disruptive change combined with the willingness to initiate it at institutions that are either brand-new or in a desperate struggle for survival. New, nonprofit colleges, of which there are few in the United States but more outside it, are usually constrained by the absence of resources and liberated by the absence of traditions; even the handful that do have resources, like Olin College of Engineering and Soka University, are more innovative than most of their established peers.[46] And when what economists call Stein's law—"If something cannot go on forever, it will stop"— goes from being a hypothesis to a stark reality, innovation can assume a whole new level of urgency. But "research reveals that stress does not inspire creative, pathbreaking thought," and stress combined with an absence of resources is a bad recipe for successful transformation.[47] Stein's law, however, seems more than a little applicable to the financial model of the majority of colleges and universities, so perhaps more schools will find incentives to innovate before it seems the only remaining response to desperation. If not, it is likely that change will come not from traditional higher education but from those whose extrinsic motivations are most clear: politicians and actors in the for-profit world.

The ideas of governors and legislators in states like Florida, Texas, Georgia, and Idaho—in fact in virtually every Republican-led state—are generally ill-formed and antithetical to free inquiry, but the motivation is absolutely clear: to get elected. Higher education in these states has become a frequent and visible punching bag not because it is among the most pressing problems in the state but because it is among the most inviting targets. For a party that has become increasingly reliant on the support of noncollege-educated voters, attacking college is a relatively low-risk, high-reward move—and higher education has been much less adept and courageous in responding to these attacks than have leaders in areas like reproductive rights, anti-racism, and gender equality. Democratic politicians, while far less aggressive and less threatening to academic freedom, are not above basing policy proposals on electoral calculations: the rush by many to support the forgiveness of student loans is less about the fairness or economic sense of such proposals than about the desire to appeal to voters in a particular demographic. The unwillingness of higher education seriously to address from within issues including rising costs, post-tenure review, and viewpoint diversity has left it particularly vulnerable to interference from without.

What I fear most of all is the disruption and eventual control of the less selective portion of the higher education market by for-profit entities for whom incentives are unambiguous and for whom contribution to the public good is a secondary concern. This also happens to be the portion of the market that admits a disproportionately high percentage of traditionally underserved students. We need only look at the largest nonprofit sector of the US economy, health care, to see how rapidly this can happen. Seventy percent of physicians in the United States are now "employed either by hospital systems or other corporate entities, such as private equity firms and health insurers." Insurance companies and private equity firms have been acquiring medical practices at a rapid rate: from the end of 2018 through 2020, the number grew by 32 percent.[48] Amazon recently purchased One Medical, a health-care provider with over seven hundred thousand patients, and most experts assume that it is just getting started.[49]

To date higher education has been of much less interest to entities like private equity firms than health care because it forms a much smaller portion of the US economy (less than 3 percent compared with about 20 percent), but even 3 percent of nearly $25 trillion is a lot of money. Eventually, if nonprofit higher education cannot fix itself, they will come.

It would be easy but wrong to be lulled into complacency by the relative incompetence of many players in the first wave of for-profit colleges: the combination of hundreds of billions of dollars, dissatisfied consumers, and a Supreme Court that never met a regulation it didn't want to eliminate will at some point draw better-funded and more skillful investors. Already this is happening in parts of the world with high demand and limited supply—headlines like "Investors Excited About Africa's Private Education Opportunity" and "Private Equity Flocks to African Education" are common—and there is reason to be concerned about the results.[50] A recent study by the National Bureau of Economic Research revealed the following: "Employing novel data on 88 private equity deals and 994 schools with private equity ownership, we find that private equity buyouts lead to higher enrollment and profits, but also to lower education inputs, higher tuition, higher per-student debt, lower graduation rates, lower student loan repayment rates, and lower earnings among graduates."[51] Look to health care for the explanation: "Private equity firms buy the practices and then their investors expect them to get their money back in roughly five to seven years at a 20% to 30% profit. . . . That's not a situation which leads to an expectation of long-term relationships and with investments in making the practices better—it's quite the opposite."[52] Just substitute "universities" for "practices" and you can foresee the impact of these predatory practices on an underserved community. Many of those who complain about the "corporatization" of higher education have never seen what *real* corporatization looks like, and it is not something we should wish on ourselves or our students.

My concern about the takeover of essential social services like health care and higher education by for-profit actors is the product not of an anticapitalist bias but of an understanding of incentives. Chip Paucek, CEO and cofounder of for-profit giant 2U, is wrong or deliberately misleading when he argues that the defining difference between for-profit and nonprofit educators is "tax status." Tax status is a sign of a more fundamental difference. "A profit motive," he writes, "does not inherently mean there can't be other, equally important motives."[53] Actually, it does. By law, "for-profit corporations hold the primary responsibility to sustain profitability and to grow the shareholders' investments."[54] Such corporations can be driven by other motivations as well, but—unless they are B Corps—those must be secondary to the profit motive. Profitability and contribution to the social good are by no means incompatible, but to date they have existed in what might be described as an uneasy marriage, with the former often coming at the expense of the latter. This is why even most free-market countries do not rely chiefly on for-profit providers in areas where the social good should be of paramount importance. Nonprofits, however, need to do more than point fingers: they need to look in the mirror. The inability of traditional health care and higher education to address their cost problems and inefficiencies has left the door wide open for the Amazons and 2U's of the world to step through it. No one who has had to navigate through the financial and logistical maze of a hospital stay or tried to figure out the price of an office procedure—or of college tuition—is likely to dismiss out of hand lower-cost and more consumer-friendly alternatives to the status quo.

The problem now is serious but simple. Those with the means to effect real change, financially secure colleges and universities, lack the incentive, while those with the incentive, financially endangered colleges and universities, lack the means. The ones with both the means (money) and the incentive (more money) are for-profit actors or nonprofits like Arizona State, Western Governors, and Southern New Hampshire, which act in many ways like for-profits. The most likely result, if nothing changes, will be higher education's version of the growing inequity that seems apparent in most aspects of our society: high-cost, high-touch education for the few and low-cost education of questionable quality for the many. The only way to alter this trajectory, as I discuss in my closing chapter, is to turn an apparent weakness into a strength—that is, to use constraint not as an impediment to but as a driver of innovation. If the current model offers a choice between quality and affordability, the answer must be to change the model.

Chapter 4

The Disciplines

We working in our silos, silos
We working in our silos, silos
Slowly, slowly, slowly, slowly.

—Falco Holmz

M ACALESTER COLLEGE ENROLLS about 2,100 students. The ratio of students to faculty is roughly ten to one (however such things are calculated, which remains something of a mystery to me). Faculty members are organized into thirty-two departments that offer thirty-eight different majors, thirty-nine minors, and ten interdisciplinary concentrations. The largest department (Math, Statistics, and Computer Science) has almost twenty tenured or tenure-track positions; the smallest (Women's, Gender, and Sexuality Studies) has two. Each department is supported by a department coordinator, or a portion of the time of a department coordinator. Each department has a budget and a chair who gets a reduction in teaching load. For the purposes of the curriculum, the departments are organized into four divisions—Natural Sciences, Social Sciences, Humanities, and Fine Arts—though in most ways they don't behave as collective entities. When I departed in 2020, the Natural Science division was the only one that had a divisional chair and regular meetings; the Fine Arts faculty met from time to time; the various departments in the Social Sciences didn't get along well enough to meet; and the only time I can remember the humanists acting as a collective is when they united to complain that the scientists were getting too many resources and too much attention.

During my time at Macalester, no department was discontinued (more on that later), though, as at many colleges and universities, enrollment patterns shifted sharply away from the humanities and toward the natural sciences. From time to time a tenure-track line was reallocated from one department to another. No new departments were added, though new majors, minors, and concentrations were added in areas including but not limited to Arabic, Applied Mathematics, Chinese, Community and Global Health, and Human Rights and Humanitarianism. The student body size grew by a couple hundred, while the student-to-faculty ratio remained unchanged.

Little of this is unusual. Earlham College, which according to its website in 2023 has 653 students, offers forty-one majors, which makes for an impressive student-to-major ratio of sixteen to one, along with forty minors and sixteen "applied minors."[1] Minnesota State Mankato, with about fourteen thousand students, offers 130 undergraduate programs and "over 85" graduate programs. Community colleges tend to be chopped up into fewer pieces: Kingsborough Community College in Brooklyn also serves about fourteen thousand full- and part-time students: its faculty is organized into only fifteen departments, though they do offer thirty-seven degree programs. One would need a calculator to determine how many departments and programs were on the menu at a flagship public or large, selective private university.

This sort of atomization at colleges and universities is not limited to the faculty. It's harder to count the number of administrative departments since they tend to overlap and interweave, but at Macalester there were dozens, running not from A to Z but at least from A (Academic Programs and Advising) to W (Web Services). Some are quite large, and some comprise only a couple of people. During my presidency, some were adept at communicating with other administrators and with faculty, while others seemed equally adept at avoiding all forms of communication beyond the walls of their offices.

Very few if any other industries are chopped into as many different, highly specialized pieces as higher education. Very few have so few interchangeable parts and so little organizational flexibility. Very few, as a result, are so agonizingly difficult to change.

The estimable Clark Kerr, first chancellor of the University of California, Berkeley, famously described the American university as "a series of individual faculty entrepreneurs held together by a common grievance over parking." For Robert Maynard Hutchins of the University of

Chicago, the unifying feature was the heating system.[2] They were not far off, though I would add two caveats: first, most faculty members are not in fact entrepreneurs—entrepreneurs by definition create new enterprises and take risks—and second, when faculty members are not acting as free agents, they do sometimes think of themselves as belonging to a "department" and a discipline. Nevertheless, the central point made by Kerr and Hutchins, that the university is less a coherent organization than a loosely connected assemblage of disparate parts, is correct.

Ask a faculty member that strange question of which Americans are so fond—"What do you do?"—and you're much more likely to get an answer like, "I'm a biologist," or "I'm a historian," than "I'm a college professor." (The exception is if the person teaches at a hyperelite institution, in which case the answer is more likely to be, "I teach at Stanford," or, to paraphrase David Sedaris, "I work at a school in the Boston area.")[3] Faculty members, in other words, are more inclined to think of themselves as members of a sort of disciplinary guild than as members of a collective body called the faculty of a college. Why is this the case, and how does it affect the operations of an institution?

To answer these questions, we need to begin by looking at the history and present nature of graduate education, the products of which make up the faculties of most colleges and universities. "Faculty . . . are formed by their graduate training," David Rosowsky and Bridget Keegan correctly observe. "That formation—a remembrance of what was—shapes expectations of what should be."[4] So let us consider the expectations.

The advanced degree of choice in academia is the PhD, which began to be offered in the United States in the middle of the nineteenth century as one of many imported features of German universities. While the degree of "Doctor of Philosophy" was awarded as early as the Middle Ages, the PhD in something like its modern form, based on excellence in research, was first awarded by the University of Berlin (now Humboldt University) in 1810 and was inextricable from the idea of the university as primarily a center of scholarship rather than a center of teaching.[5] At this and other German universities, Andrew Delbanco notes, "academic freedom prevailed, research laboratories as well as graduate seminars first attained their modern form, and 'professors could function exclusively as scholars and researchers' since they 'did not have to bother themselves with remedying undergraduate deficiencies.'"[6] For several decades American students would have to travel to Europe to obtain doctoral degrees, until Yale University awarded the first PhDs in the United States in 1861 and was followed over the next two decades by the University of Pennsylvania, Harvard, and Princeton.[7] Many students still went abroad to study, but the shift to an American-based graduate system had begun.

The PhD remained a niche degree in the United States until the formation in 1900 of the Association of American Universities. This effort to raise the standards and visibility of graduate education was led by presidents including Charles William Eliot of Harvard and Benjamin Ide Wheeler of California, who had themselves studied under the German model.[8] The association has expanded from the original fourteen members to sixty-five today, which appears to be growth at a reasonably modest pace over more than a century. In 1900, three hundred PhDs were awarded by universities in the United States; that number has risen steadily in the ensuing decades, though it appears to have peaked and has held steady during the past several years at about fifty-five thousand per year—roughly twice what it was fifty years earlier.[9] That growth is not so modest, and the plateau in recent years has come at a time when undergraduate enrollment has been declining. A number of universities have paused or reduced admissions to certain graduate programs as a consequence of the pandemic, but it remains to be seen whether this is a temporary lull or a permanent shift.[10]

Much of this explosive spread of graduate education can be explained by the needs of society, the rise in the number of college graduates seeking further training, and the creation and expansion of new fields of knowledge. But an equally important explanation has to do with the needs and priorities of the universities themselves and the faculty who populate them. While the demand for PhDs in computer science or economics is stronger than ever, it has been years—decades—since the demand for PhDs in most areas of the humanities or social sciences was anywhere close to the endless, enormous supply. In 2019, pre-pandemic, the highly ranked English department at Columbia University placed only a single PhD graduate into a tenure-track position while admitting nineteen new students into the program.[11] This is not an exception but the rule, and it is getting worse: as Leonard Cassuto, whose book *The Graduate School Mess* remains the definitive study of the graduate school mess, wryly observes, "Thousands of professors are currently in the business of preparing thousands of graduate students for jobs that don't exist."[12] Yet the cycle continues because graduate students have for a long time been the fuel that powers the engine of the modern research university, or at least of the portion that purports to be the core: the arts and sciences.

Every research university with PhD students relies heavily on those students to teach undergraduates at a cost that is much lower than the cost of full-time faculty and in order to reduce the number of part-time faculty that need to be hired. Determining the precise number of courses taught by graduate students at most universities can be challenging, since this tends not to be a number featured on admissions tours or the "Quick Facts" web page and since teaching can mean anything from having full responsibility for a course to assisting with grading. But the number is high. In 2017, about 26 percent of courses at universities including Purdue and South Florida were taught by graduate students, and in the same year, according to the Bureau of Labor Statistics, universities relied on over 135,000 graduate assistants.[13] Even with declining undergraduate enrollments, the cost of replacing these graduate instructors with other faculty would blow apart the financial model at most universities, and at the most prestigious universities undergraduate enrollment is not declining. Another option, of course, would be to increase the teaching load of full-time faculty. Good luck with that. Interestingly, and despite their receiving almost no pedagogical training, graduate instructors generally do a pretty good job: according to a study in the *Economics of Education Review*, "undergraduates are *more* [my emphasis] likely to major in a subject if their first course in the subject was taught by a graduate student."[14] Whether this tells us more about graduate instructors or about everyone else is difficult to know.

My undergraduate years were a very long time ago, but I suspect that my experience would seem familiar to a current undergraduate at the same university. My freshman seminar was taught by a grad student in comparative literature; my introductory courses in chemistry and psychology were large lectures supported by discussion sections with grad students; most of my papers in my literature surveys were graded by grad students; and nearly all my work in math and physics was done with grad students. It was not until I moved into upper-level courses in my major that my instruction and grading were provided wholly by full-time faculty members. Sometimes I got to know these grad students well, sometimes they were simply names on a graded paper or rotating assistants in a tutorial. The teaching done by these students was presumably intended to prepare them for their future careers as professors, but in fields where there are virtually no jobs as professors, it is hard to see the work as career preparation and easy to see it as comparatively inexpensive labor. This is precisely the argument being made by graduate assistants who are unionizing and sometimes striking at more and more universities: they see graduate teaching not as "preparation for a decently paying academic job that may never arrive" but as work that they do for a limited time before leaving the academy.[15] The reason it takes longer on average to get a PhD in the humanities than a PhD in mechanical engineering or biology is not because of the challenges of the discipline but because the graduate student in the humanities has no incentive to enter the job market.[16]

The second crucial role played by graduate students is to enable full-time faculty members to teach graduate courses. "Just about every professor," Cassuto writes, "wants to teach graduate school. Lots of them regard it practically as their birthright . . . which isn't so unusual when you consider that the experience invokes their own birth as professional intellectuals." Teaching within American universities has a very well-established hierarchy, "with graduate teaching perched at its summit."[17] Here is the sad peculiarity of the food chain within American higher education: the further one gets from teaching undergraduates, the less of such teaching one does, the more distinguished one is considered. Adjuncts or community college faculty who teach eight or ten courses each year and carry out what is supposed to be the core work of education are far less highly regarded within the profession than endowed professors at elite universities who teach maybe one or two courses a year, and those often to small groups of graduate students.

Graduate teaching affords benefits beyond status. Especially in the humanities and some of the social sciences, graduate curricula have few requirements and less coherence. (Though this creeps into the natural sciences as well: PhD students in chemistry at MIT have a total of zero required courses.) Within only the most flexible of boundaries, teachers of graduate students get to teach whatever they want. Undergraduate curricula in disciplines like English and history are very loosely constructed, but compared with graduate curricula they are models of forethought and coherence. Cassuto again: "Term by term, year by year, the graduate course offerings in humanities departments don't make sense together. They're a hodgepodge of specialized inquiries: snapshots of books and articles in progress by professors who know what they're determined to teach, but not what their students need most to learn. Nor do most professors know what their colleagues are teaching alongside them."[18]

My PhD dissertation was on Charles Dickens. I did not take a single course in graduate school in which a novel by Dickens was on the syllabus because the Dickens expert was on a two-year research leave (ponder that for a moment) and other faculty closest to my area of study chose to teach courses on Virginia Woolf and Thomas Hardy (but not George Eliot or Henry James), Percy Shelley and Lord Byron (but not John Keats), and John Ruskin (but not Matthew Arnold). If you're a graduate student in English, you take what you can get. If you're a faculty member in English teaching graduate courses, what a treat to be able to teach what interests you most and to combine work on your latest book or article with your class preparation. Scale back the number of graduate students and you might be forced to teach the second semester of a British literature survey to sophomores.

The organization of graduate curricula around faculty specializations creates a cadre of specialists, when both higher education and other professions are far more in need of generalists. Not once—not once—during my time in graduate school was I encouraged to think of myself as a member of a university-wide group. As someone focused on nineteenth-century British literature, I had limited contact not only with graduate students outside the English Department but with students within the department whose focus was on American literature and whose faculty were mostly housed in a different building. Despite a gesture toward breadth on my oral examinations, my area of study was extremely narrow. When I became one of the fortunate few to land a tenure-track job—at a small liberal arts college—I was immediately asked to teach introductory literature of all kinds and, naturally, a survey of British literature from the sixteenth through the eighteenth centuries. The last time I had even read *Paradise Lost* was in my own literature survey as a sophomore in college.

This crazy quilt of courses and specializations is what led Derek Bok to complain that "graduate schools are among the most poorly administered and badly designed of all the advanced degree programs in the university"—an impressive statement considered the context.[19] PhD programs somehow manage to make law schools look good by comparison.

All of this explains why *U.S. News and World Report* in 2022 listed more PhD programs in English (157) or history (146) than in economics (139). This has virtually nothing to do with external factors and everything to do with the internal dynamics of universities. If almost no graduates in English from Columbia, ranked 8th by *U.S. News* in that discipline, are getting good jobs in academia, what are the prospects for graduates of programs ranked 50th or 150th, when prestige plays so important a role in the faculty hiring process?

For here is another poorly kept secret about American higher education: faculty hiring committees are as fixated on reputation as are the avid consumers of *U.S. News* rankings. According to a comprehensive study published in *Nature*, just five universities—Berkeley, Harvard, Michigan, Madison, and Stanford—produce about one-eighth of the nation's tenure-track faculty members. Eighty percent of those faculty members earned their degrees at 20 percent of the research universities in the country. "Prestige," the authors of the study observe,

> plays a central role in structuring the US professoriate. Analyses of faculty hiring networks, which map who hires whose graduates as faculty, show unambiguously in multiple fields that prestigious departments supply an outsized proportion of faculty, regardless of whether prestige is measured by an extrinsic ranking or reputation scheme or derived from the structure of the faculty hiring network itself. Prestigious departments also exhibit "social closure" by excluding those who lack prestige, facilitated by relatively stable hierarchies over time, both empirically and in mathematical models of self-reinforcing network dynamics.[20]

Not only is the market for PhDs in most disciplines vastly oversupplied: it is effectively rigged. One of the ways for a struggling college to signal its legitimacy and quality is to announce that its new hire in English or sociology has a PhD from a university with a reputation far stronger than its own. It's difficult for even a supremely gifted graduate of a less prestigious university to get past an initial screening of candidates, let alone to get hired.

It is at this point virtually impossible for most graduate faculty in struggling disciplines to be unaware that their programs are broken.

Efforts to fix them, however, crash up against a nearly impenetrable wall of resistance to change. In 2015, the National Endowment for the Humanities began issuing grants as part of a program called the Next Generation Humanities PhD, whose "goal was to focus on what the NEH delicately called 'disparities between graduate-student expectations for a career in academe and eventual career outcomes,' and to further the role of the humanities in public life."[21] Planning or implementation grants were awarded to universities including Princeton, Fordham, Washington State, Penn State, Duke, and many others. The program was "quietly canceled" only two years later, having had an impact that might generously be described as negligible. The reasons cited by some of the participants for its failure are unsurprising:

> Many grantees reflected that curricular committees make it difficult to add new courses, especially when coordination among multiple departments was necessary. . . . [Success] would require dramatically rethinking the timeline and content of Ph.D. education—a logistically challenging and existentially fraught task that few departments are eager to tackle. . . . Attempts to transform the dissertation were even more disappointing. Several colleges expressed interest in this idea . . . but few actually tackled it. . . . Most grantees noted some degree of faculty opposition to changing graduate education, resting on a combination of unfamiliarity, overwork, and a commitment to traditional, tenure-track-oriented career prep. . . . Many faculty members felt deep discomfort in talking about the issues, and clung to the notion that preparation for nonacademic careers was something graduate students might do "personally, not as part of their training."[22]

In a novel by Richard Russo or Jane Smiley, this would be the stuff of dark comedy. Outside the world of fiction, however, it is very bad news for current and future graduate students in the humanities and in other disciplines with a shrinking number of tenure-track jobs. Steven Mintz has described the "cries of anguish" from these students, and he is not far off, given the unwillingness of graduate programs to adapt to present circumstances.[23] A survey conducted at four campuses of the University of California (Berkeley, Davis, San Diego, and Merced) found that more PhD students in the humanities reported receiving career advice from "friends and other" than from faculty or their departments.[24] Given the fact that faculty seem to have little advice to offer, this is, I suppose, unsurprising.

There is a glimmer of good news, at least for graduate students in the humanities. At a handful of universities, departments have begun incorporating preparation for nonacademic careers into their programs, mainly through the offering of internships and similar experiential opportunities. With support from the Mellon Foundation, Brandeis University began an initiative called Connected PhD that "funds professional development experiences, including fellowships (something like paid internships) on campus or at external locations identified by the candidate." The Brandeis English Department is working on curricular revision that would provide better preparation for jobs other than the tenure-track positions on which graduate programs traditionally focus.[25] While this is extremely helpful for the many graduates who will end up working outside the academy, it doesn't directly address the question of how graduates understand work within the academy itself. Preparation for work at a university press or a think tank is not the same as preparation to rethink how the university functions. It is also the case that, while Brandeis is a wonderful university, its graduate programs in the humanities are not among the most selective or prestigious in the country. At the most renowned and influential programs, the resistance to even these changes is likely to be stronger. An "Advisory Working Group" at Yale recently issued a report that revealed just how poorly PhD students in the humanities were faring in the tenure-track job market and made a number of recommendations for changes similar to those being tested at Brandeis. We shall see what follows, but, in a less than encouraging sign, one member of the Yale English Department called the report "coercion," and another noted its "hostility to departmental autonomy and self-governance."[26] Apparently autonomy includes the ability not to provide much information on job placement: the department's "Graduate Student Placement" webpage includes no actual data but a short summary of highlights. According to those highlights, the department placed two graduates in tenure-track jobs in 2020–21 and two in 2019–20. There is no information on how many sought such jobs.[27]

Notwithstanding the abysmal job market in some disciplines and the competition from higher-paying industries in others, some PhDs do make it into tenure-track positions in American colleges and universities. Though these tenure-track faculty no longer form a majority in higher education, they do form the nonadministrative group with the most power at virtually all four-year and many two-year institutions. And what has their time in graduate school taught them, aside from the requisite knowledge of their fields?

Despite the absence of many core courses in PhD programs, there is one core lesson that is inculcated into students in virtually all of these programs: research is more important than teaching. Not just more important but *much* more important.

Let me be clear. It is nearly impossible to overstate the value of much of the research and scholarship that is carried out at universities in the United States and around the world. While these institutions are not perfect, they are more adept at engaging in the disinterested pursuit of knowledge than any other organizations and have contributed enormously to the social good. The most tangible benefits, of course, come from the sciences—two of the COVID-19 vaccines authorized in the United States were developed in part at Harvard—but much of the work done in the social sciences, humanities, and fine arts has deepened our understanding of our own nature and history and shown us what it means, for better or worse, to be human. Yes, much of the work appears to lead nowhere or to be absurdly trivial, but that is the nature of the research enterprise: it often takes many failures to produce success, and it is sometimes the apparently trivial that leads to the greatest advances. These points have been made many times: "Failure is integral to research and scholarship—it is how theories are refined, discoveries are made, and innovations are developed."[28] Like so much in the modern university, these arguments do apply more easily to the sciences than to the humanities. Mark Taylor, former chair of the Religion Department at Columbia, observed wryly, "A colleague recently boasted to me that his best student was doing his dissertation on how the medieval theologian Duns Scotus used citations."[29] Perhaps there is such a thing as being *too* trivial.

The main problem with the overvaluation of research in graduate school and in the evaluation of faculty members is not the frequency of failure or even the narrowness of focus. It is, first, the distortion of the research itself. I have in my career participated in hundreds of tenure and promotion reviews in which research was centrally important (at Macalester the president is a member of the review committee), and generally the question on everyone's mind—the person under review and the reviewers—was not, "What sort of research or scholarship would be most valuable?" but "What sort of research or scholarship is most likely to lead to tenure or promotion?" In a massive survey of higher education professionals conducted by *Times Higher Education*, journal prestige was considered more important in judging the quality of research than importance to society.[30] This is unsurprising. No matter how promising the book project or experimental study, the advice to an untenured assistant professor was generally to delay or abandon it if it seemed unlikely to produce publications or grant funding within the narrow window of time before the tenure review. Of course even the most altruistic scientists and scholars will be driven in part by personal ambition, but when the chief goal of research becomes career advancement rather than the pursuit of knowledge or contribution to the social good—and can anyone argue that this is not the incentive system we have created?—the mission of the university is not strengthened.

Second, and as I noted in my opening chapter, we have decided (or the nineteenth-century Germans decided and we followed) that research and undergraduate teaching should be joined together within the same, sometimes sprawling and loosely organized institutions. If research is important to society, education is equally so—perhaps more so, since there is ample evidence that the economic and social return on the investment in education is enormous.[31] The current structure of higher education has created a situation in which we often have to choose between these two essential activities—research and education—and the nature of graduate school leads to a situation in which research too often wins. In a world with the right priorities, the work of teachers in community colleges who are educating the most underserved students in the country would command respect equal to the work of a tenured professor at an Ivy League university who was writing articles on, say, Dickens. But that is not the world in which we live.

When I was pursuing my PhD at Columbia, there was no requirement that graduate students teach, let alone a requirement that graduate students be taught how to teach. My particular fellowship provided me with the option to teach at Columbia for up to, but not more than, two years, an option of which I took advantage. As a twenty-three-year-old second-year graduate student, I was assigned to teach introductory composition in Columbia's School of General Studies, the division of the university responsible for educating "returning and non-traditional students." All of my students were older than I was. I might have received a couple of days of training, but if so I can remember none of the details. I was terrified, and I was, by any reasonably objective measure, incompetent. My teaching in the School of General Studies was not something I ever discussed with the faculty in the English Department, most of whom had never come anywhere near that division of the university. My mentors were nice enough people, but if I had shown up at an office hour and asked to chat about teaching adult students and not about my dissertation or oral examinations, I suspect that they would have been more than a little puzzled. After my two years of teaching at Columbia expired, I continued my classroom apprenticeship by teaching writing at Queens College and required courses in the humanities at the Cooper Union—motivated less by a desire to become a better teacher than by a desire to pay my rent in Manhattan. I think that I was passable at the Cooper Union, where my job was mostly to teach literature, but at Queens College my task was to teach students for most of whom English was a second language, and I was, again, ill-prepared and barely competent.

Fortunately most graduate instructors are better than I was and things have changed in graduate programs since the 1980s—but only slightly. The Columbia English Department now mandates a one-credit, ungraded course entitled Teaching Writing: Theory and Practice for all PhD students, and similar courses are offered in many disciplines at many universities. Some form of teaching is now mandated in most PhD programs. But to describe progress toward the PhD—the required degree for most *teaching* positions in higher education in the United States—as including anything like rigorous training in teaching would be an enormous overstatement, unless one considers being thrown head-first into the deep end of the pool a form of rigorous training. Graduate students are rewarded with fellowships, prizes, and general approbation not for doing a wonderful job as a teaching assistant in introductory inorganic chemistry but for the quality of their research. Graduate teaching prizes do exist, but they occupy roughly the role of congeniality awards at beauty pageants.

The nature of graduate education creates in PhD students a particular set of priorities and expectations. The crown jewel of jobs is one in which you have to do as little teaching as possible—that is, a tenure-track job at a research university. The higher the teaching load, the less desirable the job, not only because teaching can be hard work but because it is work that within virtually all disciplines is less highly regarded than research. For those fortunate enough to land a tenure-track job at a four-year institution, this hierarchy of priorities continues: the more prestigious the research university, the less relevant teaching is to tenure and promotion. Even within the universe of liberal arts colleges, which define themselves as teaching institutions, the scholarly expectations among the wealthiest and most selective, as measured by things like publications and grants, have come to resemble those at research universities at the same time as teaching loads have been reduced. All of this has created a structure of perverse incentives within which the most coveted reward a faculty member can receive is having to spend less time with actual students. Given the choice between a monetary stipend or a reduction in teaching load, many faculty members at Macalester, during my presidency, chose the latter.

Teaching at a college should be an activity that brings faculty together around a shared purpose: regardless of whether one teaches philosophy or physics, many of the goals, methods, challenges, and priorities are the same. There should be a lot to talk about. Research tends to be something that fragments faculty into small, discrete groups: the scholarly work of a historian is best understood and validated not by colleagues in biology but by other historians in the same subfield, most of whom will reside at other institutions. In this way the glorification of research in graduate school contributes to the creation of silos on college campuses and makes it less likely that faculty members, even at teaching institutions, will think of themselves as members of a *faculty* and not a department. The discipline, an intellectual construct, gets packaged into a department, an organizational construct. There exist at most colleges a smattering of programs on teaching, generally offered out of some sort of teaching and learning center, and many faculty members do participate, but for most the importance of these programs pales in comparison to their engagement with their disciplines and their departments.

In sum, as Delbanco notes, the most treasured form of academic freedom for tenured faculty is "the freedom . . . to pursue an inquiry of one's own choice and to have the results assessed by one's peers"—meaning disciplinary peers outside the institution—while "serious collaboration in the work of educating undergraduates is rare."[32] Aside from its unfortunate effects on undergraduates, this fragmentation renders serious institutional change almost impossible to achieve. Among the regularly cited requirements to be a change agent in academia is "the capacity to utilize a collaborative style to connect to diverse constituent groups and gain buy in through a process of campus involvement."[33] But a collaborative style only goes so far in an environment that is structured to be noncollaborative. Another requirement is a sense of "collective ambition" that arises from a shared set of values, priorities, and goals.[34] But within higher education it is often the case that collective ambition loses out to individual ambition in the form of personal or departmental priorities. If a campus cannot agree on a set of common goals, other than the goal of not going broke, it is next to impossible to convince people that those goals and the methods of achieving them must change.

Time and again during my years as a faculty member, dean, and president, collective ambition would come into conflict with departmental ambition, and on nearly every occasion the latter proved to be the more powerful force. This is not the fault of individuals but of the fragmented culture and siloed structure that dominate higher education and that have been getting worse as the number of departments and even the divisions within departments—specializations within specializations— have increased. William Bowen and Eugene Tobin worry that "within the faculty ranks, cherished traditions of debate, consultation, deliberation, and the search for consensus have been diminished by the compartmentalized nature of the academy and by the faculty members' loyalties to their disciplines rather than to their institutions."[35] When I was the chair of an English department, I viewed most questions through the lens of departmental interests; when I became an administrator, unattached to any department, I viewed those same questions through an institutional lens. I was the same person located at different points in the system. Propose the addition of a particular general education requirement and the first question on the minds of most faculty members will not be, "Is this good for students?" but "How will this affect my department?" The same is true for questions about shifting faculty lines, introducing a new minor, raising money for a new building, or even—as we have seen—identifying antiracism as a campus priority.[36] As a group of faculty members from North Carolina A&T University has written,

> The . . . reward structure [at universities] aggravates turf wars to
> the point that often college deans and department chairs brag
> about how they have successfully negotiated to increase their
> budget and holdings while forgetting that they are working for
> the greater good. Often loyalty to a department or college leads
> to irrational and anti-interdisciplinary decisions in an effort to
> maintain the status quo. The general interest of the students, uni-
> versity, and greater public is compromised.[37]

Train people from the moment they enter graduate school to identify
with a discipline rather than a profession, place them in an organizational
structure that reinforces that identity, and this is the natural result.[38]

A sports metaphor might be helpful here. Faculty at a college or university are less like a baseball team and more like an all-star team. Players
on the Yankees or Red Sox identify first as members of a team, a group
working in concert toward a common goal; they don't identify first as
members of the fraternity of first basemen or catchers. The success of
the team depends on the strength of this collective identity. Players on
an all-star team would of course like to win, but they are there primarily as examples par excellence of their position: the best center fielder or
shortstop. Most faculty at most colleges think of themselves first not as
members of a "team" that is the college and whose success depends on
cooperation, but as all-stars, representatives of the discipline of geology
or economics. Teamwork is secondary to individual or disciplinary excellence. Or as Matthew Reed puts it, "The culture of faculty, in which they
regard themselves largely as independent contractors on loan from their
disciplines, implies a different locus of loyalty than the culture of staff, who
regard themselves as employees of the college" (though I'm guessing that
most faculty would prefer the label "all-star" to the label "contractor").[39]

On the best sports teams, players are willing to sacrifice individual
accomplishments in the interest of team success. Rarely are faculty prepared to sacrifice departmental priorities for the larger priorities of the
college. Again, this is not about character or values, but about the way academics are trained and acculturated and the way colleges are organized.

The tension between departmental interests and the interests of the
"greater public" can slow the pace of change to a crawl. In 2020 the Harold
Alfond Foundation made a commitment of $250 million to the University

of Maine system "to bring transformative change to the state's largest educational, research, innovation and talent development asset." A portion of this gift, along with $75 million of institutional funding, is to be dedicated to the creation of a new College of Engineering, Computing, and Information Science located on the Orono campus, a response to the fact that "Maine schools will not graduate enough engineers in the next decade to keep up with projected demand, and the shortfall could hamper the state's economic growth." This seems rather important. Yet the new college, whose development has been described as "inching forward," is provoking "concerns of faculty across the system about losing autonomy over their campus-specific programs." The chair of the Electrical Engineering Department at the University of Southern Maine is worried that the new college "would erase distinct characteristics of USM's engineering program" and cautions that the university needs to "respect the differences between . . . the institutions in the system." The questions at the heart of the debate between the administration and the faculty are less about the interests of the state of Maine than about issues like the following: "How can USM engineering become a division of a college at the University of Maine? I have my own dean, my own provost and president. Who is my boss now?" This is predictable, because when departmental interests are prioritized over institutional or public interests, these are the sorts of questions people will naturally ask: Who is my boss now? A version of this scenario plays out every day in every state both within university systems and on individual campuses and makes the Alfond Foundation's goal of "transformative change" agonizingly difficult to realize.[40]

Another problem with the division of the faculty into many departments that is rarely remarked on and that is especially apparent at smaller institutions is the outsized influence the structure affords to problematic faculty members. In a large group their influence can be diluted, but when a department comprises only a handful of people, it only takes one to render the entire thing dysfunctional. A bad apple can more easily cause spoilage when the barrel is tinier. There are few things more demoralizing than being trapped for decades in a small department with an awful colleague, and, between tenure and departmental autonomy, there are not many easy ways to remedy such a situation. Change is difficult enough when things are operationally efficient; when several departments are engaged at any given time in a civil war, change is next to impossible.

And any dean, provost, or president will—in a moment of candor—admit that this situation is extremely common. I'm reasonably sure that during my time as dean of the faculty at Lawrence University and president at Macalester, we brought in an external mediator at least once each year in an attempt to get members of one department or another to work together in a way that did not cause problems for students. The limiting factor was not the number of warring departments but the amount we wanted to spend on mediators.

There is evidence that the faculty at colleges and universities recognize that the departmental structure has its drawbacks: witness the proliferation of interdisciplinary concentrations and variously titled centers, whose creation has as much to do with the desire of faculty to work outside their departments as with any curricular need. In other words, "we start with a collection of disparate scholars and fields, impose a departmental structure and then go to great lengths to create centers and institutes and cross-cutting programs that work around that departmental structure."[41] If you are in a dysfunctional department, these programs can seem like islands in a sea of despair. But interdisciplinary programs are almost always created *in addition to* rather than *in place of* disciplinary departments and usually have to fight for funding within an academic budget that is already allocated elsewhere. They work at the edges and not in the center.

While a handful of colleges have attempted to abandon the departmental structure, it has proved to be virtually impervious to change. The group from North Carolina A&T suggests that "disciplinary courses and disciplinary experts can exist in a University without an administrative unit called the Department or the College. Courses should be taught by disciplinary experts but should be owned by the office of academic affairs not by disciplinary units."[42] Rosowsky and Keegan propose that faculty "self-organize" into units of their choice, which, I must confess, is among the least feasible proposals I have ever heard.[43] Taylor argues for the abolishment of permanent departments and the creation of "problem-focused programs" on areas like mind, money, and water, each of which would draw from multiple disciplines and have sunset clauses.[44] This is an interesting idea, but—putting aside the fact that it will never happen—it is difficult even to imagine the ongoing amount of organizational and administrative effort it would require. If there is to be a move away from the dominance of the disciplines, the conflict between the interests of departments and the interests of the college or university, and the prioritization of research over teaching, it must begin where the problem begins: with graduate education. If graduate school "shapes expectations [among faculty] of what should be," the best way to change those expectations over time is to change graduate school.[45] It should be possible to inculcate a sense of the centrality of teaching and to take preparation for teaching as seriously as programs take preparation for writing a scholarly paper; it should be possible to create opportunities for graduate students to work across and not simply within departments; it should be possible to teach graduate students the basics about things such as the financial model and the social function of the institutions they inhabit. It should be possible, in other words, to shape graduate programs around the interests of the graduate students rather than around the interests of the graduate faculty without blowing up the university altogether. My guess is that a graduate program that attempted these things, especially a program in areas of the humanities and social sciences whose graduates face bleak job prospects, would find enthusiastic takers, and that the graduates of such programs, if they made their way into colleges and universities, would see their work and their institutions in new and better ways.

Chapter 5

Shared Governance

It's mine but you can have some
With you I'd like to share it
'Cause if I share it with you
You'll have some too.

—Raffi

IKE MANY COLLEGES, Macalester has a number of departments whose staffing and enrollments are misaligned. In some cases, mostly involving departments in the natural sciences and a few in the social sciences, the staffing is too low; in others, mostly involving departments in the humanities, the staffing is too high. While these imbalances have often fluctuated over time, they have in recent decades steadily grown greater as more and more students have gravitated toward the STEM disciplines and economics and as the world of work has coalesced around the management of large sets of data. When I arrived at the college in 2003, fewer than 25 percent of students were pursuing a STEM major; when I departed in 2020, that number had grown to about 50 percent. This is looking less and less like a temporary shift and more and more like a long-term reconfiguration. As any dean, provost, or college president knows, the combination of tenure, departmental turf wars, stretched budgets, and college governance makes it very difficult to respond, even over long periods of time, to challenges of this kind.

One department in particular, which I shall for the purposes of this story call Department X, had, even before these recent changes, a long history of underenrollment and of graduating a very small number of majors—small as in, "a number you could count on the fingers of one hand." The department was supposed to be allocated three tenure lines because the faculty had voted at some point before my arrival to require that any disciplinary department that offered a major have a minimum of three tenure lines—even though it was never clear that the faculty had the budgetary authority to do so. With departmental shrinkage off the table, the provost had expressed a view on this matter for some time by declining to fill the third tenure line and relying instead on non-tenure-track (NTT) hires. Each year the department would put in a request for the third line, citing the faculty-approved rule, and each year the provost would delay. And there things stood for quite some time.

One additional but very important detail: the elimination of a department at Macalester requires approval by a vote of the full faculty. This rule too was put into place before my arrival. If it appears close to a guarantee that no department will ever be eliminated, well, sometimes appearances are not at all deceiving.

During the fall of my first year at Macalester, the provost attempted to resolve the matter by proposing that, in light of changing curricular needs, Department X be eliminated and its positions reallocated to other departments over time. *No permanent member of the faculty would be let go*; rather, they would be assigned to other departments. The NTT position would be reallocated immediately and the other two reallocated over time, when the current holders retired or otherwise left the college. In addition, the positions would be reallocated within the same academic division— that is, this would be no giveaway to the sciences.

The vote was a resounding no. Welcome to Macalester, President Rosenberg. Attempt number two was made the following year. This time the matter was taken up by the faculty's own Education Policy and Governance Committee (EPAG), more or less the equivalent of a curriculum committee. The voting members of the committee include seven elected from within the faculty along with two students, though some administrators, including the provost and the registrar, are nonvoting, ex officio members. The group studied the matter for some months and finally brought back to the faculty in 2004 a proposal very similar to the previous one, though this time with the imprimatur of an elected committee— sort of. Hesitant to provoke the wrath of their colleagues, the committee brought the proposal to a faculty meeting but chose not to make a recommendation one way or another on its own proposal. (Nearly two decades later, I'm still trying to figure out where that fits into *Robert's Rules of*

Order.) After spirited debate, during which there were ample assurances that enrollments were on the cusp of turning around, the faculty voted sixty-four to fifty-two to defeat the proposal.[1] One happy faculty member was quoted in the college newspaper as feeling "heartened that faculty showed understanding that a liberal arts education cannot function under a cost-effective model, a capitalist model." I returned after the faculty meeting to my office, newly heartened, where I spent my time on matters of little importance like raising money and building a budget, trying my best not to make the mistake of being cost effective.

The next front in the multiyear battle was opened during the 2010–11 academic year. Having gotten the message that a majority of the faculty was unlikely to vote to eliminate a department, EPAG brought forward a motion to require a vote of two-thirds of the faculty to overturn a recommendation from the committee for departmental elimination. Prompted perhaps by the economic shock of the Great Recession or by a momentary burst of self-awareness, the faculty, surprisingly, voted to approve the motion. One faculty member who opposed the motion insisted that it was unnecessary because the faculty were "capable of thinking institutionally and giving rational deference to EPAG."

What might be described as the climactic confrontation came the following year. Fortified by the newly approved rule and headed by an extremely diligent faculty chair, EPAG dove back into the question of Department X. For months the committee studied data on enrollment trends and faculty staffing, held listening sessions, and issued progress reports at faculty meetings. This work culminated in March 2012 in a motion brought before the faculty, yet again, to eliminate Department X and reallocate the positions. Again, no permanent faculty member would be let go. Again, the provost (a different one now) spoke strongly in favor of the motion. This time the committee actually took a position on its own motion, and virtually every voting member stood to explain the evidence and rationale behind the recommendation. Because a tenured member of Department X was retiring and another position was (still) occupied by a NTT appointment, disbanding would mean the immediate ability to reallocate two positions and the relocation of the third to another department in which the person already held a joint appointment. As before, the department and its supporters argued that enrollments were about to increase—I began to be reminded of Mr. Micawber's optimistic insistence that "something will turn up"—and, besides, that enrollments shouldn't matter when it came to curricular integrity.

Allow me a brief aside before we get to the conclusion. Another interesting feature of faculty governance at Macalester is that fully retired emeritus faculty have full voting rights. This situation is not unique—Whitman College, for example, has the same voting policy—but it is very much in the minority. No one really seems to know when or why the faculty created this rule, and no one seems overly troubled by the question of whether it's even legal for nonemployees to vote, say, on whether a student meets graduation requirements. At this point there are so many emeritus faculty that they could, if they chose, determine the outcome of every faculty vote, but rarely do emeriti attend faculty meetings, since one of the benefits of retirement is not having to attend faculty meetings, and those who do attend rarely exercise their right to vote.[2]

At the March 2012 faculty meeting, there were in fact a good number of retired faculty in attendance, and many of them came ready to vote. Some of them were actively encouraged to attend by supporters of Department X and some were inspired to attend by a habit sharpened by decades of experience of opposing almost anything supported by the administration. It is impossible to know how they actually voted, since the faculty chose to rely in this instance on paper ballots (also not looked on kindly by *Robert's Rules*), but it is fairly easy to guess.

I have by this point removed all suspense regarding the outcome of this exercise: the final vote was one hundred to forty-seven against the motion from EPAG. The two-thirds threshold was met, Department X was saved, and a new search would begin for a tenure-track faculty member. A recommendation that was the product of months of careful work was rejected at the conclusion of a ninety-minute meeting, many of whose attendees had given the matter less than ninety minutes of thought. Perhaps the votes of the retired faculty made the difference, but the fact that it was even close revealed the will of the majority of unretired faculty, or at least the majority of those who opted to attend the meeting, clearly enough. Apparently "rational deference to EPAG" was not applicable in this instance.

The college newspaper accurately reported that there was a "gasp" in the room when the results of the vote were announced. Several faculty members remarked to me later that they voted against the motion as a show of symbolic support for their colleagues in Department X, never imagining that the motion would actually be defeated. (This was before the instructive lesson of the 2016 US presidential election.) Some worried about the dreaded domino effect: If Department X could fall, what might be next? The chair of Department X was quoted as calling the decision of the faculty to overrule the carefully formulated recommendation of its own elected committee and the provost "a miracle."

And indeed it was.

Higher education has more "third rails" than a train yard. Of these, the one with the second-highest voltage is shared governance (tenure is first). I approach this subject, therefore, with some caution, but with a determination to be as honest and as fair as possible.

Let us be clear, first, about what the term *shared governance* actually means, and does not mean, in an academic context. What it does *not* mean is governance that is truly shared by all constituencies in a college or university community—that is, all employees, students, and other relevant stakeholders. What is *does* mean is that governance is shared among three specified groups or individuals: the governing board, the president, and the faculty. The document that codified the modern idea of shared governance in higher education is the 1966 "Statement on Government of Colleges and Universities" that was jointly formulated and endorsed by the American Association of University Professors (AAUP), the American Council on Education, and the Association of Governing Boards of Universities and Colleges. That document has sections on the three aforementioned parties but asserts that "the obstacles to [student] participation [in governance] are large and should not be minimized: inexperience, untested capacity, a transitory status which means that present action does not carry with it subsequent responsibility, and the inescapable fact that the other components of the institution are in a position of judgment over the students."[3] Administrative staff aside from the president and other employees of the college or university are not mentioned at all, except to note that academic deans should be appointed by the president with input from the faculty. The document also makes no mention of any differences between tenure-track and NTT faculty, though at most institutions the practice has been to include within shared governance only or chiefly the former group.

Of course the term *shared governance* today has taken on a variety of additional or different meanings—so many, in fact, that Gary Olson worries that it has become "what some linguists call an 'empty' or 'float-ing' signifier, a term so devoid of determinate meaning that it takes on whatever significance a particular speaker gives it at the moment. Once a term arrives at that point, it is essentially useless."[4] This is fair, but it none-theless seems important to return to the term's original and still dominant meaning to make sense of how shared governance most often operates in the academy.

The 1966 statement presumes that the most effective governance of an academic institution is based on "community of interest" and "joint effort" among the three central parties. To the governing board is assigned the responsibility for obtaining and maintaining necessary resources, the "obligation to ensure that the history of the college or university shall serve as a prelude and inspiration to the future," and the right to publish "codified statements that define the overall policies and procedures of the institution under its jurisdiction." Importantly, the statement acknowl-edges that "the governing board of an institution of higher education in the United States operates, with few exceptions, as the final institutional authority."

To the faculty is assigned the "primary responsibility for such funda-mental areas as curriculum, subject matter and methods of instruction, research, faculty status, and those aspects of student life which relate to the educational process": that is, for the academic core of the institution. Beyond that, the document suggests that faculty should have broad input into "the government of the college or university," including "in the deter-mination of policies and procedures governing salary increases."

The description of the responsibilities of the president, the connecting link between the board and the faculty, is the most interesting. Unsur-prisingly, "the president's work is to plan, to organize, to direct, and to represent." Beyond that, "the president has a special obligation to innovate and initiate" and "to solve problems of obsolescence," responsibilities not assigned to the faculty despite their control over the academic program. One can see in this description the seeds of many of today's presidential challenges, since solving problems of obsolescence in a system of shared governance often requires the faculty to agree that something is obsolete. "The selection of a chief administrative officer should follow upon a coop-erative search by the governing board and the faculty"—noteworthy both for the role given to the faculty and for the absence of other voices—and "the president should be equally qualified to serve both as the executive officer of the governing board and as the chief academic officer of the institution and the faculty," an artifact of a time when nearly all college and university presidents rose from the faculty ranks.

The vulnerability of shared governance to dysfunction was built into its original definition. The board is responsible for mission and resources, the faculty for academic programs, and the president for innovating. These responsibilities are obviously interconnected and interdependent, and each party can only fulfill its responsibility effectively if their collective relationship is in fact built on a "community of interest" and "joint effort." If they work independently or in opposition to one another, the system breaks down or, more often, freezes up.

Awareness of the precise historical situation of the AAUP statement is critical to an understanding of its assumptions and goals. As Susan Resnick Pierce notes in her study of shared governance, faculty participation in governance "was not an issue on U.S. college campuses prior to the Civil War," when most were still firmly under denominational control.[5] Over the next century, questions about governance became more common, but for the most part these centered on the issue of academic freedom rather than on the control of the institution. After World War II things changed, when higher education in the United States entered what William Bowen and Eugene Tobin, among others, have called its "golden age," marked by "unprecedented growth in enrollments that . . . lasted, with some interruptions, until the end of the 1960s."[6] In this context, when the chief issue appeared to be how to manage a steady infusion of new students and new resources, it is understandable both that faculty would want to play a more central role in decision-making and that faculty and administrators could envision a governance model based, at least broadly, on shared goals and collective trust. It is also unsurprising that during this period "the biggest gains in income, power, prestige, and protections were those accumulated by the faculty," whose skills were very much in demand.[7] The "golden age," however, was in 1966 about to end with the explosion onto college campuses of the civil unrest of the late 1960s and early 1970s, when goals stopped being quite so shared and, as in so many other areas of American life, trust in authority evaporated. Students and alumni began demanding a more prominent voice in university decision-making and presidents, in the words of Clark Kerr, "were used like Kleenex"—an unpleasant image, but one that will no doubt resonate with many college presidents today.[8] The "community of interest" envisioned in the AAUP statement quickly began to erode, and by the time economic stress and the need for retrenchment hit in the 1970s, the seeds of today's conflicts around shared governance had been sown. In 1972, the AAUP published, as a sort of supplement to its earlier statement on shared governance, "The Role of the Faculty in Budgetary and Salary Matters," in which it is asserted that "the faculty should participate both in the preparation of the total institutional budget and (within the framework of the total budget) in decisions relevant to the further apportioning of its specific fiscal divisions (salaries, academic programs, tuition, physical plant and grounds, and so on)." This is a more expansive, or at least a more clearly specified, role than was suggested only a few years earlier.[9]

The operation of shared governance in higher education has from the start been criticized from virtually every angle, and the chorus of criticism has grown louder in recent years as many colleges and universities have faced unprecedented stress. Kerr was never a fan, writing, "The professoriate is not well organized to consider issues of efficient use of resources."[10] (He would no doubt have been delighted by the Macalester faculty member offended by the notion that education should be "cost-effective.") Bowen and Tobin write, "Almost every contemporary issue facing higher education . . . is impeded and frustrated by a hundred-year-old system of governance practices that desperately needs modification."[11] Larry Gerber, on the other hand, worries that faculty power is being eroded by an increasingly corporate style of governance and that "if current trends toward the deprofessionalization of faculty continue, the academic freedom and shared governance that have been so vital to the emergence of American higher education as the envy of the world are not likely to survive."[12] Timothy Kaufman-Osborn goes further, arguing, contrary not only to tradition but to the law, that the AAUP should never have conceded in 1966 that the governing board had ultimate authority over an institution, which, he insists, "concedes the American academy's constitution as an autocratic corporation."[13] (If this were true, the American academy would constitute the least efficient autocracy ever created.) In short, one can find arguments that faculty have too much and too little power in college governance and that the practice of shared governance has over time changed too much or not enough. What would be difficult to find from anyone involved is satisfaction.

Like most systems of governance, shared governance within academia has strengths and weaknesses and is better suited to some situations than to others. "The benefit of shared governance," according to Lena Eisenstein, "is that it taps the knowledge, wisdom, and experience of a variety of groups and people with the aim of sharing resources and identifying meaningful opportunities to help move the institution forward."[14] College campuses are filled with smart people whose expertise and judgment can be drawn on to solve challenging problems. People also tend to be more supportive, or at least accepting, of policies and decisions that they had a hand in shaping. A history of shared and transparent decision-making can create a reservoir of trust that can prove invaluable in moments of crisis. And taking the time to gather input from a variety of constituencies can prevent an institution from making hasty and ill-considered changes.

The flip side of these strengths is that shared governance can prevent an institution from making any substantive changes at all, even when they are urgently needed. Shared governance as practiced within higher education is far better at guarding against disruptive change than it is at encouraging and enabling such change. It proceeds at a pace that might generously be described as stately and less generously described as glacial. It was designed for an industry and is best suited for an industry whose goal is stability and gradual, deliberate evolution. That has been, in truth, the actual or desired state within higher education for pretty much the entirety of its existence, and it is among the reasons that universities are a disproportionate number of the oldest institutions in the world. The question today is whether this will continue to describe the situation of higher education in the decades ahead or whether we have reached one of those moments of more wholesale disruption that have marked so many other industries.

The explicit or implicit goal of shared governance on a campus is something approaching consensus, and there are situations in which consensus is highly desirable. At Macalester, for instance, the Faculty Personnel Committee, whose members include elected faculty and the president and provost, reaches all decisions on tenure and promotion by consensus. This can sometimes take much longer than would a simple vote, yet the time is well spent, since the outcome tends to be more broadly supported by both the committee itself and the college; unlike on most campuses, negative decisions rarely pit faculty against the administration, since both helped form the consensus view. The goal in this instance, however, is not to change something but to carry out an established procedure as carefully as possible. Generally consensus works well when the goal is to make important but incremental decisions that have the potential, if poorly managed, to be divisive.

When the goal is transformational change, however, patient attempts to reach consensus are usually much less successful. Change of this kind requires innovation, and "the tricky part of innovation is that, by definition, the result is something that hasn't been seen before. The goal is to solve a problem, or series of problems, in a way that currently doesn't exist. As an inevitable consequence, the process is going to involve considering thoughts and ideas that don't sit well with everyone in the room."[15] "Consensus," writes Jackie Dryden, "feels safe [and] safety is the opposite of innovation."[16] Shared governance relies at virtually all colleges on a complex structure of committees, task forces, town hall meetings, and working groups. I have participated in countless such groups and chaired many during my decades in higher education and can say with confidence that the ratio of time spent to great ideas generated is insanely high. The work of standing committees can easily become mechanical and routinized, and groups that are formed to take on controversial questions are inclined to veer away from controversial answers. This is almost unavoidable when consensus—reaching a conclusion that is at least partially satisfactory to all—is the goal. Perhaps it is an overstatement to say that true innovation has never been the product of a committee—but not by much.

The foundation of traditional higher education is presumably the careful consideration of evidence and deliberative study, yet—as my story of Department X reveals—that is often not the case with shared governance. A common pattern is for a small, thoughtful group to study a matter of consequence at length and then bring its conclusions and recommendations before larger and larger groups. As the concentric circles widen, the knowledge of the subject becomes more and more incomplete, until—often at a meeting of the full faculty—the least informed group makes the most consequential decision. One might expect faculty members to respect the judgment of their own elected committees—to show the "rational deference" imagined by a Macalester optimist—but too often they elect colleagues to committees and other positions of leadership and immediately begin to be suspicious of the very people they elected. This is not always the case, but I have seen it happen often enough at multiple institutions to know that it is not uncommon.

The challenges of shared governance are perhaps revealed most clearly in the strategic planning process in higher education. There is much debate about the general value of strategic plans, but the reality is that accreditors want them, as do most boards of trustees, many of whose members come from a world where firms like McKinsey and Deloitte charge millions of dollars to produce such plans. And so the pattern goes as follows: new president, new strategic plan, fund-raising campaign to support the strategic plan, departure of president. Rinse, wash, repeat. (I stayed around long enough to have the good fortune of doing this twice.) These plans are often the products not of weeks or months but of years of work, so that by the time they are finished they are liable already to be out-of-date. As attempts to predict the future, they are mostly useless: my first plan failed to anticipate the Great Recession and my second a devastating global pandemic. While the key players are usually the board, the administration, and the faculty, nearly every individual in every constituency—including students and alumni—wants a voice. Task forces are formed and open meetings—lots of open meetings—are held. Emailed messages ask for great ideas to be submitted to strategic planning websites.

Not many people find this process especially useful or inspiring. I could outline the reasons, but I came across a blog post by Stephen Heard, an evolutionary ecologist and entomologist at the University of New Brunswick, that does so more effectively than I ever could. I quote Heard's post at length because it is, undeniably, so quotable:

> Most of the university strategic plans I've seen are pretty similar. They identify some lofty but vague goals, but not how they will be attained. They promise all things to all people: we'll prioritize research, and teaching, and community service, and being an economic engine for our region. They might identify some special areas of scholarship in which the university will attempt to excel—but they'll combine that with language indicating that they don't mean it (usually, something about "while retaining comprehensive

excellence"), and they *won't* identify any area of scholarship that the university *won't* pursue. In other words: they're essentially meaningless. Prioritizing everything means prioritizing nothing; and it isn't strategic to fight a war on every front all at once.

Why does this happen? Partly because strategic planning is hard, but leaving it there is unsatisfying. More particularly, I think it happens *at universities* because of our unique governance structure. Universities are, at least in theory, run by collegial governance. This means that there's value in the strategic plan emerging, or at least being seen to emerge, from a bottom-up process and with the approval of bodies like a University Senate. Collegial governance is good at many things; but it's spectacularly bad at identifying things *not to do*—largely because no unit will ever, under any circumstances, vote for a strategic plan that doesn't identify that unit as a priority. Collegial governance is very bad at focusing a mission. (It's also, as everyone has experienced, very bad at doing anything quickly.)[17]

Exactly.

I offer as evidence in support of Heard's argument the 2021 strategic plan of Williams College. (When you are ranked number one for twenty consecutive years and have an endowment of $4 billion, you can handle a bit of gentle poking.) Williams, of course, needs no strategic plan other than "Keep Being Williams," but it has one, and it is described in detail on the requisite strategic planning website. The planning process began in the fall of 2018 and concluded at some point in 2021 (long timeframe: check). "This deliberate approach," we are assured, "allowed time to invite participation by a generous cross section of the Williams community, including faculty, staff, students, alumni, families and area residents. Our eight working groups and three strategic academic initiatives all together held more than 120 campus outreach meetings with departments, offices and student and staff groups" (inclusion of all voices, the creation of many committees, and the scheduling of hundreds of meetings: check, check, and check).[18] The six strategic priorities that emerged from this deliberate, inclusive, exhaustive, and no doubt exhausting process are the following:

- Defining a new academic excellence
- Providing a complete education
- Expanding access and affordability
- Engaging alumni
- Substantially increasing our commitments to Sustainability and Diversity, Equity, Inclusion, and Accessibility as fundamental societal challenges
- Caring for the resources we depend on[19]

There are many words that could be used to describe these entirely reasonable if wholly self-evident and generic priorities—*anodyne* comes to mind—but *strategic* and *plan* are not among them. Surely a plan with any actual strategy should include at least one priority with which some rational person would disagree. Perhaps I am wrong and there is someone at Williams arguing for an incomplete education or for treating resources carelessly.

The strategic planning process within academia demonstrates the validity of Dryden's contention that safety and consensus are the opposite of innovation. Call it the Immutable Law of Strategic Planning: the number of people involved in creating the plan is inversely proportional to the amount of actual strategy it contains. In the effort to please everyone, or at least as many people from as many different constituencies as possible, strategic plans end by being either general to the point of uselessness or a long, unfiltered wish list that includes everyone's highest priorities, or some combination of both. The process acts as a giant sifter or meat grinder—pick your metaphor—straining out any genuinely disruptive ideas as if they were impurities. David Strauss, principal at the consulting group Art & Science, "recalls a college president who told him and his colleagues how proud she was of her strategic plan. 'We asked her, "So what basis do you use to judge that it was successful?" . . . She said, "Well, it had the input of 5,000 members of the campus community." Her objective was to include people, not to devise a strategy to move the institution.'"[20] This is unsurprising, given that inclusion is a higher priority than innovation within the system of shared governance. And here is the ultimate and unfortunate irony: no matter how inclusive the process, no matter how many open meetings are held and calls for ideas are issued, those who are critical of the final product will in the end complain that their voices were not heard.

The constitution, priorities, and incentives of the professoriate have changed dramatically since the publication in 1966 of the AAUP "Statement on Governance," as has the nature of such functional areas as admissions and budgeting. NTT faculty now form the majority nationally and on many campuses; often these NTT faculty are excluded from the governance structure altogether and, when they are included, their interests are sometimes at odds with the interests of their tenured and tenure-track colleagues, making it more difficult to identify a "faculty voice." At Macalester the faculty handbook specifies that tenure-track faculty members must be in possession of the terminal degree in their fields—usually the PhD—and departments regularly lobby for more tenure-track lines. Yet many NTT faculty who are excellent teachers are not in possession of those degrees and therefore would by rule lose their jobs if their positions were converted to the tenure track.

Around the time that the AAUP statement was published, the expectations placed on and embraced by tenure-track faculty also began to change. "First, and perhaps foremost," Andrew Delbanco notes, "there is the growing premium on research as opposed to teaching as a measure of institutional and personal prestige. There has been a shift away from local loyalties that once entailed collaboration with faculty colleagues on matters of curriculum and governance toward a diffused system of national and international organizations, conferences, symposia, etc. in which reputations are made and displayed."[21] The time once spent by faculty members on institutional governance is now being spent on research—the only rational decision in a system in which research is valued and rewarded and service, while almost always listed as a faculty responsibility, is an afterthought when it comes to tenure, promotion, and salary reviews. Faculty do complain about the erosion of shared governance, but the reality is that very few would choose to take time away from their laboratories or laptops to read admissions files or review line items on a spreadsheet—and those who would tend to become administrators.

Macalester again is an illuminating case in point. Through the first half of the twentieth century, the faculty of the college focused chiefly on teaching and service; only about a third held PhDs, and faculty commit-tees were heavily involved in areas such as admissions and budgeting. In 1961, the board created the Long Range Planning Commission, whose report was presented to the full board at what has come to be known as the Stillwater Conference. (It was held in Stillwater, a lovely town on the Saint Croix River.) The report essentially marks the shift to a new style of college, one that more closely resembles a research university. Among the recommendations were that "the percentage of faculty with PhDs should move from approximately one-third to one-half as soon as possible and eventually to two-thirds," "teaching loads should be adjusted to encourage research," "a regular sabbatical leave program should be implemented," "consideration should be given to hiring graduate students as teaching assistants," and "faculty should be encouraged to seek foundation grants." In effect, the modern liberal arts college, with less emphasis on teaching and service and more on research, was conceived, though the gestation process would carry through much of the 1960s. Interestingly, the Faculty Committee on the commission was virtually silent on the question of the faculty role in college governance.[22]

By the time I left Macalester in 2020, the faculty had reduced the number of its own standing committees to four, and it was a challenge to convince a sufficient number of people to stand for election to those (a thankless job that fell to the chair of the Faculty Personnel Committee). Untenured faculty in many departments were being actively discouraged by their tenured colleagues from serving on standing committees and encouraged to devote their time instead to research and teaching in prepa-ration for reappointment and tenure reviews.[23] In fact the faculty bylaws had to be changed from requiring twice the number of candidates per open position (2x) to requiring only one more candidate than the number of open positions (x + 1): three openings would no longer require six can-didates, but only four (drawn from a faculty of about two hundred). Often even that bar was difficult to clear, particularly in the case of EPAG. For some reason interest in serving on that committee declined in the years following the vote to preserve Department X. The bylaws also had to be changed to reduce the definition of a quorum at faculty meetings from half of the faculty members then "in residence" to one-third because so many people were not showing up for the meetings at which the most consequen-tial academic decisions were purportedly made.

The two words most likely to invite derision among members of the professoriate—with the possible exception of *associate dean*—are *faculty meeting*. (The feeling among administrators is similar though more tinged with dread.) At smaller institutions these are typically gatherings to which the entire faculty is invited, though only a subset regularly accepts the invitation; at larger institutions with faculty senates, they are gatherings of faculty within colleges, divisions, or departments. Almost no one likes them. Many people aggressively avoid them. Kevin Gannon touches on one reason why when he recalls, "Our regular meetings were regularly hijacked by one vocal member with a list of grievances as long as my arm, honed to a razor's edge in his decades at the university." Douglas Whaley touches on another when he describes meetings "so boring that mice have moved out of the building rather than ever experience this again."[24] These are recurrent annoyances, but the real problem with faculty meetings is that they are a terrible place at which to make important decisions. Cass Sunstein and Reid Hastie explain why and describe a dynamic that will sound familiar to anyone who has ever attended one of these meetings:

> First, groups do not merely fail to correct the errors of their members; they can amplify these errors. Second, groups fall into herds, as group members follow the statements and actions of those who speak or act first, even if those statements and actions lead the group in unfortunate, terrible, or tragic directions. Third, groups tend to get more extreme—as, for example, when a group of people inclined to suffer from excessive optimism becomes still more optimistic as a result of internal discussions. Fourth, members emphasize shared information at the expense of unshared information and thus do not give the group the benefit of critical and perhaps disturbing information that one or a few people have.[25]

Except for the "excessive optimism" part, this is a good description of how things have tended to play out at most of the faculty meetings I've attended. The speed with which one loud voice or one erroneous assertion can derail a discussion is breathtaking. Maybe those who stay away are on to something.

Concurrent with the shift in faculty priorities has been the steadily increasing professionalization in areas including admissions, student affairs, finance, and human resources—all functions in which faculty once played an important role. Admissions is no longer simply a matter of deciding whom to admit: more and more colleges hire outside consultants to build complex predictive models in an attempt to anticipate everything from yield on offers of admissions to the diversity of the class to net tuition revenue. Student affairs staff are expected to provide support in areas, including mental health, sexual assault and harassment, and diversity, equity, and inclusion, that were on almost no one's radar in 1966. Financial management, especially of large universities, has become staggeringly complicated. Graduate school, as I have pointed out, barely teaches teachers how to teach; it certainly does not train future English professors to handle predictive algorithms in admissions or crises in mental health. Some, especially among those who entered the professoriate in an earlier time, bemoan these developments—Yale's David Bromwich (naturally, an English professor) attributes administrative growth to the university's "swollen self-image"—but we neither can nor should return to a time when mostly white, mostly male universities could ignore a range of issues that are now top of mind for students.[26] When I arrived at Macalester, there was no separate office for Title IX oversight or disability services; those areas have been added not because of an administrative lust for power but because of expectations from students and families and an expanded set of government regulations. It now makes about as much sense to rely on extensive faculty engagement in an area such as counseling services or financial aid management as it would to rely on administrative engagement in the formation of the curriculum for the biology major.

If the growth and professionalization of administrative staff have convinced some faculty that higher education has fallen from its once lofty perch, that attitude among faculty has not gone unnoticed by staff—no one really likes seeing their job attributed to a university's "swollen self-image"—and has worsened a long-standing divide. Matthew Reed has "seen a persistent confusion among some faculty between 'shared governance' and 'faculty governance.' They don't see the distinction, though to the staff the distinction is loud and clear. Pronouncements like 'the faculty are the college' are a direct slap in the face to staff."[27] Meredith Skaggs, in one of the very few actual research studies of how faculty and professional staff perceive one another, concludes that "the concept of faculty governance impacts the overall voice of the staff on campus as staff indicate feeling silenced and undervalued."[28] My favorite take on this is by Kathy Johnson Bowles, who has composed a tongue-in-cheek "manual" for staff from the Committee for Managing Faculty Expectations (COMFE). Among the topics to avoid when conversing with faculty are administrative decisions, the budget, the value of tenure, religion, and politics. Among the actions to avoid: "Asking faculty to do anything they don't want to do." Among the attitudes to avoid are confidence and a show of expertise.[29] The irony here is profound: calls to dismantle a hierarchical structure through shared governance are often based on an unspoken but very real hierarchy (faculty essential, staff not) that exists on nearly every college and university campus. It is difficult to overstate the pervasiveness of this situation or the extent to which it affects the cohesiveness of academic communities.

Another impediment to the effective functioning of shared governance is a long-standing conflict between some of the widespread political and economic views of the faculty, especially those in the humanities and social sciences, and the financial realities of running a college or university, a conflict exemplified by the Macalester faculty member who celebrated the rejection of a "cost-effective" and "capitalist" model. If external observers like Kevin Carey are quick to make ethical judgments about the business practices of higher education, many internal stakeholders among the faculty are even quicker. The harshly critical voices might not be in the majority, but they are loud and persistent, and their less anti-capitalist colleagues tend to prefer avoidance to confrontation. Some of the criticism is warranted. Columbia spending $600 million on a new business school campus designed by a celebrity architect while the central campus in Morningside Heights slowly falls apart is more than worthy of blame.[30] But as I have been saying repeatedly, most of higher education has almost nothing in common with an institution like Columbia, and the chief worry of most presidents and CFOs is not about where to spend the next $600 million: it is more likely to be about where to find revenue to meet expenses and how to balance priorities like employee compensation, financial aid, and deferred maintenance. Let me say again what I said in my opening chapter: we speak of higher education as a public good, fund it as if it were a private good, and then blame it for developing strategies for maximizing revenue in an increasingly competitive environment. If you are going to argue, like James Rushing Daniel—yet another English professor[31]—that colleges should "liberate" themselves from wealthy donors and focus less on endowment returns, you also need to suggest how they are going to pay for the things about which you care, such as faculty salaries, endowed professorships, scholarships, and central heating.[32] You need to be able to explain this position to tuition-paying families. And at some colleges you need to suggest how to reject cost effectiveness and still keep the doors open. I am all in favor of increasing public financing of higher education, but there is no sign that it is likely to happen. Under the current system, the vast majority of colleges do not need to be liberated from wealthy donors; they need, desperately, to find them.

This divergence in faculty and administrative priorities and expertise has reshaped the nature of shared governance, which might now be more accurately described as divided governance. Two groups charged with the completion of two tasks can choose to "share" this responsibility in a couple of different ways: each can be assigned to the completion of one task, or both can work on both tasks together. Depending on the nature of the tasks, and the groups, one or the other of these approaches might prove the more effective. Shared governance at most colleges has evolved into a model that more closely resembles the first than the second of these approaches. It is nearly always the case that the faculty is charged with the design, oversight, and teaching of the curriculum, with some minimal level of input from administrators. Virtually all other matters—co-curricular programming, student life, and, above all else, decisions about the spending of institutional dollars—are chiefly the purview of administrators, with some minimal level of input from faculty. We have, that is, a system of sharing through division more than a system of sharing through regular collaboration. Each side has little power to direct but some power to obstruct the other: administrators can decline to fill tenure-track positions, as my tale of Department X demonstrates, or provide inadequate funding for an approved program; faculty can refuse to cooperate in the reallocation of resources, also seen in the Department X saga, or vote no confidence in a president. Bowen and Tobin acknowledge this situation and argue that "what is most needed on the part of all parties, including both faculty and administrators, is not just a willingness to reject 'we' versus 'they' thinking, but an eagerness to embrace good ideas generated by others."[33] This is a hard statement with which to disagree, and, as someone who has spent much time on both sides of the faculty-administration battle line, I would embrace such an attitudinal shift. But basing one's hope for improvement on people simply behaving better is rarely a realistic idea, especially when so many are under so much stress. And judging from the turnover of presidents and the almost daily anti-administrative articles in the *Chronicle* and *Inside Higher Education*, such comity does not seem to be on the horizon. The following passage exemplifies the way many faculty members see administrators and themselves:

> Budget managers occupy positions with the most compensation and status. It is not lost on faculty that the next level of advancement beyond the rank of full professor is typically a deanlet position that can build the résumé necessary for further advancement into what some of us call the administrati. When excellence in teaching is not affirmed or incentivized in the way that excellence in budget management is, teachers feel another painful blow to their sense of responsibility for the enterprise.[34]

The tropes here are familiar to anyone within the academy: the belittling of those who take on administrative work (imagine what would happen to a dean who referred to a professor with a term comparable to "deanlet"), the dismissal of those who actually worry about finances (does anyone really believe that "budget managers" have more status within the university than full professors?), the sense of grievance. This is an enthusiastic embrace rather than a rejection of "we versus they" thinking. The good news is that there was an op-ed published in the *Chronicle* in 2021 entitled "Administrators Are Not the Enemy." The bad news is that I wrote it (because I regularly do foolish things) and that the reaction was more or less what one would expect. Blog posts during that same year by faculty members bore such titles as "Administrators Are the Enemy, You Know" and "Administrators Are the Enemy, but Staff Members Aren't." And there we sit.[35]

There are actually two professional domains within which shared governance is regularly practiced and studied: higher education and nursing. In fact, if you do an internet search for "shared governance," the vast majority of results will pertain to nursing. The differences between the two forms of shared governance are instructive. In nursing the idea arose in the 1980s and refers to "teamwork among nurses, healthcare providers, and their patients." It operates chiefly within and across nursing units in a hospital and is designed to provide nurses with more agency and responsibility within a clinical care setting; it has nothing whatsoever to do with, say, the construction of a new parking ramp or additional funding for a new oncology practice.[36] Applied to higher education, this model would essentially describe teamwork within and across academic departments in order to provide a better education to students: in other words, it is a much more narrowly focused concept. Even with this form of shared governance, however, "administrators, researchers, and clinicians have struggled to understand what shared governance is, how it works, and whether it in fact works," and a research study reached the conclusion that "the organizational, work environment, and job satisfaction outcomes of shared governance have not consistently supported its anticipated benefits."[37] Sharing governance seems in almost any setting to be challenging, and in neither higher education nor health care, two of the most change-resistant industries in existence, has it sparked innovation.

While shared governance poses some challenges that are peculiar to higher education, disruptive innovation is very difficult to find within almost any organization. Thousands of books and articles have been written on this topic, only some of which are at all applicable to higher education and most of which would confirm the worst fears of the most traditional faculty members in the humanities about the corporatization of the academy. But there is a whiff of arrogance in dismissing everything that's been learned and proposed by researchers in organizational theory, however corporate they sound, and higher education might benefit in particular from consideration of a model sometimes referred to as the "ambidextrous organization."

The idea of the ambidextrous organization has been around since the 1970s and is rooted in an observation with which it is difficult to argue: while many organizations, including colleges and universities, are pretty good at slow, incremental innovation, very few are good at more rapid, widespread, and disruptive innovation. The former feels relatively safe and can be advanced through the efforts of small units or even individuals; the latter, for all the reasons I've discussed, feels quite risky and even frightening and is likely to affect nearly everyone in the organization. The former can be incorporated into the ordinary flow of work; the latter requires time and energy that are often incompatible with carrying out the work of business as usual. "Companies fail to innovate," according to Villanova professor Steve Andriole, "because their business models, organizational structures and leadership teams find it 'difficult' to adjust to new ways of thinking and doing. The fear is driven by uncertainty. Will the new ideas really work? If they don't, will I get egg on my face? And why am I risking anything when things are just fine the way they are?" If there were any doubt that "universities" could be substituted for "companies," Andriole goes on to say that "a good example of this is education. For decades the old business model persisted until a tsunami named Covid blew into town. Now the business model is under attack. How should it respond? How should it disrupt itself? Or is the pull to 'get back to normal' just too overwhelming? . . . Will the leadership of [this industry] chase disruptive innovation or will they try to harvest existing business models for as long as they can?"[38]

Ambidextrous organizations confront this challenge by creating "structurally independent units" within the larger ecosystem: in effect, they create their own internal start-ups that are insulated from having to carry out the day-to-day business and insulated from the instinct of the larger organization to squash disruptive innovation.[39] These units—composed not of volunteers but of people chosen for their capacity and willingness to be truly creative—are presented with an important problem or set of problems and given free rein to come up with innovative solutions without initially having to worry about seeking consensus or persuading the skeptics. The best of these solutions, rather than being nipped in the bud, are in this context given an opportunity to develop into something that might be compelling and persuasive. Perhaps there is an opportunity to demonstrate on a small scale that an idea works before attempting to implement it on a larger scale. Only after the evidence of improvement is clear does the work of bringing along the rest of the organization begin: no guarantee of success, to be sure, but better odds than if one were presenting a barely formed and untested idea.

Research has shown that this approach to major change is more effective than working within the established organizational structure.[40] While it is not certain that the approach would work within higher education, with its especially complex and diffuse governance system, there is some evidence that it might. A Dutch researcher has applied the concept of ambidexterity to "excellence programs"—what in the United States we would call honors programs or honors colleges—and investigated whether these might, as at least semiautonomous units, function as "a testing ground for educational innovations." His conclusion after studying five universities is that "the testing ground [in honors programs] does indeed produce innovation that can renew regular education, and as such functions as an explorative unit." Innovation in areas including student-driven learning and assessment were more common than in the university as a whole and potentially transformational. When asked what the most important factors were in advancing innovation, participants in the study identified the most important, "by far," as "freedom."[41]

On a more personal level, I have had experience recently working within an ambidextrous structure at the African Leadership University, a very young institution that has neither the resources nor the traditions of most universities in the United States and western Europe. I will write at more length about the African Leadership University in my final chapter, but here I will simply note that it is remarkable what can be accomplished when a small group of creative and motivated people are given the opportunity—more, are encouraged—to come up with new ways of doing things in a situation of constraint. Such people exist on every college and university campus in the United States, and my hope is that more of them will be provided with the chance to innovate. Shared governance might be the final hurdle that transformational change in higher education must clear, but it is unlikely to be the place where such change begins.

Chapter 6

Tenure

Some days won't ever end
And some days pass on by,
I'll be working here forever,
At least until I die.

—Huey Lewis and the News

T HIS IS NOT A CHAPTER that I have been especially anxious to write.
For someone like me, who rose up through the ranks of the tenure-track faculty, criticizing tenure in any way feels like violating the ultimate taboo and being unfaithful to my own history. There are far too many people, mostly politicians and pundits on the right, who are attacking tenure for all the wrong reasons: who have little interest in real issues like academic freedom or fair compensation and are simply trying to score points in the culture war against the "woke left" and to misuse the term *critical race theory* as often as possible. Attempts by Republican legislatures or governors in states including South Carolina, Louisiana, Georgia, Missouri, Wisconsin, Texas, and Florida—especially Florida—to weaken or eliminate tenure deserve to fail because the alternative they envision, greater legislative control over everything from hiring to the curriculum, is far worse than any problems created by tenure itself.

My own participation in the tenure review process, moreover, has been among the most inspiring experiences in my career. I have been a part of hundreds of confidential tenure reviews at three institutions and, almost without exception, have seen faculty rise to the importance of the moment and make responsible and thoughtful decisions. Faculty governance has on these occasions worked extremely well. Granted, I have never been part of such reviews at a research university or a public institution;

there has never been an instance in which a tenure recommendation made by a faculty committee on which I've served has been overturned by an administrator or a board. My experience has been fortunate but, I know, incomplete. As a student I was able to glimpse a darker side of the process when both my undergraduate and graduate faculty mentors were denied tenure despite the fact that each was a wonderful teacher and had published a book with a major university press. The problem, I suppose, was that they had not published two books. Nevertheless, I am convinced that anyone who believes that faculty take the responsibility of awarding tenure lightly is wrong.

It is, however, impossible to talk about impediments to change in higher education without talking about the impact of tenure. The institution of tenure has strengths and weaknesses, advantages and disadvantages for the colleges and universities that award it, but clearly one of its effects is to make rapid or dramatic changes in staffing, curriculum, and organizational structure more difficult. Whether one perceives this as a feature or a bug depends, I suppose, on the extent to which one believes that higher education needs something beyond slow, incremental change. I am among those who believe that it does, and so it is important that I examine the challenges posed by tenure. When almost the only ones defending a privilege, moreover, are the ones in possession of it, a careful examination of that privilege seems appropriate.[1]

Here goes.

Richard Chait argues convincingly that, given the variety of ways in which tenure processes and practices are implemented across the United States, it is misleading to talk about a single tenure "system." Chait notes that a 1996 report from the National Center for Education Statistics identifies almost 1,300 four-year colleges and over 665 two-year colleges that award tenure to faculty. In the center's most recent report, the percentage of institutions that award tenure had declined slightly, but a 2022 survey conducted by the American Association of University Professors (AAUP) suggests that Chait's numbers remain reasonably accurate.[2] Given that there are "monumental differences with respect to governance, mission, structure, programs, curricula, culture, wealth, admissions criteria, and student life" among these colleges and universities, it makes sense that there would be differences as well in how they understand and implement tenure.[3] Still, what seems to me most noteworthy are not the variations among tenure policies but the consistency with which tenure is understood among so many colleges and universities of so many different kinds and the stability of this understanding over time. Most of the differences relate to the criteria used to award tenure and the degree to which a successful tenure review is the norm or the exception. At Macalester, the vast majority of faculty who went through a tenure review were successful; the occasional denial was a very big deal, sometimes provoking outrage among students and alumni as well as threats of legal action. I suspect that this is the case at most liberal arts colleges. Teaching and research were given roughly equal weight in the review process, with perhaps a slight bias toward teaching, and service was, as expected, an afterthought. At some community colleges, tenure is awarded wholly on the basis of teaching and time in service. At most research universities, tenure is awarded chiefly on the basis of research, and at the most elite research universities, it is awarded almost exclusively on the basis of research (handbook language notwithstanding) and to a minority—sometimes a small minority—of candidates. The percentage of successful tenure reviews at these institutions can be misleading, since, in the words of the *Harvard Crimson*, the "weeding out process" begins years before the actual tenure review is initiated.[4]

Once tenure is awarded, however, the variations become less significant. The document that defines the nature of tenure at most colleges and universities remains the "1940 Statement of Principles on Academic Freedom and Tenure," authored by a joint committee of the AAUP and the Association of American Colleges, "an organization composed of undergraduate academic institutions and run by their top administrators." (This somewhat peculiar partnership seems the result of indifference or hostility to the labors of the AAUP among presidents from the Association of American Universities, the more prestigious association of research universities.) As Walter Metzger has noted, "One of the arresting features [of this statement] is its exceptional durability."[5] More than eighty years after its publication, the statement has, according to the AAUP, gained the endorsement of more than 250 scholarly and higher education organizations.[6] "Three-quarters of four-year colleges with a tenure system base their academic freedom policy on the 1940 Statement."[7] Though it does not have and never has had the force of law, it is included in or referred to in the faculty handbooks of countless institutions and therefore becomes relevant in almost any legal dispute over a tenure case. The majority of AAUP investigations today have to do with alleged violations of the principles and practices spelled out in the 1940 statement, whose "words and phrases," Metzger observes, continue to be recited by officials of the AAUP "with a reverence usually reserved for the hymning of a doxology" and pondered "with an exegetical skill that invites comparison with that of gospel hermeneuts and Talmudic scholars."[8] I can think of no other document that has had so wide and long-standing an influence on how higher education functions in the United States.

The 1940 statement did not come out of the blue but was built on earlier AAUP statements published in 1915 and 1925 known respectively as the "Declaration of Principles" and the "Conference Statement on Academic Freedom and Tenure." Both of these earlier statements, however, focus more on academic freedom than on tenure, and the 1925 statement is both long-winded and vague in its description of tenure itself. It also failed to have much impact on the way colleges and universities handled faculty appointments. Before the issuance of the 1940 statement, Metzger writes, "tenure as we know it today—as a set of due process rights that go with the acquisition of a certain status after serving a fixed number of years—did not exist or existed only in seed even in the mainstream universities."[9] It took time for "tenure as we know it today" to become widespread, but its birthday was in 1940.

The explanation of the importance of tenure in the 1940 statement is admirably clear and succinct: "Tenure is a means to certain ends; specifically: (1) freedom of teaching and research and of extramural activities, and (2) a sufficient degree of economic security to make the profession attractive to men and women of ability. Freedom and economic security, hence, tenure, are indispensable to the success of an institution in fulfilling its obligations to its students and to society."[10] The word "hence" does a lot of work in that last sentence, since it suggests that tenure is not separable from academic freedom or economic security and also not separable from the ability of an institution to "fulfill its obligations to its students and to society"—that is, its mission. This set of contentions—that tenure is inseparable from academic freedom, that faculty have a special right to economic security, and that having a tenured faculty is the best way for a university to serve students and society—has sat at the heart of debates for more than eight decades, debates that have grown both more heated and more consequential as the economic and political pressures on institutions have intensified.

Though the 1940 document is entitled a "Statement of Principles," it is actually a statement of principles and rules, or, in its own words, "In the interpretation of this principle [of academic tenure] it is understood that the following represents acceptable academic practice." "The following" describes many of the practices that are widespread today, including the length of the pre-tenure probationary period (no longer than seven years), the time between a tenure denial and dismissal (one year), and the procedures surrounding termination for cause (extensive). Some of these practices, especially related to termination, are described in much more detail than one would normally expect in a statement of principles. "Comments" added to the document in 1970 go into even more detail on various procedures and definitions: "moral turpitude," for example, is defined as "behavior that would evoke condemnation from the academic community generally," which has, in my experience, not proved to be exceptionally helpful in specific cases. The extent to which these rules remain influential is demonstrated in the "2022 AAUP Survey of Tenure Practices," where the mean length of the pre-tenure probationary period among all institutions was shown to be 5.7 years.[11] At Macalester, the exact process described in the 1940 statement is the one followed in those rare cases in which a tenured faculty member is being considered for dismissal.

One subject on which the 1940 statement is completely silent is the nature of the tenure review process itself. In fact it is silent on the question of whether there should even be a tenure review, though a passage in the 2022 survey makes the position of the AAUP clear:

> Although it was not the original intent of the 1940 Statement, which proposed that tenure be obtained by virtue of reappointment after the conclusion of the probationary period rather than as a result of a promotion-like review, the tenure system has today become identified with an extensive review process. While the AAUP continues to hold that tenure is acquired due to length of service, which is at times referred to as de facto tenure, it has issued a number of policy statements related to the tenure review process.[12]

An important deviation in practice from the AAUP position is clearly the rarity of de facto tenure based wholly on length of service, which is granted in some two-year but virtually no four-year colleges. Tenure is commonly awarded or denied on the basis of some sort of qualitative evaluation of performance that involves, to different degrees and in different ways depending on the institution, departmental colleagues, other faculty, student evaluations, outside evaluators, administrators, and board members. Unfortunately, and despite the fact that "courts have been skeptical . . . about finding de facto tenure,"[13] many colleges have relied on the rule as an excuse to dismiss full-time, non-tenure-track (NTT) faculty after six or seven years regardless of the quality of their performance. This was for a long time the case at Macalester, though, happily, it is not any longer. The practice remains widespread.[14]

The single most important deviation from the position of the AAUP has been the steady increase across the profession of NTT appointments. For several decades the story was one of rapid decline in the proportion of full-time, tenured, and tenure-track faculty and rapid growth in the proportion of part-time, NTT faculty. In 1969, the former group made up over 78 percent of the total; by 1975 it was already below 60 percent and by 2009 it was under 40 percent. The latter group grew from 30 percent of the whole in 1975 to nearly 50 percent in 2009. The growth in full-time, NTT positions during this period was much more modest.[15] More recent data tell a story that is somewhat different. According to the information included in the AAUP's *Annual Report on the Economic Status of the Profession, 2020–21*, the proportion of full-time "contingent" faculty (their term) increased across all institutions from 15.5 percent in the fall of 2006 to 20 percent in the fall of 2019. The proportion of tenured and tenure-track faculty declined from 38.5 percent to 37 percent—noteworthy, to be sure, but not exactly a collapse. Over the same time period, moreover, the proportion of part-time contingent faculty actually declined from 46 percent to 42.9 percent. As the report acknowledges, "one reason for the shift is that some institutions are taking actions to improve the working conditions for contingent faculty members, recognizing that those who teach a full load deserve to be classified as full-time employees and to receive commensurate benefits and support." This is, I would venture to say, a good thing. The AAUP's faint praise, moreover, misstates the reality of the transition, if Macalester is in any way typical. We never denied NTT faculty who were teaching a "full load" full-time status or benefits. What we did over the past decade is shift away from part-time faculty by giving more teaching assignments to our continuing NTT faculty, enabling more of them to qualify for college benefits and higher salaries.[16]

Also worth noting are differences across different classes of institutions. The largest increases in the proportion of full-time faculty not tenured or on the tenure track can be seen from 2006 to 2019 at doctoral institutions (22 to 32 percent) and master's institutions (24 to 33 percent). At baccalaureate institutions there was no change during the same period (32 percent), and at associate's institutions there was a small change (from 44 to 47 percent). There is too much variation across each category to make sweeping generalizations, but it does appear that full-time contingent faculty use has increased the most at larger universities and at universities that have graduate and professional programs. Obtaining information on contingent faculty from individual institutions is notoriously difficult—it's another of those data points that is not featured in promotional materials— but one would expect to find greater use of such faculty at schools with fewer resources, many of which are public comprehensive universities.

The reasons for the increase in the proportion of NTT faculty have been rehearsed often enough to require little elaboration here. They cost institutions less than tenure-eligible faculty in salary and benefits; their numbers can be adjusted up or down more easily with the ebbs and flows of budgets and enrollments; they are easier to terminate for poor performance or misbehavior (though not quite so easy if they are unionized); they have less of a say, sometimes almost no say, in college governance. If you're a dean faced with a tight budget, unpredictable admissions numbers, and a cranky tenure-line faculty, what's not to like? If you're one of those tenure-line faculty, what's not to hate? The exact effect of this tug-of-war on students is difficult to gauge. Common sense would suggest that they benefit more from tenured and tenure-track faculty; the research, as is often the case, paints a more nuanced picture. There are studies that appear to show that students fare worse when taught by adjuncts, and there are studies that appear to show that students fare better when taught by adjuncts, and there are studies that show little difference. One consistency that seems to emerge across these studies, Jordan Weissmann observes, is that what matters most is not whether a faculty member is tenured, but whether a faculty member is full or part time: "Students, and especially at-risk students like young freshmen and community colleges attendees, appear to be better off with a full-time professor, whether they're tenured or not."[17] It seems sometimes as if the arguments in favor of hiring more full-time faculty—for which the foregoing data provide a glimmer of hope—get buried beneath the much more heated arguments about tenure. The real victims in this saga are the thousands of part-time, NTT faculty who are, even at the wealthiest universities, essentially treated as abysmally underpaid gig workers.

So is Richard Vedder, indefatigable conservative critic of higher education, correct when he writes that "tenure is dying"?[18] Sort of. As with almost everything else in this industry, it depends on the kind of college or university about which one is speaking. The most immediate threats, as I mentioned earlier, are to tenure at public systems in Republican-controlled states. None of the attempts to end tenure completely in these states has, as of this writing, succeeded, though the Board of Regents in Georgia did approve a policy that makes it easier to fire tenured faculty members and the University of West Virginia has drafted a similar policy.[19] But the target is too tempting for the effort to be abandoned, and I suspect that if one state succeeds, others will follow: as we have seen with efforts to stifle teaching on subjects like race and gender, the race to the bottom can move pretty quickly. Otherwise very few colleges with tenure systems will simply eliminate them but, rather, will continue the gradual process of replacing tenure lines with non-tenure-eligible ones: Chait's observation— "Tenure reform consumes too much political capital at too fast a pace with too uncertain a payoff to justify the effort"—will continue to hold true for the foreseeable future, as will higher education's preference for the slow and incremental over the rapid and disruptive.[20] Predictably, the least change will happen at the most affluent institutions. There is absolutely no evidence that well-resourced private colleges and universities or public flagships in more education-friendly states are thinking about ending tenure. Even if such a move provides a subject for the daydreams of some president, provost, or trustee, the costs in money, time, energy, and bad publicity would cause anyone with any sense to stay away from it.

The 1940 statement asserts that tenure is essential for two reasons: to safeguard academic freedom and to provide a level of economic security that will attract people to academia. Without the latitude to explore and give voice to unpopular ideas, the academy cannot fulfill its social purpose, and without the particular form of economic security provided by tenure, the academy could not recruit and retain the requisite talent. Each of these justifications has been the subject of debate from the start.

By far the strongest and most frequently invoked argument in support of tenure is its necessity as a protector of academic freedom, a concept that is—like tenure itself—understood in many different ways. The 1940 statement defines academic freedom as meaning "full freedom of research and in the publication of results" and "freedom in the classroom in discussing [the relevant] subject." Each of these forms of freedom, however, is subject in the statement to qualification: freedom in research is "subject to the performance of other academic duties," and teachers are free in the classroom "but should be careful not to introduce into their teaching controversial matter which has no relation to the subject." Academic freedom, moreover, carries with it "special obligations": faculty "should at all times be accurate, should exercise appropriate restraint, should show respect for the opinions of others, and should make every effort to indicate that they are not speaking for the institution."[21] Or, to borrow from multiple Spider-man movies, "with great freedom comes great responsibility."

It seems fair to say that, at least for many, the definition of academic freedom has become much more capacious than it was in the 1940 document. Academic freedom is certainly used often these days as a justification for bringing into the classroom "controversial matter which has no relation to the subject."[22] It is used as an argument against everything from being pressured to attend diversity training sessions to being censured for comments or actions inside or outside the classroom that many might find offensive. It is used in defense of social media posts, the right to bring to campus speakers whose goal is merely to outrage, and the right simply to act like a jerk.[23] Too often it is confused, even by many within higher education, with freedom of speech, to which it bears some relation but from which it is materially different. Freedom of speech is a right guaranteed by the First Amendment, has nothing specifically to do with the academy, and has been declared by the courts to be subject to certain restrictions. Academic freedom, on the other hand, "is at best a quasi-legal concept. It is not well defined and has never been convincingly justified from legal principles."[24] Though the AAUP asserts that the Supreme Court "extended First Amendment protection to academic freedom" in 1967 in the case of *Keyishian v. Board of Regents*, the reality, as expressed through many rulings of the court over the years, is much less straightforward.[25] It would be more accurate to say, with William Van Alstyne, that academic freedom as defined by the AAUP "is an example of very soft law. Generally speaking, the 1940 Statement is not policed by courts."[26] Some of this confusion might arise from the difference between the obligations imposed on private and public universities, the latter of which are generally defined as public property and subject to a stricter interpretation of free speech laws.

However one defines academic freedom, the vast majority of tenured professors would argue that tenure is a powerful way to protect it. This argument seems to me unassailable, so long as one adds a few qualifications. First, as the actions of legislators during the era of McCarthyism and during our own era of ideological purging reveal, tenure is no guarantee against challenges to academic freedom when they come from powerful and politically motivated actors in particular. The State of Florida, the current epicenter of the attack on the independence of higher education, is arguing in a legal case that "faculty members' curriculum and in-class instruction at public universities is 'government speech' and 'not the speech of the educators themselves'" and therefore "fair game to be regulated by state lawmakers."[27] The general counsel for the University of Idaho has warned faculty members that the expression of any views on the subject of abortion could result in "prosecution, imprisonment, and 'a permanent bar from future state employment.'"[28] This is awful, Orwellian stuff against which tenure seems to provide little to no protection in our current legal and political environment.

Second, tenure is not the *only* way to protect academic freedom, and the explicit linkage of academic freedom to tenure has had the perhaps unintended consequence of suggesting that those not in tenured positions lack the right to academic freedom and the right to protection against retaliatory behavior. "Tenure," Greg Afinogenov writes, "does afford speech protections to a shrinking minority of academics, but why should such protections be exceptional?"[29] This argument, in its most emphatic form, goes as follows:

> The oft-argued link between academic freedom and tenure is a myth. All tenure does is convert the faculty from an employee "at will" to one who cannot be removed without "just cause."

Tenure does not guarantee academic freedom, but only contract/ protected rights. This is not to say that tenure is a bad thing, but simply that academic freedom and tenure are not as intertwined as is often asserted. Academic freedom is not linked to the employment status; rather, it is a right or moral imperative bestowed by virtue of being a member of the professoriate. To defend tenure as a branch of academic freedom devalues it and seeks to deny it to non-tenured members of the professoriate.[30]

As I said, emphatic. This does not, I believe, represent the views that either the AAUP or most tenured faculty members intend to express, but it does suggest the impact that those views often have on NTT faculty. The relevant section in the Macalester *Faculty Handbook*, as an example, is entitled "Tenure and Academic Freedom" and draws verbatim from the 1940 statement in its linkage of academic freedom to tenure. The subsequent section begins as follows: "As affirmed above, Macalester College faculty members are entitled to full freedom in research and publication" and "freedom in the classroom," but since the section "above" describes only tenured and tenure-track faculty members, an NTT faculty member might be left feeling a bit overlooked. The intention, I believe, is to guarantee academic freedom to all faculty members, but the language is vague, and language matters.[31]

Stanford's Emily Levine synthesizes all this into an especially powerful argument that relates to the original 1915 "Declaration of Principles" and subsequent statements and actions of the AAUP. "By focusing on protection from removal, the AAUP created what the philosopher Isaiah Berlin called a negative rather than positive liberty—a freedom from rather than a freedom for. It never spelled out exactly what scholars were gaining freedom to do." The linkage of academic freedom to tenure has had the effect of linking it to "an increasingly small share of academia," and "the absence of a positive vision for academic freedom untethers its beneficiaries from responsibilities to society or citizenship. Academic freedom and tenure are instead linked in a circular logic: Academic freedom is expressed through tenure, and tenure is justified by the need for academic freedom." This, she argues, is how we end up with "racism masquerading as scholarship" and "dubious public health recommendations" being defended on the grounds of academic freedom.[32] Julie Reuben makes a similar point, noting that academic freedom "does not mean that academics are free to say anything they please in professional contexts" and that "the content of academic speech matters."[33] To be fair to the AAUP, the 1940 statement does describe "special obligations" that come with academic freedom, including such things as accuracy, restraint, and respect for others, but these have over time been given much less attention than the "freedom" part.[34]

Academic freedom—that is, the freedom to explore even the unpopular in teaching and research without fear of being silenced—is essential to the mission of the university. But a commitment to the pursuit of truth through judging the accuracy and credibility of speech—the quality of speech—is equally essential and forms the heart of every class and research project. Sometimes these two fundamental principles will come into conflict, and it is a mistake always to prioritize the first over the second. As Judith Shapiro has pointed out, the uncritical commitment to academic freedom over everything else is "part of a wider, uncritical celebration of freedom" over responsibility that seems to be a distinctive and destructive American trait.[35] Academic freedom should not mean the freedom to do or say anything you want, short of breaking the law, without suffering any professional consequences.

Let me be clear: there is a difference between the freedom to say things that are unpopular or uncomfortable and the freedom to say things in one's academic role that are demonstrably untrue. We can argue about the extent to which academic freedom protects the right of a professor to say derogatory things about Africa, but not about whether a professor can teach that the land mass of Africa is smaller than that of Europe (Africa is about three times as large). Academic freedom protects one's right to argue in class that Donald Trump was America's greatest president; it does not protect one's right to teach that the 2020 presidential election was decided by massive voter fraud or that the COVID-19 pandemic was a hoax, any more than it protects the right of a geographer to teach that the world is flat.

Few things demonstrate the extent to which the understanding of tenure and academic freedom has expanded more clearly than the ongoing saga of Amy Wax, Robert Mundheim Professor of Law at the University of Pennsylvania. The only two jobs in America from which Wax would not long ago have been fired are tenured faculty member and Newsmax commentator.[36] The list of Wax's racist, sexist, homophobic, and xenophobic comments in a variety of settings is too long and too offensive to be repeated here. The important point to make is that she has made many of these comments to students and to colleagues in the course of performing her duties as a faculty member and that she has often ignored or misrepresented factual evidence. If this were exclusively extramural speech made on talk shows or social media, a case could be made that she is protected by freedom of speech, but when it comes to actions performed and remarks made in the course of her work at a private university, freedom of speech is not the relevant standard. Wax has trampled over every caveat about academic freedom in the 1940 AAUP statement: she has "introduce[d] into [her] teaching controversial matter which has no relation to the subject"; she has failed to be "accurate," to "exercise appropriate restraint," and "to show respect for the opinions of others." After years of this behavior, the dean of the law school has initiated a process that could lead to "major sanctions" of an unspecified nature, but so far as I can tell, her only "sanction" to date has been to be assigned less work for full pay. Naturally the Foundation for Individual Rights and Expression has complained that Penn "is creating a chilling process bound to haunt other faculty members" (which sounds more like *The Turn of the Screw* than sanctions for a racist), and Keith Whittington of the Academic Freedom Alliance has argued that Wax's behavior merits no punitive action.[37] Thus far the AAUP has remained officially silent on Wax's case, which is preferable to rushing to her defense but far worse than stating that her actions might in fact fall outside the protection of academic freedom: doing so from time to time in cases of this nature might lend more credibility to the AAUP in cases where academic freedom is more legitimately at issue. As it is, the general perception is that tenured faculty will defend the right of tenured faculty to do or say almost anything.[38] Missing from the concerns of organizations like the Foundation for Individual Rights and Expression and the Academic Freedom Alliance are the interests of the group higher education is actually meant to serve, the students, and, to quote a columnist in the *Harvard Crimson*, "under such a system, it's the students that lose."[39]

Is there a better or at least an equally good way to protect academic freedom than through the guarantee of a lifetime appointment (more on that in a moment)? For the shrinking minority of tenured faculty in the United States, the answer is "probably not." For the profession as a whole, the answer is "perhaps." William Deresiewicz argues that all faculty—tenured and untenured, public and private—should unionize, which ignores the fact that the Supreme Court ruled in 1980, in the case of *National Labor Relations Board v. Yeshiva University*, that tenured faculty at private institutions were part of management, an uncomfortable surprise to many of them, and therefore ineligible to join a union.[40] Tenured faculty at public institutions in many states, and NTT faculty nationally, are eligible to unionize, and it is certainly possible to include a guarantee of academic freedom in a union contract. In a number of European countries—Ireland, Sweden, Denmark, and Austria, for example—academic freedom is protected by the constitution or by legislation, a stronger protection than tenure but one highly unlikely to pass through the dysfunctional legislative system in the United States.[41] After tenure was eliminated in the United Kingdom in 1988, "academe continued much without major structural change" and "most observers [saw] . . . the abolition of tenure as more of a symbolic loss than a real one."[42] Neither Olin College of Engineering nor Bennington College offers tenure. Olin includes the support of "freedom in inquiry" among its "core institutional values,"[43] and Bennington makes a commitment in it faculty handbook to "the principle of free expression and exploration of ideas in an atmosphere of mutual respect and civility."[44] A study of the small number of private institutions in the United States that do not award tenure concludes that "term contracts provide both academic freedom and economic security."[45]

David Helfand has been an astronomer at Columbia for a half century. He refused tenure when offered it and instead worked on a series of five-year contracts. He left Columbia from 2008 until 2015 to serve as president of Quest University in Canada.[46] "Tenure," he has written, "does more to deprive the academic freedom of those who lack it—now approaching three-quarters of instructional faculty—than it does to protect the freedom of those who have it."[47] His observation should not be dismissed out of hand.

One last point on this subject: it is not a stretch to argue that the pressures of the tenure process actually constrain the academic freedom of tenure-track faculty members early in their careers. Most are far more concerned about gaining the approval of the tenured members of their department and of other tenured colleagues than they are about gaining the approval of any administrator, up to and including the president. They are less likely than are tenured faculty members to speak at faculty meetings, and certainly less likely to challenge the views of a senior colleague. (Full disclosure: I was unusually and perhaps foolishly outspoken as an assistant professor and was told by the holder of an endowed chair, "You can always leave if you don't like it here." I didn't leave.) They are less likely to take their research in unorthodox directions and less likely to undertake projects that cannot result in publication within a short time frame. When the most consequential moment in your career takes place within its first handful of years, the pressure to conform can be enormous.

Whatever its weaknesses, the argument that tenure is a protection of academic freedom is far stronger than the argument that its guarantee of what amounts to lifetime employment is necessary to "make the profession attractive to men and women of ability." The contention here is essentially that tenure is compensation for the fact that salaries for well-trained professionals are lower in higher education than in other fields and that absent such compensation, talented people would stay away. This is a case made on the basis of the economics of the marketplace rather than on principle, which is fine so long as it's a case made on the basis of evidence. According to the 2020–21 AAUP faculty salary survey, the average salaries across institutions of all types are about $144,000 for a full professor, $98,000 for an associate professor, and $85,000 for an assistant professor, the three ranks that typically exist on the tenure track. Variations across sectors are predictably very large, with full professors at doctoral institutions averaging $163,000 and at associate's institutions averaging $92,000.[48] These salaries are indeed very low when compared with those in sectors like finance, technology, and consulting—though competition from those sectors has driven up faculty salaries in disciplines like computer science and economics. Compared with other service or nonprofit industries, however, they look considerably better. To become a nurse practitioner, for example, one must "be a registered nurse (RN), hold a Bachelor of Science in Nursing (BSN), complete an NP-focused graduate master's or doctoral nursing program and successfully pass a national NP board certification exam." This adds up to many years of combined undergraduate and graduate education and clinical training leading to an extremely demanding profession, whose average salary across all levels of experience is $111,000. A public defender with a law degree and at least twenty years of experience can expect to earn about $76,000. A clinical psychologist with a doctoral degree and two years of clinical training is paid on average $83,000. It is fair to critique an economic system that structures its financial rewards in this way—essentially, capitalism—but inaccurate to claim that tenured faculty are disproportionately affected relative to professionals in other essential service industries. The egregiously underpaid faculty within higher education are not those on the tenure track, but those who are not.[49]

Most supporters of tenure would challenge my earlier description of it as a guarantee of lifetime employment. Aeon Skoble asks us to "dispense with a common misconception, that tenure means 'can't be fired.' Tenure is not intended to protect people who have plagiarized their research, or who have harassed students or colleagues, or who fail to perform contractually mandated duties, or who turn out to be serial killers."[50] That is quite the list. Serial killers I will grant, but termination of tenured faculty on the basis of plagiarism, harassment, or failure to carry out mandated duties is very far from a sure thing. There are no reliable data on the number of tenured faculty members annually terminated for cause because the circumstances surrounding these terminations are often confidential, but I am certain that the number is very, very small.[51] During my seventeen years as president at Macalester and five as dean of the faculty at Lawrence, no tenured faculty member was terminated for cause. We reached negotiated buy-outs with a couple, paid a few *not* to work, offered early retirement packages to some, but terminated none. A single effort to terminate a tenure-track but untenured professor on the basis of a Title IX violation, which I mention only because it is part of the public record, followed AAUP procedural guidelines yet went all the way to the Minnesota Supreme Court—and cost the college hundreds of thousands of dollars in legal fees—before it was successfully concluded. Instances of plagiarism, harassment, and failure to carry out duties were very uncommon and generally resulted in a sanction of some sort, but they did not result in termination because the cost of such an effort in time, energy, and social media flogging would be too high. Any college or university president or provost would, if speaking candidly, say exactly the same thing.

The hyperbole around this issue is really quite extraordinary, in part because the dismissal of a tenured faculty member is so rare, and in part because the ones that make news tend to be the ones that are least justified. English professor Daniel Pollack-Pelzner appears to have been fired by Linfield University without due process or just cause and is currently suing the university. From his case a writer in *Inside Higher Education* extrapolates the following: "In the corporate university, tenure has no meaning, whistle-blowers can be fired, rich and influential donors determine who is granted tenure or not, and faculty have become at-will employees. And just like any at-will employee, faculty members can also be sacked anytime and without cause."[52] This seems . . . overstated. In an even more highly publicized case, Princeton classicist Joshua Katz was fired by the university on the basis of what the university describes as a Title IX violation; Katz and others argue that he was dismissed because of his expression of unpopular views. A piece in the *Chronicle of Higher Education* critical of Princeton begins with the question, "How does tenure end?"[53] Not, I would reply, through this particular case and not at Princeton any time soon. I know only what I have read about the specifics of this case, but one thing I have learned, and wish others would learn, is never to make pronouncements about the justice of a Title IX investigation whose details are for very good reasons kept confidential.[54] The truly pressing question to ask in higher education is not, "Why are so many tenured professors being fired?" but, with Aisha Ahmad, "Why is it so hard to fire a tenured sexual predator?"[55] Because the truth is that it is *hard*.

Until 1994, higher education was permitted, through a special exemption from the Age Discrimination in Employment Act, to establish a mandatory retirement age of seventy for tenured faculty. In that year the exemption was allowed to lapse, based on a number of reports in which it was concluded that the effect on colleges and universities would be negligible. This conclusion has proved to be incorrect. The professoriate is aging because tenured faculty are retiring later. A 2020 report on faculty demographics paints a clear picture: 23 percent of all US workers are fifty-five and older, compared with 37 percent of faculty; 6 percent of US workers are sixty-five and older, compared with 13 percent of faculty. The number of faculty who are sixty-five is about the same as the number who are thirty-five. Unsurprisingly, this older group is whiter, more male, and more highly compensated than the professoriate as a whole. A detailed study of law school faculty shows that the percentage over seventy rose after 1994 from 1 percent, where it had held for a long time, to 14 percent in 2017.[56] "Lifetime employment" has taken on a whole new meaning, putting pressure on college budgets and at many institutions constraining tenure-track hiring, since a seventy-year-old full professor is likely to cost about twice as much as an entering assistant professor. At Macalester, an early retirement program helps mitigate the impact of this phenomenon, though faculty are eligible to take "early" retirement up until the age of seventy.

A final argument often used to defend tenure but not articulated in the 1940 statement is that, as Richard Greenwald suggests, "efficient university operations actually depend on it. Simply put, colleges and universities need tenured and tenure-track faculty to get our important work done." The important work to which he refers includes advising, service on committees, and participation in other ways in the shared governance of the university. Since tenure-eligible faculty are the only ones permitted to engage in such work, and since NTT faculty "are not situated or compensated" to perform it, we need more tenure-eligible faculty.[57] The problem he describes is real and growing as the proportion of faculty on the tenure track shrinks. There is, however, another, fairly obvious solution to this problem, which is to make more NTT faculty full time, give more of them multiyear contracts, permit them to participate more fully in activities like advising and governance, and compensate them appropriately for doing so. The logic of Greenwald's argument forms an almost perfect circle.

I get it: tenure is an extraordinary privilege that is granted to no other sizable class of workers in American society, and most faculty members do not abuse that privilege. No one who has it or aspires to it would want it to go away. When I received tenure, it felt as if I had received a gift of incalculable value. It is possible to make the case that, even with its downside, the benefits of tenure mean that it is worth preserving. What it is not possible to do is to make the case that tenure and disruptive change are easily compatible.

To an even greater extent than shared governance, tenure is expressly designed to prevent change: change in individual positions, change in departments, change in colleges and universities. If the goal is preservation and very slow, very incremental evolution, tenure is a tool of enormous value. Once tenured, faculty members in particular disciplines with particular specializations and particular ways of teaching are frozen in place for as long as they choose to be. If the goal, or even the necessity, is transformational change to a curriculum, a business model, or a way of thinking about the role of higher education, tenure is a nearly impenetrable barrier. I have heard the argument that tenure is the one thing preventing administrators from running roughshod over the values and traditions of the academy, whatever those happen to be, and this is an argument with some force. But the important word in the previous sentence is *preventing.* When it comes to institutional as opposed to individual power, tenure mostly confers the ability to say no: no confidence in a president, no to a change in governance structure, no to almost any mandatory training program. It is far better suited to preventing than inventing.

Tenure makes it next to impossible to add new disciplinary or interdisciplinary programs without taking many years or adding to the size of the faculty. In a period of growth this might have seemed feasible. Today, for most institutions, it is not. A provost might be able to chip away at a position here or there as faculty members retire or otherwise depart, but more wholesale change would require the elimination of an entire department—which, as my story of Department X demonstrates, carries its own set of major challenges—or a declaration of financial exigency, which is not a good talking point on admissions tours. Even within departments, the hiring of a specialist in eighteenth-century British literature in 1990 means that you are likely to have someone teaching eighteenth-century British literature today, whether or not there is any demand. College faculties are among the most highly compartmentalized and specialized workforces found anywhere, and tenure is designed to lock those specialized pieces in place. To put a slightly different spin on Emily Levine's description of tenure as a "negative liberty," tenure mostly defines what a university *cannot* do: it cannot interfere with a faculty member's scholarship or teaching; it cannot, except under the most extreme of circumstances, dismiss a tenured faculty member. It is silent on the question of what a university *can* do to respond to shifts in the contours of disciplines, to advances in pedagogy or technology, or to changes in the needs or interests of students. Most of the institutions that are replacing tenure-track with NTT faculty are not doing so because their administration is power-hungry or mean; they are doing so to work around the cost and rigidity of tenure in a moment of precarious finances and rapid change in enrollment patterns. This does not justify underpaying those NTT faculty or keeping so many of them part time, but it explains why they look preferable in the eyes of a dean to tenure-track hires. It is what Greg Afinogenov means when he says that tenure "institutionalizes a hierarchy of privilege and impunity whose chief victims are other academics."[58]

As an old person myself, I am also intimately familiar with the reality that old people find it especially difficult to change. There is scientific evidence to support this observation—apparently a study of mice revealed that "a key brain circuit that allows mammals to adapt to change fades with age"—but experiential evidence is more than convincing enough.[59] There are exceptions, but as a rule new ideas about teaching, new areas of research, new disciplinary interests, and more flexibility in general are much more likely to be found among incoming faculty than among faculty who have been employed in the same position since 1985. Younger faculty are more likely to be comfortable with the newest forms of technology and with the nature of contemporary undergraduates. Physicians are required to do continuing medical education, or CME, to retain their licenses. Attorneys in most states and territories are required to do continuing legal education, or CLE, to retain their licenses as well. The same is true for clinical psychologists, nurses, accountants, and, in many states, cosmetologists. Admittedly, all of these are fields in which laws and the standard of care are constantly changing, whereas in a university, as I have argued, the "standard of care" is not. Many tenured faculty members do elect to remain current in their fields by attending conferences and reading journals, but this is entirely by choice and, at colleges and universities where teaching loads are very high, can be extremely difficult. At many institutions, research is required to be promoted to the rank of full professor, though this can happen as early as twelve or fifteen years into a much longer career. One could imagine ongoing education in the latest research about effective teaching, but since no education about teaching is required of college faculty in the first place, it doesn't make much sense to require that it be "continued." Plus anything that even remotely resembled a CME or CLE requirement would crash against the rocks of academic freedom, which even its defenders must admit includes the freedom to be uninformed.

The truth is that tenured faculty members entering their fourth or fifth decade of service have almost no extrinsic incentives to support either individual or institutional change beyond the incremental. As economist Steven Levitt notes, faculty hired on the tenure track have "strong incentives early in their career (and presumably work very hard early on as a consequence) and very weak incentives forever after (and presumably work much less hard on average as a consequence)."[60] This is a system almost without parallel anywhere else in the economy: enormous pressure to perform and produce during the initial six or seven years, followed by relatively little to produce for the remaining thirty or forty or fifty. Associates in a law or accounting firm face some of the same early pressure, but if they make partner, the need to be productive does not stop; poorly performing partners can be fired, and many firms include mandatory retirement ages in their partnership agreements. Unless a college is hanging by a thread, the older members of the tenured faculty can acknowledge the truth of even the most dire forecasts and assume, rightly, that they can "wait it out" rather than go through the difficult process of disruptive change. Younger faculty are of necessity more invested in the long-term health of the colleges at which they are employed and therefore more likely to be moved by evidence of upcoming changes in financial stability or demographic patterns. An industry in which sixty-five-year-olds are equal in number to thirty-five-year-olds is simply not one that is likely to be easy to alter in profound ways.

The only parallel within the United States to the job guarantee of tenure exists within the federal judiciary. Like tenured professors, federal judges have lifetime appointments with no mandatory retirement age. In fact, as Adam Sitze has explained, the origins of and logic behind tenure in the 1915 and 1925 AAUP documents are intertwined with arguments about an independent judiciary that go back to the founding of the republic. Both judicial and academic employment protections, he argues, are more about safeguarding the public good than about the benefits to particular individuals. "In just the same way that judicial tenure is the means by which the independent judiciary protects democracy's ongoing capacity for justice, so too academic tenure is the means by which the autonomous university protects democracy's ongoing capacity for truth."[61] It seems worth observing that lifetime appointments to the federal bench are not in fact doing an especially good job of protecting democracy or justice and that tenure is not doing very well at protecting the capacity for truth. Beyond that, the comparison between federal judges and justices and tenured professors is on shaky ground. There are a total of 870 federal judges and justices: 9 on the Supreme Court, 179 on the courts of appeal, 673 on district courts, and 9 on the Court of International Trade. Even with the rise of NTT faculty, there are tens of thousands of tenured or tenure-track faculty, so we are talking about protections that operate on totally different scales. Federal judges and justices, moreover, have typically been appointed midcareer (at least until Donald Trump and the Federalist Society began appointing partisans with almost no relevant experience), whereas faculty earn tenure only six or seven years into theirs. Even these days, it is very rare for a member of the federal judiciary to have the four or five decades of guaranteed employment that is common among tenured faculty. Bad actors within the former group are clearly more consequential, but bad actors in the latter usually take longer to go away.

Since 1983, an organization known as the Annapolis Group, now with 120 members, has been a vehicle for sharing best practices among liberal arts colleges, promoting the value of the liberal arts, and providing a form of therapy through shared pain to the presidents and chief academic officers of member institutions. Every June, those presidents and CAOs meet, unsurprisingly, in Annapolis, and during my twenty-two years as a dean and president I attended a good number of those meetings. At one, late in my presidency, the following question was posed to a room full of college presidents: If you could start a college from scratch, which current practices and structures would you keep and which would you eliminate?

By far the most popular candidate for elimination was tenure.

In a recent and more formal survey of chief academic officers, slightly more than half expressed a preference for "a system of long-term contracts over the current tenure system," and this is a group most of whose members are or were at some point tenured members of a faculty.[62]

If one puts aside for a moment the enormous difficulty of changing the tenure system and the utter ferocity with which it is defended, it becomes obvious that there are alternative models that could protect academic freedom, provide a reasonable degree of financial security, create more space for new hires, yet not guarantee people employment for life regardless of performance or institutional needs. Long-term contracts following an initial probationary period and with a contractual guarantee of academic freedom would probably be the system that most colleges would adopt if given the opportunity to do so. Even *very* long contracts—twenty-five or thirty years—would far exceed what virtually any other professionals are offered yet would be preferable to the current system.

Of course it is easy to dismiss this daydream, as it is easy to dismiss much of this chapter, as a sign that tenure is achieving its desired end by frustrating the desires of power-hungry administrators. But it is also worth asking whether maybe—maybe—presidents and provosts, many of whom were formerly tenured faculty members, are on to something when they identify tenure as a problem. Academic freedom and economic security for faculty are or should be among the essential goals for any college or university. But there are ways of protecting academic freedom without a guarantee of lifetime employment—a guarantee afforded to no other class of workers in American society—and the economic security of those with tenure is helping to create economic insecurity for those without it. Freezing departments, specializations, and individual faculty members in place for decades is making it agonizingly difficult for institutions that are facing powerful headwinds and calls to diversify to respond with much more than symbolic change. And almost lost in the incessant battles over tenure is the question that should be top of mind for both faculty and administrators: What is best for students? Tenure, which makes it nearly impossible to replace poor teachers and sometimes nearly impossible to keep and appropriately compensate good ones, is, like much of American higher education, founded on the notion that the most important constituency in a college or university comprises not the students, who at major research universities are sometimes treated as a necessary inconvenience, but the tenured faculty. A possibly apocryphal story that appears in various versions tells of an exchange between Dwight D. Eisenhower, newly installed as president of Columbia, and (maybe) the physicist Isidor Rabi. Eisenhower made the mistake of addressing the assembled faculty as "employees of the university," to which Rabi replied, "Mr. President, we are not employees of the university. We are the university."[63] Even if we give Rabi the benefit of the doubt and assume that he was not speaking in the most literal sense (someone was issuing those paychecks), his statement captures in a nutshell the challenges facing any institution for which business as usual is not an option. If tenured faculty *are* the university, if they don't see themselves as in service to the university and its students, how much change can happen when the top priority of that group is the preservation of the status quo? The answer, to date, has been "not much."

Chapter 7

The Path to Change

Ch-ch-ch-ch-changes
Turn and face the strange.

—David Bowie

FRED SWANIKER WAS BORN in Ghana and raised in four different African countries. His mother, a teacher and founder of a school, appointed him as principal when he was eighteen years old. Then came a bachelor's degree from Macalester College, where he majored in economics; a short stint at McKinsey; and an MBA from Stanford. His friend and colleague Veda Sunassee was born in Mauritius and decided, after seeing the movie *A Beautiful Mind*, that he wanted to study with John Nash at Princeton. The fact that he received the highest score in the country on his O-level exam in additional mathematics didn't hurt. Study at Princeton he did, though he graduated not with a degree in mathematics but with a degree in political science. Both experienced American higher education at its most rarified level. Both returned to Africa to work on improving the quality of and access to a postsecondary education. And both knew at least one big thing: the economic model and pedagogical approach of the system within which they had succeeded would not work in the very different context of a very different continent.

Swaniker is now the founder and executive chairman of the African Leadership University (ALU), as well as the head of the larger African Leadership Group. Sunassee is the chief executive officer of ALU. Both are getting a chance to answer in the real world the hypothetical question posed to the liberal arts college presidents gathered together in Annapolis: If you could start a college or university from scratch, which current practices and structures would you keep, and which would you eliminate or change? The added challenge is to do so in a context of far more daunting constraints than those faced in most of the United States; the distinctive opportunity is to do so in a context unbound by the traditions, assumptions, and orthodoxies of American higher education.[1]

Swaniker and Sunassee are appreciative of what they received during their own journeys and keenly aware both of what they did not receive and of what is unlikely to work in Africa. For Swaniker the only choice for Africa is not to emulate Western systems but to create systems that are better and more efficient. Higher education, he says, "has the potential to unlock tremendous progress for society . . . and for individuals, yet today it costs too much, it takes too long, and it is not accessible to millions of people who need it to progress in life." Like Eric Mazur, he believes that higher education still "has not caught up to the fact that we no longer live in a world where access to information is scarce."[2] The absence of a developed system of higher education in Africa creates the space to build something new and better. When you are starting from behind, he says, "you can't move at the same speed as the rest of the world and expect to catch up."[3] You have to be more creative, more agile, more motivated. The results so far have included the African Leadership Academy for high school students (2004), ALU (2015), and ALX (2018), a low-cost "online accelerator for young professionals that . . . helps them launch careers of impact."[4]

Sunassee never set out to disrupt higher education when he left New Jersey to teach at the African Leadership Academy outside Johannesburg. What he discovered, however, was that he was learning as a teacher "the things that I never got despite all my education, that is, precisely those kinds of lessons that prepare you to be a good, caring, compassionate, values-driven human being—things that, I suspect, higher education does not see as being its responsibility." The university he envisions would graduate people who are prepared, intellectually and temperamentally, to seek solutions to problems for the greater good: one shaped by the traditional African concept of *ubuntu*, "I am because we are." At Princeton he was steered away from following his interests and passions because they did not align closely enough with the interests of his professors: he wrote his honors thesis not on the topic of his choice but on the topic of his adviser's book in progress. "When Fred came around with the idea for the African Leadership University, which really put students at the center of their learning, that was extremely appealing, because by then I had language and a framework to reflect on my own experience and understand what I had been missing."[5]

It would be reasonable to argue that American higher education has little to learn from a small African university that is less than a decade old and has campuses in Mauritius and Rwanda and "hubs," or small group gathering spaces, in countries including Uganda, Kenya, and Nigeria. It would also be wrong. Generally the assumption is that intellectual innovation starts at the top and trickles down: from Harvard to lesser colleges and universities, from Apple to lesser technology companies, from the more developed to the less developed world. Often this is true—but not always. Sometimes ideas flow in the opposite direction, from the less developed and affluent to the more, through a process that has been called reverse innovation. The logic behind this process is straightforward: in situations of constraint, companies and organizations have no choice but to figure out solutions to problems that are less expensive and simpler to implement. As Swaniker has said, "At the African Leadership Group we live by the mantra 'constraint drives innovation.'"[6] Handheld electrocardiogram devices and portable ultrasound machines were developed in rural India and rural China because there was simply no way to afford or access more expensive machines; eventually these devices filtered back into more developed economies.[7] Scholars at Northeastern University have argued that the United States and Europe could learn much about how to combat COVID-19 from some countries in Africa or Asia, where more experience in dealing with epidemics has led to better outcomes during the pandemic.[8] Higher education, with its very high cost and inability to meet the needs of many of the most underserved communities, would seem ripe for innovation of this kind. If a scalable version of low-cost, high-quality higher education is to be developed, it will not come from institutions that spend $80,000 or more per year on each student. That model might (or might not) produce wonderful results, but it is simply irrelevant as a model for just about everyone else.

If the United States is facing a demographic cliff, Africa is in the process of climbing a steep demographic mountain. The median age in Africa is under twenty. This compares with a median age in Japan of forty-eight, in Germany of forty-six, in the United States and China of thirty-eight, in South America of thirty-two, and in India of twenty-eight. By the year 2050, one-quarter of the world's population will be African, and Nigeria will overtake the United States as the third most populous nation in the world. The fifteen fastest-growing cities in the world are all located in Africa.[9] It really doesn't matter which statistic you pick, since they all tell the same story: Africa has an enormous and rapidly growing population of young people, and the economic and political future not just of the continent but of the world will be shaped in large part by the extent to which higher education can prepare that population both for employment and for engagement and leadership in civic life.

The current barriers to achieving that goal are daunting. The United States, with a population of about 330 million and a median age of thirty-eight, has, depending on how one counts, between 4,000 and 5,000 colleges and universities. Africa, with a population of about 1.4 billion and a median age of under twenty, has just over 1,200. Nigeria, the most populous country on the continent with over 200 million people, has fewer than 200 universities. Between 2010 and 2015, only about one in four Nigerian applicants to those universities gained admission, meaning that on a national level, tertiary education in Nigeria is more selective than Macalester College,[10] and unlike the students who are not admitted to Macalester, those not admitted in Nigeria essentially have nowhere else to go: there are no "safety schools."[11] According to the World Bank, about 9 percent of eligible students in sub-Saharan African were enrolled in tertiary education in 2019, the lowest percentage of any region in the world, and only about half of those students graduate.[12] And this is the current state of affairs, *before* the explosive growth in population forecast for the next several decades.

This problem has been identified by many inside and outside Africa, but some of the proposed solutions—build more traditional universities, provide more government funding for higher education—are based on the assumption that a Western model designed to be exclusive and expensive can somehow operate at scale in a region where the GDP per capita is about $1,600 USD, compared with $64,000 in the United States and $40,000 in the United Kingdom, and where the middle class, however defined, still forms a very small percentage of the overall population.[13] Given the enormous imbalance between supply and demand, it is not surprising that low-cost online higher education offered by both for-profit and nonprofit providers is expanding rapidly across the continent; however one feels about the quality of such education, it seems preferable to none at all. Even online education, though, faces challenges in Africa, since many people do not have access to reliable internet service or even to reliable electricity, and while about half the population of sub-Saharan Africa has cell phone access—a surprising statistic—most online courses are not designed to be taken on a phone.[14]

This is where the work of ALU becomes interesting and where it becomes relevant in broad terms as a model for American higher education. The *kinds* of questions that a new university in Africa has to ask—fundamental questions about the purposes and practices of education—are at least as important and instructive as the particular answers to those questions. The key to providing high-quality tertiary education at scale in a situation of constraint is not to offer a partial or lesser version of the traditional model but to reimagine the model from the ground up—to question many of the implicit assumptions that have shaped higher education for a millennium and gone largely unchallenged and unchanged. The answer in Africa is not to build more American-style universities or for American or European universities to open African outposts; rather, the answer is to design a university that acknowledges the constraints and takes advantage of the assets of the particular context. Purely online education, by offering a less expensive, more widely accessible product, moves in this direction, but too often it simply reproduces on a screen a traditional pedagogical approach, and too often it simply isn't very good. Too often it is operated by for-profit entities whose goal, by definition, is to make money, and if more money can be made with a lesser product, that is considered success. Much of it resembles the earlier example of moving the *Encyclopedia Britannica* onto CD-ROM.

The specific goals and strategies of ALU are detailed on its website and are worth a read.[15] In brief, the mission of the university is to achieve what it calls "Excellence at Scale" within a region desperately in need of both, a mission that can only be accomplished by sharply lowering the cost of education and radically altering the method of delivery: by creating neither a wholly online university, which usually sacrifices excellence, nor a wholly campus-based university, which isn't scalable, but an *experiential* university, which combines the lower cost, flexibility, and access to information of the former with the community and culture of the latter and shifts the emphasis from passive listening to active learning. To the original campuses the university is adding "hubs" across Africa, and even outside it, where students can receive online and in-person instruction, connect with one another, and work with employers and communities all over the continent.

For the ALU model to work, it has to upend some of higher education's most long-standing and widespread assumptions.

(1) *The faculty are the university.* Isidor Rabi's response to Dwight Eisenhower is a fair description of the prevailing view at most American universities, where the faculty are considered the one absolutely essential group and where learning is organized around the expertise and preferences of the faculty. It is difficult to overstate the strength of this belief or the tenacity, even ferocity, with which many faculty members cling to it. "The heart of a college or university," writes Joshua Doležal, "used to be its faculty. These were the scholars, scientists, and musicians who defined their cities and towns in the way that Michael Jordan once *was* Chicago."[16] I have no words in response to this claim except, maybe, *What?* It is tempting to reminisce about the days when Lionel Trilling battled Joe DiMaggio for dominance of New York City, except that I don't think there ever were such days in New York, Chicago, or any other large or small town.

Even if one agrees that the faculty are the heart of the university—why is it always the heart and never the brain?—what happens when there are not enough of them to go around? The PhD or equivalent is the required degree for most permanent faculty in the United States, but in Africa there are not enough individuals with that degree to staff existing universities, let alone to allow for growth. David Dunne, director of the Cambridge-Africa program, estimates that to meet international standards, "Africa needs a million new PhD researchers over the next decade." South Africa, which produces by far the most PhDs on the continent, graduates forty-six PhD holders per one million people, roughly one-tenth the number of Switzerland or the United Kingdom.[17] And African countries cannot afford to pay PhD holders from abroad enough to attract them in meaningful numbers. Increasing access to higher education by building it around traditional faculty members, even if it were the ideal end, is at present impossible.

What this means, as Fred Swaniker has said many times, is that universities in Africa and in other underserved regions must be built around a resource that is abundant rather than scarce: that is, students. The implications of this shift for everything from the organization of disciplines to methods of instruction are profound. It means entertaining seriously the notion that even new high school graduates, with the right guidance, can be more adept at self-directed learning than is commonly assumed. It means rethinking how information is accessed, how a curriculum is structured, how a university is staffed, how technology is used, and how learning outcomes are measured. Maybe most fundamentally, it means asking whether traditional pedagogy is our only or our best option.

Studies of self-directed learning have a long history but have become more widespread and influential as technology has come to play a major role in education during the past several decades. Most of these studies have two things in common: a focus on adult learners and the use of some of the clumsiest-sounding words in the English language. *Andragogy*, *autodidaxy*, *heutagogy*, and *technoheutagogy* (really a thing) do not exactly trip off the tongue, but they are terms that have been used to describe various forms of learning that rely less on the teacher and more on the motivation and interests of the student. In plainer English, all are attempts to answer important questions: How much can individual students learn on their own, perhaps guided by but not formally instructed by a teacher? Is learning determined by a fixed curriculum more or less effective than learning driven by the particular interests of the student? Given the right tools, proper assistance, and almost unlimited access to information, what can students accomplish without traditional classes? Is self-directed learning as suitable for young adults as for older adults? Answering these questions could provide a path to educating more students more effectively at lower cost—or not. But we will never know the answers if we do not ask the questions and test new educational models. This is most likely to happen at a place like ALU, where the more traditional model is not feasible.

There is a lesson here for American higher education: if the big questions don't get asked, they can't get answered. Let's grant that the traditional pedagogical model is best: a great teacher (of which there are some) with small groupings of engaged students. This is what President James Garfield, a Williams College graduate, idealized as legendary professor "Mark Hopkins on one end of a log and a student on the other." This model will continue to exist for the foreseeable future at the wealthiest liberal arts colleges and in some upper-level classes at the wealthiest universities.[18] But it simply fails to address the need to lower the cost of higher education and to reach more people who have neither the money nor the time required to spend four years on an idyllic campus. There are not enough logs to go around.[19] We need to know what can be accomplished through andragogy (facilitated, self-directed learning) and heutagogy (even more fully self-managed learning) because the more we know, the better we will be able to make higher education more accessible. Few institutions in the United States have shown a willingness to experiment seriously with these models, so they should watch what happens in regions like Africa, where experimentation is of necessity actually occurring.

I understand the stark implication of this argument: fewer teachers for more students. As harsh as it sounds, the truth is that the purpose of higher education is not to provide jobs for as many faculty and staff as possible, just as the purpose of health care is not to provide jobs for as many doctors and nurses as possible; the purpose of health care is to improve individual and public health, while the purpose of higher education is to educate students. If this can be done effectively with fewer people and at lower cost, and if the people who are employed are fairly compensated, what is the counterargument? We've tried the high-cost, high-staffing model for a long time and by many important measures, including college-going and college-completion rates, it is not working very well. What is the justification, other than tradition and a resistance to change, for refusing to explore every opportunity to improve it?

(2) *Higher education is a meritocracy.* Higher education is now and has always been elitist. By this I do not mean simply that name-brand institutions are snooty or that rankings matter too much. I mean that the history of higher education across the globe is a history of providing a special form of instruction and enrichment to a small, privileged group. In Western countries, the system has from the start been more about "weeding out" than about welcoming in, either explicitly on the basis of race, class, religion, or gender or implicitly on the basis of cost, scarcity, and lack of accessibility. Even the widespread practice of "holistic" admissions began as a strategy to limit the number of Jews at Ivy League universities.[20] The great exception is the American system of community colleges, many of which are either formally or informally open access, but as I have pointed out, these are also the colleges that attract the least funding and the least respect within the education hierarchy—which makes my point about elitism. Selective colleges will argue today that they are admitting those who are elite based on intellect and accomplishment; many others will

argue that the scales are heavily weighted in favor of the socially and economically privileged. The so-called golden age of American higher education after World War II did see increased emphasis on expanding access through the passage of the GI Bill, the development of community college systems, and new state and federal investments, but that period can now be seen, for education as for so many other areas of American life, more as an aberration than as the rule. Today, even colleges and universities that admit virtually all of their applicants usually go through an application and selection process that is more theater than reality because this is what respected institutions are expected to do. They act as what Jacques Steinberg calls "gatekeepers" even though the gate is wide open.[21]

The most meaningful response to this situation is not, as some have argued, for elite institutions to admit more students.[22] They could certainly do so, and it would not be a bad thing: Princeton's endowment is equivalent to over $4.5 million for every student, so letting a few more in and maintaining academic quality would not seem like a stretch. But Noah Millman's answer to the question, "Why not let more in?" is right: "The true answer is that doing so would defeat the entire purpose of the institution. Harvard is selective because selectivity is its purpose." The brands of Harvard and Princeton have exceptional value precisely because they don't let more in.[23] Even if the population of every Ivy League institution were to double, however, the effect on access to higher education in the United States would be negligible: those universities serve too small a percentage of students, and the additional ones they admit would otherwise have gone to Michigan or Colgate. "Princeton and Yale are lovely," Matt Reed notes, "and they serve a purpose. But if we care at all about the majority of Americans, they're irrelevant."[24]

Africa's social, political, and economic future depends on a very different emphasis: inclusivity rather than selectivity as the purpose of higher education. The goal at ALU is to grow from fewer than 1,500 to 10,000 or 15,000 students in several years, and doing so means rethinking not only recruitment and admissions processes but the operations of the university itself to make it more affordable, accessible, and effective: changing not just the nature of sales but the nature of the product being sold. Many colleges and universities in the United States, increasingly desperate to meet enrollment and revenue targets, are focusing on the former—sales—by hiring consultants and yield managers and by getting clever on social media. What very few are doing is looking seriously at the latter—that is, the form of education they are actually providing. The two changes that could actually make American higher education more inclusive would be to lower the cost, which means changing the model in fundamental ways, and to become more flexible and creative in modes of delivery so that more students outside the eighteen-to-twenty-two-year-old demographic can be served. Rather than looking down on community colleges, more four-year institutions might want to learn from them. New programs like Concourse and Sage Scholars, which allow high school students to create profiles, skip the application process, and be admitted directly into colleges, are probably a sign of what is to come for the majority of nonselective institutions.[25]

(3) *The university stands "at a slight angle to the world."* This phrase comes from an essay written by William Bowen when he was president of Princeton and describes, better than a phrase like "ivory tower," the generally assumed relationship between the activities inside and outside the walls of the university.[26] Very often those walls are literal: the architecture and geographical location of many American colleges and universities express in physical form their presumed separation from what Dickens, in the great final sentence of *Little Dorrit*, describes as "the roaring streets" where "the noisy and the eager, and the arrogant and the froward and the vain, fretted, and chafed, and made their usual uproar." College and university campuses are often surrounded by brick barriers or wrought-iron fences—"At Yale," Nick Burns writes, "castle-like architecture makes the campus feel like a fortified enclave"—and many of the earliest were established far from the centers of population in order to isolate young men from the moral corruption that was ostensibly rampant in cities. This move both failed to preserve masculine virtue and has had some unfortunate side effects, including the perception that academic life is different from "real" life and the exclusion from the academic work of the university of much of the wisdom and experience that exist beyond the campus. Burns again: "What students and faculty gain in the enhanced sense of academic community that comes from campus life, they can lose in regular interaction with people who don't dwell in the world of the academy. The campus, by design, restricts opportunities to encounter people from a wider range of professions, education levels and class backgrounds."[27] Most would agree today that the absence of such encounters has created fissures within American society that have become dangerously deep.

The separation of the university from the surrounding world is particularly ill-suited for an African context. Most universities in Africa have imported a Western curriculum and organization and in doing so have turned away from traditional forms of education that have long been developed within and adapted to the continent. "African education emphasized social responsibility, job orientation, political participation, spiritual and moral values": not a bad description of what are supposed to be some of the central goals of college. "Children learnt by doing, that is to say, children and adolescents were engaged in participatory ceremonies, rituals, imitation, recitation and demonstration." Babs Fanfuwa writes that "education in old Africa was not rigidly compartmentalized as is the case in the contemporary system today. Educators are beginning to talk about Universities without walls, schools without classes and subjects without grades."[28] Sometimes the past can inform the future. ALU is an attempt to blend this more traditional form of African education with instruction in many of the skills and ideas required to succeed in the contemporary world. At the core of its model is the concept of "learning by doing," or experiential learning, which has grown in importance within American higher education but remains very much on the periphery, usually confined to co-curricular rather than curricular activities.

The absence of experiential learning is one of the factors that is limiting the effectiveness and driving up the cost of American higher education. John Dewey was the most influential early proponent in the United States of learning by doing, though his focus was mostly on the education of young children: "As a child discovers by doing, the child is explicitly realized as the main actor of the entire learning process."[29] Subsequent research has made a strong case that human beings of all ages learn more from challenging experiences than from coursework and that the benefits of this approach are particularly apparent for traditionally underserved students.[30] For the most part, "learning by doing" has been much less prominent at both the K–12 and postsecondary levels than what might be called "learning by being spoken to" and "learning by reading." Experiential learning has begun to make steady inroads in primary and secondary education and is central to something like the Montessori model, but higher education remains more resistant, as the frustrations of scientists like Eric Mazur and Scott Freeman, strong proponents of learning by doing in science, make clear. I have already explored some of the reasons for the pedagogical ossification in higher education, but I would add here the common complaint that experiential learning is more difficult to assess and the unavoidable reality that it would shift some importance away from precisely those people, traditional faculty, who have to decide on its relevance. Assessing the outcomes of experiential learning is certainly more challenging than grading an exam or an essay, since one needs "to assess both the process and the product," but it is far from impossible, and there is a growing body of literature on how to do it.[31] And if shifting some emphasis away from the teacher in the classroom means bringing a new set of people and resources into the learning process through activities such as internships and entrepreneurial projects, that is not at all a bad thing—especially if it benefits students, benefits the larger community, and reduces costs.

One other point, about which John Dewey did not need to think: shifting to more experiential learning is one way to respond to the effects of artificial intelligence on higher education. Chatbots like ChatGPT have become increasingly adept at producing research papers and answering exam questions, but they cannot (at least for now) replicate actual human experiences. If Inara Scott is correct in warning that the evolution of artificial intelligence means that "we need to dramatically change the scope, structure and purpose of higher education," then adding more learning by doing would be a good place to begin.[32]

(4) *Students need a major.* The major, usually in a discipline and occasionally in an interdisciplinary area, is "the most prominent and significant structural element of the American baccalaureate degree."[33] General education requirements are widely varied, as are first-year programs and the availability of minors, but the major is nearly ubiquitous. Arizona State is innovative, in both interesting and questionable ways, but it still offers four hundred undergraduate majors, almost all of which are in traditional disciplines. Northeastern, another innovator, offers more than ninety majors and concentrations. Brown and Harvard have no majors—they have concentrations, which are majors that they've decided not to call majors. Whatever they happen to be called, these clusters of disciplinary courses have been the chief organizing principle at American colleges and universities since the nineteenth century.

Majors are not the worst way to structure undergraduate studies. They require students to go into some depth in a particular subject and, sometimes, to deal with increasing levels of sophistication and complexity. Majors in some disciplines tend to be highly structured and to follow a clear path: generally these are in STEM fields. Majors in other disciplines can be a hodgepodge of courses that bear no particular relation to one another, with students sometimes taking introductory-level courses in their senior year. Generally these are in the humanities. But nearly all majors have one thing in common: unless you choose from a very small set of career paths, your major will have little to do with the things you need to know and the work you need to do when you graduate from college. This is especially true in the humanities and social sciences, where majors continue to be designed as if most students will be going on to pursue PhD study in the discipline. But even in STEM disciplines, majors become decreasingly useful as you get further from an academic career. The work you do as a biology major has little to do with the work you will do in medical school and even less to do with the work you will do as a physician.

If majors are okay but far from ideal, why are there not a variety of ways in which colleges choose to structure undergraduate education? Consider that a rhetorical question because the answer is so obvious: majors are built around the interests and training of faculty, not around the needs or priorities of students. If you have a history department staffed by people with history PhDs, you are going to offer a history major—it really is as simple as that.

I'd imagine that there would be any number of interesting ways to focus an undergraduate education if majors were not so baked into the system. At ALU, the choice is to have students choose not a major but a "mission." Students organize their education around one of fourteen "grand challenges and great opportunities" for the African continent, including urbanization, education, climate change, governance, agriculture, women's empowerment and gender equity, conservation, and arts, culture, and design. This eliminates the need for and fragmentation created by disciplinary departments, more closely approximates the issues with which students will need to deal after they graduate, prepares them to make an impact, and speaks directly to their passions. It also shifts the emphasis of education away from what Scott calls "content specialties" and toward "critical thinking, problem solving, ethical decision-making, applying context, communicating and working with other humans."[34] It is not a system for everyone—if you plan on going to graduate school in astrophysics, there are better choices—but it is the sort of variation from the standard path that more American colleges and universities should be attempting.

(5) *Offer lots and lots of different stuff.* As I pointed out earlier, even small, underresourced private colleges and comprehensive universities in the United States almost always offer an extensive menu of programs and majors. The original basis for this was the model of the liberal arts and the emphasis on breadth that has been more characteristic of higher education in America than in any other country. And at an earlier time, when there were fewer colleges and less redundancy in the system, this probably made sense. Today it results in institutions in a highly competitive market that are indistinguishable from one another and whose resources are stretched in an attempt to be all things to all people. Knox College in Galesburg, Illinois, founded in 1837, enrolls fewer than 1,200 students and offers forty-two majors and fifty-seven minors; Monmouth College, sixteen miles away in Monmouth, Illinois, was founded in 1853, enrolls fewer than 800 students, and offers thirty-nine majors and thirty-eight minors. Most of the majors and minors at these two long-standing but struggling colleges are the same. "Whatever your personal and professional ambitions may be," reads the Monmouth website, "Monmouth has an academic program to match." There, in a nutshell, is the pitch of the majority of colleges and universities in the country. Most are so worried about whom they won't attract that they never ask whom they are best situated to attract. Somehow we have developed a system within which nearly everyone looks to institutions that are large or wealthy or both for the template and then tries, with far less capacity, to emulate it. Rather than trying to be a miniature version of the University of Illinois or a much less wealthy version of Grinnell, with a program to match every interest, Monmouth should be trying to offer something different and better suited to its size and resource base.

ALU is equally aware of what it is and what it is not, what purpose it intends to serve and what purpose it will leave to other institutions. It's right there in the name: the African *Leadership* University. The mission is to educate "ethical and entrepreneurial leaders" for a continent whose future depends on the work of such people. This is the particular problem it is trying to solve. It is not a research institution. It has no majors in chemistry and Latin. It currently offers a very small number of undergraduate degrees, including a bachelor of science in entrepreneurial leadership and a bachelor of science in software engineering—the latter to meet a pressing need in the region. Prospective students can distinguish it easily from other universities in Africa and know precisely what they will be getting and what they will not be getting. More colleges and universities in the United States need to follow the same path by asking what they are positioned to do distinctively well, what the local or national community needs, and what will resonate in a competitive market. *What problem are you as an institution trying to solve?* "Staying in business" is not a compelling answer. I often think about how desperately we need an American Leadership University and what would happen if some institution were bold enough to make that its mission—not in website language but in reality. This strategy comes with risk, but—as about a thousand different people have said, all claiming to be original—sometimes the greatest risk lies in doing nothing. Right now too many colleges are doing nothing, and it is not working out very well for many of them or for much of society.

(6) *Higher education can't change.* I have spent the entirety of this book arguing that this is the case and attempting to explain why. But here's the truth: absent the structural and cultural impediments to transformation present in the United States, it can.

When ALU was founded in 2015, the intention from the start was to offer an alternative to the traditional university model. But within a short period of time, the university—by remaining small and paying a premium—was able to hire PhDs as faculty and hire seasoned academics, some from the United States, as administrators. Given the powerful gravitational pull of the traditional in higher education, the result should not have been surprising: ALU began to look and function more and more like a small, American liberal arts college. The pedagogy was traditional, the student-to-faculty ratio was very low, and—most troublesome—the cost grew to a level that almost no African students could afford. Thanks to generous philanthropic support, 95 percent of students were on full scholarship. Majors began to develop and proliferate. The model was not sufficiently innovative or scalable and was certainly not financially sustainable. Essentially ALU found itself in the position of many colleges in the United States, only in a context of even greater constraints.

If ALU had been any of a thousand different American colleges, it would have had two choices: shift to a focus on the most affluent families in Africa or, within a short period of time, close. But without the inflex-ibility created by shared governance, tenure, and nostalgic alumni, it did have another option: change, dramatically and rapidly. Building on the idea of the ambidextrous organization, a small group began to design a new model more suited to the university's mission and setting even as most of the faculty and staff continued to carry out the old model. There was a lot of input from inside and outside ALU, but the actual decision makers were few. When the new model was rolled out, every employee was evaluated to determine suitability for that model. Some chose to leave, some were let go, some were shifted to new positions, and some new ones were hired. The goal was to ensure that the people and the program were aligned, and the focus always was on having the desired impact on the students and the continent. Once the necessary personnel decisions were made, the effort to create the right culture and to build enthusiasm for the mission was relentless. Within less than two years, ALU had become in many ways an entirely different and better university. This rapid and sharply focused process of transformation would be horrifying to most of the academics with whom I've spent my career—where are the committees and task forces? the listening sessions? the online surveys?—but it was the only viable choice. Stasis and inefficiency are luxuries that a young institu-tion on the African continent simply cannot afford.

In September 2022, five faculty members at MIT published a white paper entitled "Ideas for Designing an Affordable New Educational Institu-tion." The paper attracted a good deal of attention in the higher education press as well as an article in *Forbes* because, well, MIT. It described in the-ory almost exactly what ALU had been in practice at that point for more than a year: an institution with an emphasis on teaching over research, a more student-centered learning model, a more holistic curriculum, a nar-rower focus, less reliance on traditional infrastructure, and stronger con-nections to partners beyond the campus. It even called for the absence of tenure and a trimester calendar, both features of ALU. My point is not that the authors of the MIT paper should have been aware of ALU (though that might have been nice), but that when five professors at a university that *Forbes* described as "exceedingly well positioned to speak from a position of knowledge, success, broad and deep expertise, innovation, and both indus-try and global partnerships" attempted to reimagine higher education, they came up with something almost identical to a start-up in Africa.[35]

There is no guarantee that the ALU experiment will succeed. The motto of the university is Fred Swaniker's favorite catchphrase, "Do hard things," and there are few harder things than building a sustainable model of high-quality education at scale on the African continent. But the strategy is sound, it has attracted an enormous amount of philanthropic support from those who understand its potential, and it is inspiring others around the world to think differently about higher education. Tim Knowles, president of the Carnegie Foundation for the Advancement of Teaching, describes the ALU model as "rigorous, affordable, experiential, career aligned, and scalable" and hopes that it can inspire "a new model of post-secondary education in the United States."[36] Lawrence Schall, president of the New England Commission of Higher Education—the accreditor of Harvard and MIT—wrote recently that "I have worked in Higher Education for more than thirty years and have been exposed to hundreds of colleges, but I can honestly say I've never witnessed anything like the African Leadership University. . . . [I] count myself incredibly fortunate to witness what's happening there."[37] ALU might not be too big to fail, but it is I think too important to fail.

To travel from Sterling College to Middlebury College, you begin in the extremely tiny, unincorporated village of Craftsbury Common—part of the somewhat less tiny town of Craftsbury—and drive southwest through the back roads of Vermont. It's a trip of about eighty miles or of enormous distance, depending on how it is measured. The two schools are geographically proximate but, in almost every other way, are so far apart that they might as well exist on different planets. Sterling is one of the smallest colleges in the country, with about 125 students. Its endowment stands at not much over $1 million, and its total revenues in fiscal year 2020 were about $5.3 million. It employs fewer than two dozen faculty and offers four majors and six minors, including a minor in draft animal power systems. A single building, Simpson Hall, holds the science labs, the art spaces, the gym, classrooms, and faculty offices, and the dining hall was constructed in 1962, in part by students at what was then a boys' boarding school. All Sterling students are required to work, and none compete in varsity intercollegiate sports. The comprehensive fee for 2022–23 is $49,600, and 98 percent of the students receive some form of financial aid. *U.S. News and World Report* places Sterling in its bottom category for national liberal arts colleges, an unranked group that runs from number 168 to number 222. (Presumably the editors figured that by that point, nobody reading the list really cared.)

Middlebury College enrolls about 2,500 undergraduates and another 750 graduate students at its Institute of International Studies in Monterey, California. Its endowment is about $1.5 billion, and its total revenues in fiscal year 2020 were over $400 million. The student-to-faculty ratio is 8:1, meaning that there are well over 300 faculty members, and 850 courses are offered in forty-four majors. The campus infrastructure is enormous for a college of its size, with eight arts and performance venues and eight indoor athletics facilities alone. The college has thirty-one NCAA varsity teams that together have won thirty-five national championships since 1995. The comprehensive fee for 2022–23 is $80,260—we have indeed crossed the $80,000 barrier—and only 51 percent of the students receive financial aid, meaning that about half the students can afford to pay over $80,000 a year—despite the fact that Middlebury is "need-blind" for all domestic applicants. Go figure. In the 2022 *U.S. News* rankings, Middlebury is tied for ninth (with Carleton) among national liberal arts colleges.

This comparison is going to make what I am about to say seem deeply counterintuitive: a promising future path for most colleges in the United States runs not through Middlebury but through Sterling. Middlebury is by many measures a superb college, but it is a very, very expensive college whose student body is disproportionately composed of very, very wealthy students. It will almost certainly thrive and continue to do what it is presently doing well into the future—though it is worth noting that the college was forced to reduce its staff size by about 10 percent in 2008, when the Great Recession hit, in order to balance its budget, a reminder that no matter how wealthy one is, the money going out cannot exceed the money coming in.[38] The truth is that the Middlebury model, like the models of other rich, highly selective colleges and universities, is simply not reproducible at scale and is an unobtainable fantasy for most institutions. It will never be the answer to the problems confronting American higher education broadly or a way to increase access among the populations that are the most underserved, just as concierge medicine will never be the answer to the broken economics and inequities in our health-care system. It is now and will remain a luxury good.

The Sterling model is distinctive and scalable and has a good deal in common with the model at ALU. The focus of the college is precise: rather than trying with limited resources to have a program to match every "personal and professional ambition," the college is very clear about what it does and what it does not do. Its mission is "to advance ecological thinking and action through affordable experiential learning that prepares people to be knowledgeable, skilled, and responsible leaders in the communities in which they live"; its vision is to use "education as a force to address critical ecological problems caused by unlimited growth and consumption that is destroying the planet as we have known it."[39] Matthew Derr, formerly president at Sterling for nearly a decade, notes that the college "has been uncompromising in what it believes a good education requires, and what that good education looks like is informed by what the creators of the college believed the world needed. Students and alumni tend to associate that kind of education with value. When we used phrases that a lot of other colleges used it was true, it wasn't marketing."[40] While Sterling teaches many of the competencies and habits of mind associated with the liberal arts, it is not trying to appeal to those who want to major in mathematics or a foreign language. Like ALU, it is founded on the belief that it is better to do a few things very well than to do many different things adequately.

Sterling has chosen as its focus a problem of enormous importance, without question the defining global challenge of our time. If "ethical and entrepreneurial leadership" is critical to the future of Africa, environmental stewardship is critical to the future of the planet. Imagine how different American higher education would look if instead of having hundreds of colleges and universities trying to stretch their limited resources to offer essentially the same, extensive suite of majors and areas of study—the Sterling website likens them, with some basis, to big-box stores—we had more that elected to create a narrower and more problem-based curriculum: perhaps one built around the study of urbanization, or sustainable democracy, or population health. Here is Christina Goodwin, Sterling's vice president for advancement and a Sterling graduate: "Higher education as a whole has fallen into the same trap as most of the economy in developed countries and specifically the United States, that is, bigger is better, and you, the service provider, should be able to offer everything to everyone instead of leaning into the thing you're really good at. So we've created this market where it's pretty challenging to compete against the behemoths. That's a strategy that's destined for failure."[41]

To the extent that we have more specialized institutions, they tend to be career focused rather than issue focused. Schools of engineering, business, and the arts serve an important function, but there are additional forms of specialization that could be tied very directly to the challenges students will confront once they graduate, that would make it easier to distinguish one college from another, and that might appeal to prospective students in a way that many generically organized colleges do not.

This is not, I want to emphasize, an argument against the liberal arts, in whose power and formative potential I deeply believe. Rather, it is an argument in favor of being open to teaching the liberal arts in a different way. Students at a college like Sterling or ALU still read literature, still consider philosophical problems, still use scientific methods, but they do so in pursuit of answers to a particular set of questions and in combination with other forms of learning. If anything, exposure to the humanities and social sciences has the potential to be especially powerful if the relevance of those disciplines is made evident as they are brought to bear on a clearly defined set of practical challenges. We need to acknowledge, at the very least, that if the goal is to encourage students to engage with the humanities and social sciences, the current, major-centric model is failing. Humanities graduates are "a dying breed"—there are now as many students majoring in computer science as in all the humanities disciplines combined—and nearly half of those who do major in the humanities regret having done so.[42] The preservation of the study of literature and history in college will not come from a fruitless fight to preserve withering majors, but from reconceiving the place of such study in a comprehensive education.[43] Surely reading Thoreau or Emerson might seem more and not less meaningful at a college built around ecological thinking and action.

The learning model at Sterling is far more experiential and student centered than the model at traditional universities. "Through the high-impact practices of place-based and experiential learning, students are actively engaged in collaborative processes of self-discovery, self-direction, and long- and short-term goal setting." Note the similarities to ALU: rooted in a particular place, learning through doing, student agency. The "guiding philosophy" of the college echoes the thoughts of Veda Sunassee about the African concept of *ubuntu*: it "encourages compassion, care, and reflection, focusing on student development through individual growth and accountability for behavior."[44] I am because we are. Or in Goodwin's words, "How do we structure educational experiences that are holistically educational? There's the knowledge piece, the relationship piece, the experiential piece, and when all of those things come together, that's when something special happens."[45] While similar language can be found on the websites of many colleges, practices and requirements that grow out of such language are rare. Work related to the learning model is required of all students at Sterling, which is one of only ten federally designated "work colleges" in the United States.[46] Students are paid for that work, which is tied directly to learning competencies and to community well-being. Virtually every course includes a serious experiential component, and only a handful of faculty members have PhDs. Nearly all are practitioners as well as educators. Each student works with an adviser to create an "individualized learning plan."

One of the fascinating things about Sterling is that it is simultaneously rooted in deeply traditional agricultural and ecological practices that reach back centuries—students can take Introduction to Foraging Ecology—and engaged with the possibilities newly created by technology. Despite the courses on draft horses, this is not an anachronistic institution. Technology continues to expand the possibilities for self-directed and experiential learning by enabling the creation of larger networks and the development of more sophisticated assessment tools. A program called EcoGather "combines Sterling's place-based approach to education with a suite of online tools to foster collaboration."[47] These online tools, partially developed in-house, connect Sterling students and faculty with partner organizations in Puerto Rico, Bhutan, Colorado, and India and enable collaboration around best practices and community-based projects. A group of online, project-based courses is being cocreated by the organizations on topics like food systems thinking and water management. This is how a tiny college achieves outsize impact without spending a fortune or relying on growing its faculty. For about $10 million, Middlebury was able to expand by purchasing the Monterey Institute for International Studies. It appears to have been a good deal, but again, it is not the sort of deal that is realistic for the vast majority of colleges and universities in the country.[48] That group will need to try, like Sterling, to be innovative.

I have dwelled at length on these two institutions because it seems more helpful to show the beginnings of innovation than merely to speculate about it and also because neither conforms to the most widely held beliefs about how disruption will come to higher education. Neither ALU nor Sterling is a big, online purveyor of degrees or certificates. Neither is a nonprofit behemoth like Arizona State, Southern New Hampshire, or Western Governors University or a for-profit provider like Coursera, now a publicly traded, multibillion-dollar company. Neither has the sheen of Minerva, a Silicon Valley start-up that boasts a lower acceptance rate than Harvard and whose globetrotting model is impossible to operate at scale. All of these organizations have a role to play, and all are bringing pressure to bear on the traditional educational model. But none really offers struggling colleges and universities a way to transform themselves: they exist to out-compete those colleges, not to provide them with promising ideas. Every institution in search of enrollment and revenue, it seems, is looking to move somehow into the world of online education, but in doing so they are stepping into the world of bigger, better-known, more well-funded providers or contracting with for-profit online program managers, who take up to 50 percent of online revenue and have a less than admirable history.[49] There are some indications that online program managers, which promised to help colleges "achieve the elusive dream of doing well while doing good," might, like the massive open online courses of a decade ago, be losing their allure, but there will always be a new technological bauble for which to grab.[50] The latest is the "metaversity"—that is, "an immersive virtual reality platform where remote faculty and students don VR headsets and meet synchronously as they would on a physical campus." What could possibly go wrong when publicly traded technology companies gain access to enormous amounts of private data through virtual reality tools and students who spend hours, alone, gazing at make-believe reality created by software engineers? Nir Eisikovits, founding director of the Applied Ethics Center at the University of Massachusetts at Boston, does not believe that virtual college "is just going to end up as a supplement. I think on-campus education is going to be the supplement."[51] If that doesn't send you in search of alternative forms of innovation, nothing will.

ALU and Sterling are clear examples of constraint driving innovation and reminders that it doesn't take venture capital investors, online program managers, VR headsets, or a huge marketing budget to build a better, more accessible and effective college. Rather than relying on either technological wizardry or deep pockets, they are attempting to build new models around things that can't be measured in gigabytes or dollars: the innate human capacity to learn and the urge to seek answers to important questions. The education at both institutions is more student centered, more experiential, more narrowly focused, and more problem oriented than the form of higher education that began a millennium ago and continues to be accepted as the only viable one by most colleges in the United States and around the world. Both sit in a middle ground between the very expensive, campus-based, faculty-centric model at colleges and universities from Michigan to Macalester to Monmouth and the much less expensive, wholly online, and machine-centric model of Coursera. The former model is too costly to allow many students to enter; the latter model is too ineffective and isolating to enable many students to finish. Neither ALU nor Sterling attempts to combine a research enterprise with undergraduate education, let alone professional schools, hospitals, and intercollegiate sports. Neither has a large cadre of PhDs or elaborate facilities. Both leverage technology, but they leverage even more the untapped potential of human beings. They attempt to build caring, responsible communities and cultures while being efficient with limited resources. They are the inverse of the metaverse.

The examples of ALU and Sterling do raise what is perhaps the central question in this discussion: Is it even feasible to expect "legacy" institutions, with years of accumulated structures and cultures, to emulate colleges that are essentially start-ups? My short answer is "probably not." ALU was founded in 2015. Sterling began in 1958 as a boys' boarding school, transitioned into a two-year college, and did not become an accredited four-year college until 1997. The majority of colleges that deviate in major ways from the traditional model are, by the standards of higher education, youthful; rather than changing, they were different from the moment of inception. Olin College, a deeply experiential school of engineering, was founded in 1997. Soka University in California, which offers only interdisciplinary majors, admitted its first freshman class in 2001. College Unbound, which has pioneered an experiential model for adult learners, was founded in 2009 and only recently received preliminary accreditation. Minerva opened in 2012. It is worth noting that even schools like Olin and Soka, which were established with very significant funding, did not attempt to replicate the traditional structures and practices of higher education. Their answer to the question, "What would you do if you could start a college from scratch?" was definitively, "Not what all those other colleges are doing."

Given all the impediments to change that I have discussed—fixed reputations, the absence of incentives, the domination of disciplinary thinking, shared governance, tenure—it might be unrealistic to expect higher education to generate from within a truly transformational process. It is also probably overly dramatic to say that higher education will be abruptly disrupted from without, given the role of college as a rite of passage to adulthood and the desire among students and their parents to continue that rite. College occupies a very different place in our national culture than does any particular version of a phone or automobile and will not be so rapidly displaced. Still, the status quo cannot continue for very much longer; to paraphrase Paul Friga, the days of "just getting by somehow" are for many institutions probably numbered. Even if one is inclined to dismiss the inequities and inefficiencies and pedagogical flaws, the internal and external financial trends are plainly too powerful to ignore. On a systemic level, higher education has simply become too expensive: too expensive for institutions to provide and too expensive for consumers to afford. The exogenous changes that could alter this situation—sharp increases in public funding, a reversal of the decades-long growth in income inequality—are nowhere on the horizon. The internal changes, as I noted earlier, have consisted mostly of discounting and cutting programs rather than altering the model that has created the cost problem. If innovation doesn't change higher education, economics will. I realize that this has been forecast for a long time and that futurists, like stock-market experts, are almost always wrong about the future, but I truly believe that predictions of a financial breaking point have been premature rather than erroneous. Stein's law will hold: "If something cannot go on forever, it will stop."[52]

Steven Mintz has for years been writing, with what I would describe as a tone of measured urgency, about the need for higher education to change and its inability or unwillingness to do so. Despite being consistently disappointed, he continues, admirably, to suggest possible paths for endangered and nonendangered institutions to follow, even as he concedes that most do not "strik[e] me as likely." These include a "total curricular and service redesign"; "pedagogy that includes active learning, collaborative assignments, maker projects, and intensive writing"; and "an education for the future of work," each of which describes in many ways places like ALU and Sterling. He is appropriately skeptical of the quality of the online education offered by "for-profit providers and their imitators," yet at the same time he seems to accept as a given that "institutional change . . . takes place incrementally, one department or one unit or one faculty or staff member at a time." The scale of change for which he argues and the process of change he describes are fundamentally incompatible. "A college without a vision," he writes, "is a college without a future." A college in which each department or unit or individual faculty member goes their own way and changes, or not, at their own pace is, I submit, a college without a vision.[53]

Jason Wingard, former president of Temple University, writes with a greater sense of urgency. Borrowing an image from the former CEO of Nokia, he argues that higher education is on a "burning platform" and that it must "change or die." If your platform is on fire, it would seem, the reaction must be rapid and dramatic. Yet Wingard's response is to suggest that "we must tweak and adapt our curriculum *at least* [his emphasis] every single year" and "get back to basics." While no prescription in response to a burning platform should include the word "tweak," Wingard seems to be acknowledging the realities of the industry he inhabits. He also argues, correctly, that "we need to address affordability" but stops short of advocating for the kinds of deep reimagining that would truly reduce the cost of educating students. I can't blame him: for a then-sitting president to go even as far as he did took courage.[54]

The most likely scenario going forward is that slow, incremental change will continue to be the rule. The impediments to rapid transformational change from within seem simply too powerful and deeply entrenched to overcome. "Faculty choosing to resist change at struggling institutions," Derr observes, "is a cultural issue. They're able to understand the problem and maybe how they can contribute to its solution, but there isn't a culture to support that. To take on that shared responsibility is contrary to the place they believe they hold in the institution."[55] Under these circumstances, what is most important is that the small changes move colleges gradually in the right direction. Toward more experiential learning. Toward less disciplinary rigidity. Toward a more clearly defined, more limited, and more genuinely distinctive mission. Toward more focus on the issues that matter in the world. Above all else, toward more emphasis on students as the highest priority of the college and as the drivers of their own learning. All of these goals have the potential both to bend the cost curve of higher education and to make it better. Technology has a critical role to play in these changes, but it is one tool to be used in pursuit of improved education and not an end in itself. Absent an emphasis on the human capacity to learn, an emphasis on technological innovation will lead us down some of the same ethically and qualitatively questionable paths as those blazed by Facebook and Amazon. It is common to hear that we have only scratched the surface of what technology can do. Let us not forget that we have, in our educational system, only scratched the surface of what people can do, especially people who have historically been underserved.

If these gradual, beneficial changes came to pass, it would mean different things for different kinds of institutions. For the most selective and financially secure, it would mean slowly improving the quality and utility of the education they provide to the students fortunate enough to have access to their considerable resources. For less elite colleges and universities, incremental change, even in the right direction, would probably, as Mintz acknowledges, lead to a future in which both their economic security and educational quality "gradually, progressively deteriorate".[56] declining resources would almost inevitably outpace improving practices. For the most vulnerable institutions, whose number is much larger than their upbeat websites and admissions brochures would have you believe, this would possibly mean closure, merger, or partnership with an online provider, especially once the demographic decline really hits in the latter half of this decade. These schools cannot afford to change slowly. Under the current delivery model and pricing structure, there is simply more supply of than demand for colleges that are not name brands, and so the market would make the necessary adjustments.

Slow, nearly indiscernible change will also continue to create opportunities for those who want to remake higher education from without. Some of these attempts will be productive, but the majority—especially from elected officials—will not be. Most of those attacking higher education from within statehouses and gubernatorial mansions know little and care less about the enterprise itself. What they possess is an almost preternatural ability to identify and direct their umbrage at easy targets, and higher education, in failing to address its own vulnerabilities, has made itself far too easy a target. When Bernie Sanders and Ron DeSantis can both generate enthusiasm among their supporters by criticizing your work, you have a real problem.

Here is where I am again inclined to borrow from Dickens, this time from Scrooge's question near the end of his visit with the Ghost of Christmas Yet to Come: "Are these the shadows of the things that Will be, or are they shadows of things that May be, only?"

Nothing is absolutely certain. While things might turn out worse than I just described—that is, no real change at all—they might also turn out better. As I noted earlier, higher education is an industry in which winning initiatives are quickly copied, so it might take only a few successful experiments in transformation to begin to affect a good portion of the sector. Right now innovators are either effectively start-ups, like Sterling or ALU, or massive and commercial, like Arizona State or Southern New Hampshire. The mantle of being that traditional, mission-driven college or university genuinely willing to do the hard work of disruption is there for the taking. While the barriers to change will not go away any time soon, they are difficult but not impossible to overcome. With the right confluence of circumstances—brave and creative leadership within the administration and the faculty, external pressures that demand a response, and good ideas—it is feasible to imagine a college or university that offers to the world an education that is more affordable, more student centered, more experiential, and more holistic: one that doesn't attempt to replicate the offerings and practices of countless institutions all over the country or default to less effective, prepackaged online courses. I genuinely believe that the market would respond well to the first colleges that go down this path. I hold out hope that somewhere there are educational leaders who, when presented with the opportunity and the risk of challenging orthodoxies and changing for the better, will decide—unlike the version of me with which I began this narrative—that yes, it is worth it.

Notes

Preface

1. Jeff Denneen et al., "The Financially Sustainable University: The Lost Decade," Bain and Company, July 15, 2022, https://bain.com/insights/financially-sustainable -university-the-lost-decade-infographic/.

Chapter 1

1. David Figlio and Morton Shapiro, "Staffing the Higher Education Classroom," *Journal of Economic Perspectives* 35, no. 1 (Winter 2021): 149. See also John Hattie and H. W. Marsh, "The Relationship Between Research and Teaching: A Meta-analysis," *Review of Educational Research* 66, no. 4 (Winter 1996): 507–42. A 2017 study done at the University of Maastricht in the Netherlands actually finds a negative correlation between research productivity and teaching evaluations at the undergraduate level, though admittedly the focus of the study was very narrow. See Ali Palali et al., "Are Good Researchers Also Good Teachers? The Relationship Between Research Quality and Teaching Quality," *Economics of Education Review* 64 (June 2018): 40–49.
2. *Macalester College Faculty Handbook*, 47, accessed March 22, 2023, https://docs .google.com/document/d/1jrZ3No-idNNOYiqV2pBT9HghQs_2utJRFY_eFl5mLbs /edit.
3. Esat Braveboy, "English Faculty Vote to Change Name to 'Department of Literatures in English,'" *Cornell Daily Sun*, October 14, 2020, https://cornellsun.com/2020/10/14 /english-faculty-vote-to-change-name-to-department-of-literatures-in-english/.
4. Jim Collins, *Good to Great and the Social Sectors* (self-published, 2005), 23.
5. Michael Larrson, CEO of Duet, a Boston-based educational nonprofit, quoted in Scott Kirsner, "College Presidents Are Leaders, but Why Not Innovators?," *Boston Globe*, November 6, 2022, https://bostonglobe.com/2022/11/06/business/college -presidents-are-leaders-why-not-innovators/?s_campaign=8315.
6. See Rosabeth Moss Kanter, "Ten Reasons People Resist Change," *Harvard Business Review*, September 25, 2012, https://hbr.org/2012/09/ten-reasons-people-resist -chang.

7. C. J. Holden, "True Disruption Comes When You Step Outside Your Industry," LinkedIn, December 18, 2018, https://linkedin.com/pulse/true-disruption-comes -when-you-step-outside-your-industry-cj-holden-1d.

8. Kevin Gannon, "Let's Disrupt the Calls for 'Disruptive Innovation,'" *Chronicle of Higher Education*, October 26, 2022, https://chronicle.com/article/lets-disrupt-the -calls-for-disruptive-innovation.

9. Johann N. Neem, "The University in Ruins," *Chronicle of Higher Education*, March 21, 2022, https://chronicle.com/article/the-university-in-ruins.

10. See Hank Tucker, "How America's Wealthiest Colleges Are Getting Richer Faster Than Schools with Small Endowments," *Forbes*, February 19, 2022, https://forbes .com/sites/hanktucker/2022/02/19/how-americas-wealthiest-colleges-are-getting -richer-faster-than-schools-with-small-endowments; and Emma Whitford, "College Endowments Boomed in Fiscal 2021," *Inside Higher Education*, February 18, 2022, https://insidehighered.com/news/2022/02/18/college-endowments-boomed-fiscal-year -2021-study-shows.

11. See Josh Moody, "A Guide to the Changing Number of U.S. Universities," *U.S. News and World Report*, April 27, 2021, https://usnews.com/education/best-colleges /articles/how-many-universities-are-in-the-us-and-why-that-number-is-changing.

12. The best and most comprehensive analysis of the rising cost of college remains Robert Archibald and David Feldman, *Why Does College Cost So Much?* (New York: Oxford University Press, 2011).

13. See Lee Gardner, "Why Does College Cost So Much?," *Chronicle of Higher Education*, May 16, 2022, https://chronicle.com/article/why-does-college-cost-so-much.

14. W. J. Baumol and W. G. Bowen, "On the Performing Arts: The Anatomy of Their Economic Problems," *American Economic Review* 55, no. 1–2 (March 1965): 495–502. It is only fair to note that there is widespread though not universal acceptance of the role of cost disease in driving up the cost of higher education. For a skeptical view, see Andrew Gillen, "Does the Baumol Effect Explain Rising College Costs?," *Education Next*, July 18, 2019, https://educationnext.org/does-baumol-effect-explain-rising -college-costs/.

15. Cost disease, more than a loss of interest in the performing arts, explains why orchestras and theatrical companies were struggling badly even before the pandemic. According to Robert Flanagan, "Even if every seat in every symphony hall was filled for every concert, the vast majority of U.S. symphony orchestras would still face significant performance deficits." To college CFOs, this will sound depressingly familiar. Quoted in Mary Carole McCauley, "Why Is It So Hard to Keep an Orchestra Afloat? The Baltimore Symphony Orchestra Is Not Alone in Its Woes," *Baltimore Sun*, August 2, 2019, https://baltimoresun.com/entertainment/bs-fe-orchestras -afloat-20190802-7m7y5q2swnhyjc56rlelz6azt4-story.html.

16. William J. Bennett, "Our Greedy Colleges," *New York Times*, February 18, 1987, https://nytimes.com/1987/02/18/opinion/our-greedy-colleges.html.

17. Donald E. Heller, *Does Federal Financial Aid Drive Up College Prices?* (Washington, DC: American Council on Education, April 2018), 18, https://acenet.edu/Documents /Heller-Monograph.pdf. For alternative views, see Andrew Gillen, "Introducing Bennet Hypothesis 2.0," Center for College Affordability and Productivity, February 2012, https://files.eric.ed.gov/fulltext/ED536151.pdf; and Richard Vedder, "The

Bennet Hypothesis Confirmed—Again," *Forbes*, July 21, 2015, https://forbes.com/sites/ccap/2015/07/21/the-bennett-hypothesis-confirmed-again.

18. See Kevin Carey, "The Single Most Important Thing to Know About Financial Aid: It's a Sham," *Slate*, July 25, 2022, https://slate.com/business/2022/07/college-financial-aid-sham.html; and Jordan Weissman, "Master's Degrees Are the Second Biggest Scam in Higher Education," *Slate*, July 16, 2021, https://slate.com/business/2021/07/masters-degrees-debt-loans-worth-it.html. Carey is interviewed in the Weissman piece.

19. Juliana Menasce Horowitz, Ruth Igielnik, and Rakesh Kochhar, "Trends in Income and Wealth Inequality," Pew Research Center, January 9, 2020, https://pewresearch.org/social-trends/2020/01/09/trends-in-income-and-wealth-inequality.

20. Jon Boeckenstedt, "Will Your College Survive the Demographic Cliff?," *Chronicle of Higher Education*, March 22, 2022, https://chronicle.com/article/will-your-college-survive-the-demographic-cliff.

21. Nathan D. Grawe, *Demographics and the Demand for Higher Education* (Baltimore: Johns Hopkins University Press, 2018).

22. Boeckenstedt, "Demographic Cliff."

23. Tanya Lewis, "The Pandemic Caused a Baby Bust, Not a Boom," *Scientific American*, August 30, 2021, https://scientificamerican.com/article/the-pandemic-caused-a-baby-bust-not-a-boom/; "The US Population Is Aging," Urban Institute, accessed March 22, 2023, https://urban.org/policy-centers/cross-center-initiatives/program-retirement-policy/projects/data-warehouse/what-future-holds/us-population-aging. One bit of positive news: the baby bust of 2020 seems to have been followed by a slight "baby boom" in 2021. See Max Witynski, "A Pandemic 'Baby Boom' is Happening in the U.S., Study Finds," https://news.northwestern.edu/stories/2022/10/the-united-states-is-experiencing-a-pandemic-baby-bump/.

24. Institute of Education Sciences, *Report on the Condition of Education 2022* (Washington, DC: National Center for Education Statistics, May 2022), https://nces.ed.gov/pubs2022/2022144.pdf; Stephanie Saul, "College Enrollment Drops, Even as the Pandemic's Effects Ebb," *New York Times*, May 26, 2022, https://nytimes.com/2022/05/26/us/college-enrollment.html; Maria Carrasco, "Fewer High School Graduates Go Straight to College," *Inside Higher Education*, January 10, 2022, https://insidehighered.com/admissions/article/2022/01/10/fewer-high-school-graduates-are-going-straight-college; Brianna Hatch, "Why Fewer High-School Graduates Are Going to College," *Chronicle of Higher Education*, June 16, 2022, https://chronicle.com/article/why-fewer-high-school-graduates-are-going-to-college. The most recent data confirm that the trend has slowed but not reversed. See Audrey Williams June, "Higher Ed's Enrollment Fell Again This Fall, If a Bit More Slowly," *Chronicle of Higher Education*, October 20, 2022, https://chronicle.com/article/higher-eds-enrollment-fell-again-this-fall-if-a-bit-more-slowly. Doug Shapiro is quoted in the piece in the *New York Times*.

25. Karin Fisher, "The Shrinking of Higher Ed," *Chronicle of Higher Education*, August 12, 2022, https://chronicle.com/article/the-shrinking-of-higher-ed. Thelin is quoted in this article.

26. *CFO Outlook for Higher Education* (Syntellis, 2022), https://syntellis.com/sites/default/files/2022-01/2022_Education_Outlook_2022_0.pdf; Doug Lederman, "Business

Officers Upbeat Despite Major Headwinds," *Inside Higher Education*, July 13, 2022, https://insidehighered.com/news/survey/college-business-officers-upbeat-despite -worrisome-outlook.

27. Colleen Flaherty, "Saint Mary's of Minnesota Plans Program Closures, Layoffs," *Inside Higher Education*, May 12, 2022, https://insidehighered.com/quicktakes/2022 /05/12/saint-mary%E2%80%99s-minnesota-plans-program-closures-layoffs.

28. Jon Marcus and Kirk Carapezza, "As Small Private Colleges Keep Closing, Some Are Fighting Back," GBH, April 15, 2019, https://www.wgbh.org/news/education/2019/04/15 /as-small-private-colleges-keep-closing-some-are-fighting-back. To be fair to Hiram, their move to trademark "The New Liberal Arts" looks reasonable in comparison to the successful effort by Ohio State to trademark the word *The*. Excuse me—The Ohio State.

29. Colleen Flaherty, "Cuts Reversed at Stevens Point," *Inside Higher Education*, April 11, 2019, https://insidehighered.com/news/2019/04/11/stevens-point-abandons -controversial-plan-cut-liberal-arts-majors-including-history.

30. National Association of College and University Business Officers, *The 2019 NACUBO Tuition Discounting Study* (Washington, DC: National Association of College and University Business Officers, 2020), https://nasfaa.org/uploads/documents /NACUBO_Tuition_Discounting_2019.pdf.

31. Audrey Williams June, "Tuition-Discount Rates Continued to Climb at Private Colleges," *Chronicle of Higher Education*, May 19, 2022, https://chronicle.com/article /tuition-discount-rates-continued-to-climb-at-private-colleges.

32. Gordon C. Winston, "Why Can't a College Be More like a Firm," *Change* 29, no. 5 (1997): 34. Winston arrives at that number because the cost of providing an education at a college like Williams, where he taught, far exceeds even the full tuition price.

33. Jessica Dickler, "Amid the Covid Crisis, This College Is Cutting Tuition in Half Next Year," CNBC, December 21, 2020, https://cnbc.com/2020/12/21/colleges-slashing -tuition-for-2021-22.html; Mike Morken, "Tuition Will Drop at Concordia as School Going with New 'School' Structure," Valley News Live, September 24, 2020, https:// valleynewslive.com/2020/09/24/tuition-will-drop-at-concordia-as-school-going-with -new-school-structure/.

34. Wendel Clark, "What Is a Psychological Pricing Strategy?," Bizfluent, October 25, 2018, https://bizfluent.com/about-7421400-psychological-pricing-strategy-.html.

35. Ry Rivard, "Price Goes Down, Price Goes Up," *Inside Higher Education*, October 9, 2013, https://insidehighered.com/news/2013/10/09/two-years-after-dramatic-price -drop-sewanees-tuition-has-climbed-back.

36. Robert Zemsky, Susan Shaman, and Susan Campbell Baldridge, "Will Your College Close?," *Chronicle of Higher Education*, February 7, 2020, https://chronicle.com /article/will-your-college-close/.

37. Noah Askin and Matthew S. Bothner, "Status-Aspirational Pricing: The 'Chivas Regal' Strategy in U.S. Higher Education, 2006–2012," *Administrative Science Quarterly* 61, no. 2, published ahead of print, January 29, 2016, https://journals.sagepub .com/doi/abs/10.1177/0001839216629671.

38. Sandy Baum and Sarah Turner, "'Free Tuition' Is the Opposite of Progressive Policymaking," *Washington Post*, May 3, 2019, https://washingtonpost.com/outlook/free -tuition-is-the-opposite-of-progressive-policymaking/2019/05/03/4767edc8-6c1b-11e9 -a66d-a82d3f3d96d5_story.html.

39. See Scott Carlson, "The Backlog That Could Threaten Higher Ed's Viability," *Chronicle of Higher Education*, March 31, 2023, https://chronicle.com/article/the-backlog-that-could-threaten-higher-eds-viability.

40. *State of Facilities in Higher Education*, Gordian, https://gordian.com/uploads/2023/03/2023-State-of-Facilities-Report.20230321205652466.pdf.

41. Jonathan Zimmerman, *The Amateur Hour: A History of College Teaching in America* (Baltimore: Johns Hopkins University Press, 2020), 11.

42. The first Mazur quote is from Aleszu Bajak, "Lectures Aren't Just Boring, They're Ineffective, Too, Study Finds," *Science*, May 12, 2014, https://science.org/content/article/lectures-arent-just-boring-theyre-ineffective-too-study-finds. The second is from Craig Lambert, "Twilight of the Lecture," *Harvard Magazine*, March–April 2012, https://harvardmagazine.com/2012/03/twilight-of-the-lecture. Nobel Prize–winning physicist Carl Weiman has also been an evangelist for moving away from lectures and toward more active modes of learning in science and has created the Science Education Initiative. Maybe we need to pay more attention to physicists. See Carl Weiman, *Improving How Universities Teach Science* (Cambridge, MA: Harvard University Press, 2017).

43. Bajak, "Lectures."

44. Mazur quoted in Lambert, "Twilight."

45. Bajak, "Lectures."

46. Steven Mintz, "A Glance Backward," *Inside Higher Education*, April 24, 2022, https://insidehighered.com/blogs/higher-ed-gamma/glance-backward.

47. Molly Worthen, "Lecture Me, Really," *New York Times*, October 17, 2015, https://nytimes.com/2015/10/18/opinion/sunday/lecture-me-really.html.

48. Mazur quoted in Lambert, "Twilight."

49. Janna Quitney Anderson, Jan Lauren Boyles, and Lee Raine, *The Future Impact of the Internet on Higher Education* (Washington, DC: Pew Research Center, July 27, 2012), 4, https://files.eric.ed.gov/fulltext/ED534048.pdf.

50. Anderson, Boyles, and Raine, 3.

51. Saskia de Melker, "Agrarian Roots? Think Again. Debunking the Myth of Summer Vacation's Origins," PBS News Weekend, September 7, 2014, https://pbs.org/newshour/education/debunking-myth-summer-vacation.

52. Norene Malone, "Gimme a Break," *Slate*, December 30, 2009, https://slate.com/news-and-politics/2009/12/why-do-college-students-get-such-long-winter-vacations.html.

53. Jon Marcus, "Momentum Builds Behind a Way to Lower the Cost of College: A Degree in Three Years," Hechinger Report, April 15, 2022, https://hechingerreport.org/momentum-builds-behind-a-way-to-lower-the-cost-of-college-a-degree-in-three-years/.

54. "'College in 3' Project Teams Up with 13 Institutions to Explore Three-Year Degree Options," Penn GSE News, University of Pennsylvania, November 17, 2021, https://www.gse.upenn.edu/news/college-3-project-teams-13-institutions-explore-three-year-degree-options.

55. David M. Quinn and Morgan Polikoff, "Summer Learning Loss: What It Is, and What We Can Do About It," Brookings Institute, September 14, 2017, https://brookings.edu/research/summer-learning-loss-what-is-it-and-what-can-we-do-about-it.

56. Quinn and Polikoff, "Summer Learning Loss."

57. Andrew Delbanco, *College: What It Was, Is, and Should Be* (Princeton, NJ: Princeton University Press, 2012), 79.

58. Kara Gavin, "How Academic Medical Centers Came to Be," Michigan Health Lab, University of Michigan, January 27, 2020, https://labblog.uofmhealth.org/industry -dx/how-academic-medical-centers-came-to-be.

59. Delbanco, *College*, 85.

60. Henry Zhang, "More Departments Face Over-enrollments as Course Loads Decrease," *Swarthmore Phoenix*, February 14, 2014, https://swarthmorephoenix.com /2014/02/14/professors-course-loads-to-be-decreased/.

61. *Digest of Education Statistics* (National Center for Education Statistics, 2022), table 326.10, https://nces.ed.gov/programs/digest/d21/tables/dt21_326.10.asp.

62. Jon Marcus, "Most College Students Don't Graduate in Four Years, So Colleges and the Government Count Six Years as 'Success,'" Hechinger Report, October 10, 2021, https://hechingerreport.org/how-the-college-lobby-got-the-government-to -measure-graduation-rates-over-six-years-instead-of-four/. Marcus provides a nice summary of how the six-year graduation rate became the standard for reporting purposes.

63. "Fast Facts: Undergraduate Graduation Rates," National Center for Education Statistics, accessed March 22, 2023, https://nces.ed.gov/fastfacts/display.asp?id=40.

64. Matt S. Giani, Paul Attewell, and David Walling, "The Value of an Incomplete Degree: Heterogeneity in the Labor Market Benefits of College Non-completion," *Journal of Higher Education* 91, no. 4 (August 2019): 514–39, https://tandfonline.com /doi/full/10.1080/00221546.2019.1653122.

65. Marcos Aguiar et al., "What AI Reveals About Trust in the World's Largest Companies," Boston Consulting Group, May 20, 2022, https://bcg.com/publications/2022 /trust-index-analyzing-companies-trustworthiness.

66. Kim Parker, "The Growing Partisan Divide in Views of Higher Education," Pew Research Center, August 19, 2019, https://pewresearch.org/social-trends/2019/08 /19/the-growing-partisan-divide-in-views-of-higher-education-2/; Jeffrey M. Jones, "Confidence in Higher Education Down Since 2015," October 8, 2018, https://news .gallup.com/opinion/gallup/242441/confidence-higher-education-down-2015.aspx; Rachel Fishman, Sophie Nguyen, and Louisa Woodhouse, "Varying Degrees 2022," New America, July 26, 2022, https://newamerica.org/education-policy/reports /varying-degrees-2022/.

67. Fishman, "Varying Degrees."

68. Rahul Choudaha, "America's Most Trusted Universities, and the Need to Bridge Gaps in Public Trust," Morning Consult, August 2, 2022, https://morningconsult.com /2022/08/02/most-trusted-universities-gaps-public-trust/.

69. Will Bunch, *After the Ivory Tower Falls: How College Broke the American Dream and Blew Up Our Politics—and How to Fix It* (New York: William Morrow, 2022), 5–6.

70. Duncan et al., "Will Schools and Universities Ever Return to Normal? Nine Experts on the Future of Education after the Pandemic," *Foreign Policy*, September 5, 2020, https://foreignpolicy.com/2020/09/05/education-schools-universities-future-after -pandemic/.

71. John C. Mitchell, "As Students Return to Campus, Higher Ed Must Build on What We Learned During the Pandemic," Hechinger Report, August 22, 2022,

https://hechingerreport.org/opinion-as-students-return-to-campus-higher-ed-must
-build-on-what-we-learned-during-the-pandemic/.

72. "Pandemic Innovations & the Future of CS Assessments," Stanford Computer Science Department, May 2022, https://cspedagogy.stanford.edu/.

73. Mitchell, "Students Return."

74. Jon Marcus, "Urgency of Getting People Back to Work Gives New Momentum to 'Microcredentials,'" Hechinger Report, June 2, 2020, https://hechingerreport.org /more-students-start-earning-stackable-credentials-on-their-way-to-degrees/.

75. Lindsay McKenzie, "2U Announces Layoffs, Spending Cuts to Counter Decline in Online Learning Business," EdScoop, July 28, 2022, https://edscoop.com/2u-layoffs -spending-cuts-edx-focus/.

76. Marcus, "Urgency."

77. For those who are not fans of classic rock, that's the Who, "We Won't Get Fooled Again."

78. Vijay Govindarajan et al., "Resist Old Routines When Returning to Campus," *Harvard Business Review*, June 24, 2021, https://hbsp.harvard.edu/inspiring-minds/resist -old-routines-when-returning-to-campus.

79. *2021 Survey of College and University Chief Academic Officers* (*Inside Higher Education* and Hanover Research, 2021), https://www.insidehighered.com/system/files /booklets/IHE_2021_Provost%20Survey_with_Appendix.pdf; Lederman, "Business Officers."

80. Doug Lederman, "Hopeful Despite Headwinds: A Survey of College Presidents," *Inside Higher Education*, April 11, 2023, https://insidehighered.com/news/governance /executive-leadership/2023/04/11/hopeful-despite-headwinds-survey-presidents#.

81. Both McClure and Staisloff are quoted in Lederman, "Hopeful Despite Headwinds."

82. Quoted in Lederman, "Business Officers."

83. Quoted in Marcus, "Momentum Builds."

84. Quoted in Chris Burt, "Could 5, 50, or Even 200 New Colleges Help Save Higher Ed from Freefall?," University Business, June 16, 2022, https://universitybusiness.com /could-5-50-or-even-200-new-colleges-help-save-higher-ed-from-freefall/.

Chapter 2

1. Quoted in Brianna Hatch, "College Rankings Are 'a Joke,' Education Secretary Says," *Chronicle of Higher Education*, August 11, 2022, https://chronicle.com/article/college -rankings-are-a-joke-education-secretary-says.

2. Colin Diver, *Breaking Ranks: How the Rankings Industry Rules Higher Education and What to Do About It* (Baltimore: Johns Hopkins University Press, 2022), 40.

3. "Malcolm Gladwell & the US News Rankings," Substack, CTAS Higher Ed Business, July 20, 2021, https://ctas.substack.com/p/malcolm-gladwell-and-the-us-news.

4. Molly Alter and Randall Reback, "True for Your School? How Changing Reputations Alter Demand for Selective U.S. Colleges," *Educational Evaluation and Policy Analysis* 36, no. 3 (September 2014): 346–70.

5. I will not take the time to review all the absurdities of the *U.S. News* rankings, though it is worth pointing out that at a time when the cost of higher education is a major national problem, *U.S. News* actually rewards financial inefficiency: spending more

per student leads to a higher rank. Diver's book, cited earlier, is a good summary of the problems with and created by *U.S. News*.

6. Anemona Hartocollis, "U.S. News Releases New Rankings for Law and Medical Schools, Despite Boycott," *New York Times*, April 11, 2023, https://nytimes.com/2023/04/11/us/us-news-law-school-rankings.html.

7. The misreporting around this issue is so egregious that it might lead one to think that newspapers and magazines choose deliberately provocative headlines. Here is the *New York Times*: "Yale and Harvard Law Schools Withdraw from the U.S. News Rankings," https://nytimes.com/2022/11/16/us/yale-law-school-us-news-rankings.html; and *Forbes*: "Yale Law School Withdraws from U.S. News Rankings over Methodology," https://forbes.com/sites/annaesakismith/2022/11/16/yale-law-school-withdraws-from-us-news-rankings-over-methodology/?sh=71f6140926c7; and the *Guardian*: "Yale, Harvard and UC Berkeley Law Schools Withdraw from US News Rankings," https://www.theguardian.com/us-news/2022/nov/17/yale-harvard-law-school-us-news-world-report-rankings. This sounds better, I suppose, than saying that Yale will stop submitting data but will almost certainly continue to be ranked.

8. See Melissa Chen, "New Book Details How Several USC Scandals Almost Went Untold," *Daily Trojan*, September 19, 2022, https://dailytrojan.com/2022/09/19/new-book-details-how-several-usc-scandals-almost-went-untold/.

9. This line is regularly attributed to Franklin, but I have been unable to locate its actual source.

10. The Wallace gift, after the initial public offering of *Reader's Digest* stock, was worth about $250 million in 1990, the equivalent of about $600 million today.

11. In 1990, Allegheny made the bold move of increasing tuition for incoming students by almost 20 percent, with the goal of investing in faculty and signaling to the market a higher level of quality. The market was having none of it. Applications fell by 20 percent, the incoming class came in dramatically below the target, and major budget cuts had to be made. Additional large-scale budget cuts have followed, most recently in 2021.

12. David Steele, "The Prestige Name Game," *Inside Higher Education*, May 27, 2022, https://www.insidehighered.com/news/2022/05/27/changing-college-university-driven-image-prestige.

13. Marguerite Clarke, "Weighing Things Up: A Closer Look at *U.S. News & World Report*'s Ranking Formulas," *College and University* 79, no. 3 (Winter 2004): 3.

14. Columbia was initially ranked number two, until Columbia math professor Michael Thaddeus analyzed the data for the university published in *U.S. News* and found that much of it ranged from the implausible to the simply impossible. See Jordan Ellenberg, "Did Columbia Game the U.S. News College Rankings with Sketchy Data?," *Washington Post*, March 23, 2022, https://washingtonpost.com/outlook/2022/03/23/columbia-usnews-rankings-college-methodology/. After first pushing back against Thaddeus's analysis, the university announced in June 2022 that it was taking the extraordinary step of submitting no data to *U.S. News* for the 2023 rankings while it conducted an internal investigation. "We will take no shortcuts," the provost announced, "in getting it right." *U.S. News* responded by removing Columbia from the 2022 rankings, and a recent graduate responded by suing Columbia. Eventually Columbia admitted that it had submitted false data because it has "relied on

outdated and/or incorrect methodologies" and because, well, the data collection was so complicated—though the mistakes always seemed to benefit the university. *U.S. News* dropped Columbia to number eighteen in 2023, the publication's equivalent of sending a misbehaving toddler for a time-out. The whole episode is a case study of the warping effect of the Mother of All Rankings. Sarah Brown, "Columbia U. Won't Submit Data to 'U.S. News' Rankings After Professor Alleged False Information," *Chronicle of Higher Education*, June 30, 2022, https://chronicle.com/article/columbia-u-wont-submit-data-to-u-s-news-rankings-after-professor-alleged-false-information.

15. There are of course a number of organizations that rank universities around the globe, and the results are equally consistent and predictable. The best known of these is probably the *Times Higher Education* world rankings, but my favorite is done by an organization called Round University Ranking, based in Tbilisi, Georgia, which groups universities into "leagues," beginning with Diamond, running through Golden, Silver, Bronze, and Copper, and ending with simply "World"—a polite alternative, I suppose, to Tin. See "About Us," Round University Ranking, accessed March 23, 2023, https://roundranking.com/about-us.html.

16. In addition to the publications cited in this paragraph, those that now rank colleges and universities include *Money, Forbes,* The *Wall Street Journal/Times Higher Education* (one sees a theme there), and, appropriately, something called *College* magazine. *Princeton Review* has of course been publishing dozens of ranked lists for years, including some in such categories as "Reefer Madness" and "Lots of Beer." Despite the growing list of imitators, *U.S. News* remains the reigning and still undefeated rankings champion.

17. "2021 University Rankings," *Washington Monthly*, accessed March 23, 2023, https://washingtonmonthly.com/2021college-guide/national/.

18. Heartland Forward, *Research to Renewal: Advancing University Tech Transfer* (Heartland Forward, May 2022), https://heartlandforward.org/wp-content/uploads/2022/05/ResearchToRenewal.pdf.

19. For those unfamiliar with New York City dining, Le Bernardin regularly receives three stars from the Michelin Guide. Reservations fill about ten minutes after they become available.

20. Billy Duberstein, "If You Invested $1,000 in Bershire's IPO, This Is How Much Money You'd Have Now," Motley Fool, November 24, 2019, https://www.fool.com/investing/2019/11/24/if-you-invested-1000-in-berkshires-ipo-this-is-how.aspx.

21. David E. Sanger, "College Endowments Grow by Millions with Surge in Markets," *New York Times*, July 23, 1983, https://nytimes.com/1983/07/23/us/college-endowments-grow-by-millions-with-surge-in-market.html; John S. Rosenberg, "Harvard Endowment Increases $11.3 Billion to $53.2 Billion, and University Operations Yield $283-Million Surplus Despite Pandemic," *Harvard Magazine*, October 14, 2021, https://www.harvardmagazine.com/2021/10/harvard-endowment-surges-11-3-billion-university-surplus.

22. Dan Bauman, "Some Colleges Pay for Space on a Classic Board Game. It Ain't Monopoly Money," *Chronicle of Higher Education*, June 10, 2022, https://chronicle.com/article/some-colleges-pay-for-space-on-a-classic-game-board-it-aint-monopoly-money.

23. "What Is Search Good," IGI Global, accessed March 22, 2023, https://igi-global.com/dictionary/search-good/53799.

24. Dave Wieneke, "Customer Strategy Foundation: Search, Experience, and Creedence (SEC) Analysis Determines How Customers Buy," Rutgers Business School, January 29, 2019, https://www.business.rutgers.edu/business-insights/customer-strategy-foundation-search-experience-and-credence-sec-analysis.

25. Asher Wolinsky, "Competition in Markets for Credence Goods," *Journal of Institutional and Theoretical Economics* 151, no. 1 (1995): 117.

26. Gordon C. Winston, "Why Can't a College Be More Like a Firm?," *Change* 29, no. 5 (1997): 34.

27. Wieneke, "Customer Strategy Foundation."

28. David Dranove, "Credence Goods," ScienceDirect, accessed March 22, 2023, https://sciencedirect.com/topics/economics-econometrics-and-finance/credence-goods.

29. Winand Emons, "Credence Goods and Fraudulent Experts," *Rand Journal of Economics* 28, no. 1 (Spring 1997): 107.

30. Dan Friedell, "Will Scandal Change How People View College Rankings?," VOA Learning English, February 19, 2022, https://learningenglish.voanews.com/a/will-scandal-change-how-people-view-college-rankings-/6443074.html.

31. Rick Blizzard, "Healthcare Panel: How Do People Choose Hospitals?," Gallup, October 25, 2005, https://news.gallup.com/poll/19402/healthcare-panel-how-people-choose-hospitals.aspx.

32. "2018 Domaine de la Romanee-Conti Romanee-Conti Grand Cru," Wine Searcher, accessed March 22, 2023, https://www.wine-searcher.com/find/dom+de+la+grand+cru+cote+nuit+romanee+conti+vosne+burgundy+france/2018.

33. Aaron Goldfarb, "How Pappy Van Winkle Became a Wildly Expensive, Impossible-to-Find Unicorn," *Wine Enthusiast*, March 30, 2020, https://www.winemag.com/2020/03/03/pappy-van-winkle-expensive/.

34. "College Acceptance Rates, Then and Now," Ivywise, June 12, 2012, https://www.ivywise.com/blog/college-acceptance-rates-then-and-now/.

35. See Eric R. Eide, Michael J. Hilmer, and Mark H. Showalter, "Is It Where You Go or What You Study? The Relative Influence of College Selectivity and College Major on Earnings," *Contemporary Economic Policy* 34, no. 1 (January 2016): 37–46.

36. Abe Harraf, Brandon William Soltwisch, and Kaitlyn Talbott, "Antecedents of Organizational Complacency: Identifying and Preventing Complacency in the Work Environment," *Managing Global Transitions* 14, no. 4 (Winter 2016): 385.

37. Quoted in James D. Walsh, "The Coming Disruption: Scott Galloway Predicts a Handful of Elite Cyborg Universities Will Soon Monopolize Higher Education," *New York Magazine*, May 11, 2020, https://nymag.com/intelligencer/2020/05/scott-galloway-future-of-college.html. Lest I give Galloway too much credit, I will add that he offers so many pronouncements and predictions that some of them have to be right some of the time. Many of them are wrong. In the Walsh article cited here, for instance, he predicts that elite universities will in the very near future partner with large corporations. Why? "Their trustees aren't going to want them running inefficient businesses, where they have to dip into their endowment every year." This is what you say when you have no understanding of the culture, governance structure, or financial model of such institutions.

38. Thanks to Matt Reed for drawing my attention to this bias in the *Times* and to the relevant tweets of Akil Bello. See Matt Reed, "Friday Fragments," *Inside Higher*

Education, July 15, 2022, https://insidehighered.com/blogs/confessions-community
-college-dean/friday-fragments-237.

39. Quoted in Eliza Gray, "Are Liberal Arts Colleges Doomed?," *Washington Post Maga-zine*, October 21, 2019, https://washingtonpost.com/magazine/2019/10/21/downfall
-hampshire-college-broken-business-model-american-higher-education/.

40. "A Look at Trends in College Consolidation Since 2016," *Higher Ed Dive*, April 22,
2022, https://highereddive.com/news/how-many-colleges-and-universities-have-closed
-since-2016/539379/. Some colleges appear to be gone and then, like zombies, come back
to some sort of strange version of life. Antioch College, an institution with a distin-guished history, was limping along in the fall of 2020 with just over one hundred stu-dents; Hampshire College, also in the fall of 2020, enrolled ninety-six first-year students.

41. Sarah Butrymowicz and Pete D'Amato, "Analysis: Hundreds of Colleges and Uni-versities Show Financial Warning Signs," Hechinger Report, August 4, 2020, https://
hechingerreport.org/analysis-hundreds-of-colleges-and-universities-show-financial
-warning-signs/. The analysis by startup Edmit that claims that one-third of private
colleges are at risk is deeply flawed. See Karen Gross, "Lists; Good Ones and Bad
Ones; Edmit's Is Flawed List," Medium, November 21, 2019, https://medium.com/age
-of-awareness/lists-good-ones-and-bad-ones-edmits-is-flawed-list-e54b6ec30b8f.

42. Jeff Denneen et al., "The Financially Sustainable University: The Lost Decade,"
Bain and Company, July 15, 2022, https://bain.com/insights/financially-sustainable
-university-the-lost-decade-infographic/.

43. Quoted in Jon Marcus and Kurt Carapezza, "As Small Private Colleges Keep Closing,
Some Are Fighting Back," GBH, April 15, 2019, https://www.wgbh.org/news/education
/2019/04/15/as-small-private-colleges-keep-closing-some-are-fighting-back.

44. Matthew D. Henricks, "The Plight of Mills College Should Be an Alarm for American
Higher Education," *American Prospect*, April 20, 2022, https://prospect.org/education
/plight-of-mills-college-american-higher-ed-alarm/; Emma Whitford, "A House
Divided," *Inside Higher Education*, August 18, 2021, https://www.insidehighered.com
/news/2021/08/18/mills-college-alumnae-are-split-over-lawsuit; Nanette Asimov,
"Students Sue Mills College, Accusing School of Misleading Them About North-eastern Takeover," *San Francisco Chronicle*, May 12, 2022, https://sfchronicle.com
/bayarea/article/Students-Sue-Mills-College-saying-it-misled-them-17169370.php.

45. Quoted in Gray, "Are Liberal Arts Colleges Doomed?"

Chapter 3

1. The line actually appears in a work by Hippocrates entitled *Of the Epidemics*. See
Robert H. Schmerling, "First, Do No Harm," *Harvard Health Blog*, June 22, 2020,
https://health.harvard.edu/blog/first-do-no-harm-201510138421.

2. Scott Kirsner, "College Presidents Are Leaders, but Why Not Innovators?," *Bos-ton Globe*, November 6, 2022, https://bostonglobe.com/2022/11/06/business/college
-presidents-are-leaders-why-not-innovators/?s_campaign=8315.

3. Kathleen Teltsch, "Macalester's Endowment Rises to $320 Million," *New York Times*,
October 17, 1990, https://www.nytimes.com/1990/10/17/us/education-macalester-s
-endowment-rises-to-320-million.html.

4. See Greg McRay, "Who Owns a Nonprofit?," Foundation Group, May 10, 2019, https://501c3.org/who-really-owns-a-nonprofit/.

5. See David Burkus, "Extrinsic vs. Intrinsic Motivation at Work," *Psychology Today*, April 11, 2020, https://psychologytoday.com/us/blog/creative-leadership/202004/extrinsic-vs-intrinsic-motivation-work.

6. "The Board of Directors Duties of Care and Loyalty," LawInfo, accessed March 22, 2023, https://lawinfo.com/resources/business-law/the-board-of-directors-duties-of-care-and-loy.html.

7. "Measuring a Company's Entire Social and Environmental Impact," B Lab, accessed March 22, 2023, https://bcorporation.net/en-us/certification.

8. Jim Collins, *Good to Great and the Social Sectors* (self-published, 2005), 5.

9. The Reverend Timothy Healy, late president of Georgetown University, was reported to have said, "Every search committee is looking for God on a good day." Quoted in Shelly Storbeck, "College Presidents Need Help Lately, Too," *Chronicle of Higher Education*, January 25, 2021, https://chronicle.com/article/college-presidents-need-help-lately-too. In February 2023, Hilary L. Link, previously president of Allegheny College, was selected as Drew University's next president.

10. Eric Kelderman, "The Silent Treatment," *Chronicle of Higher Education*, July 26, 2022, https://chronicle.com/article/the-silent-treatment.

11. Holden Thorp correctly points out that the guise of presidential neutrality on political issues is both "a charade" and "a gift to forces that seek to undermine science and other objective analysis." But his proposed solution—"It should be possible for the president to state their views as an individual without reprisal from the board or political leaders"— seems to envision some world in which we simply are not living. Holden Thorp, "The Charade of Political Neutrality," *Chronicle of Higher Education*, September 16, 2022, https://chronicle.com/article/the-charade-of-political-neutrality. The handful of presidents who are outspoken—Michael Roth at Wesleyan and Patricia McGuire at Trinity Washington come to mind—tend to lead institutions that are private and on the small side. They also tend to have the security that comes with long service: McGuire has been president at Trinity Washington since 1989. At the other extreme, public college and university presidents in Florida have remained completely silent in the face of gubernatorial and legislative attacks on academic freedom in their state.

12. A recent survey of the college presidency by the American Council on Education provides another relevant data point: the average length of service among presidents surveyed was 5.9 years, down 2.6 years from 2006. Also noteworthy: more than half planned to leave their position within five years, and one in four planned to leave their position "within the next year or two." *The American College President: 2023 Edition*, American Council on Education and TIAA Institute, 8, 13, https://acenet.edu/Documents/American-College-President-IX-2023.pdf.

13. Karen Doss Bowman, "The Erosion of Presidential Tenure," *Public Purpose*, Summer 2017, 6–9; Lizette Navarette, *CEO Tenure and Retention Study* (Community College League of California, August 2018), https://ccleague.org/sites/default/files/publications/CEO/2018-ceo_tenure_retention_study_cclc.pdf.

14. Megan Zahneis, "What's Behind the Surge in No-Confidence Votes?," *Chronicle of Higher Education*, May 18, 2022, https://chronicle.com/article/whats-behind-the-surge-in-no-confidence-votes.

15. Kirsner, "College Presidents Are Leaders."

16. Richard P. Chait, "Gleanings," in *The Questions of Tenure*, ed. Richard P. Chait (Cambridge, MA: Harvard University Press, 2005), 318.

17. McRaven famously described leading a university as "the toughest job in the nation"—hyperbolic, to be sure, but a sign of the depth of his frustration. And that was in 2018, before things became tougher. Lindsay Ellis, "UT System's McRaven: College Leadership 'Toughest Job in the Nation,'" *Houston Chronicle*, May 1, 2018, https://chron.com/news/houston-texas/houston/article/UT-System-s-McRaven -College-leadership-a-12879700.php.

18. Quoted in Casey Quinlan, "Universities Run into Problems When They Hire Presidents from the Business World," ThinkProgress, March 20, 2016, https://archive .thinkprogress.org/universities-run-into-problems-when-they-hire-presidents-from -the-business-world-a66b2739c1a/.

19. Jeremy Bauer-Wolf, "Can Business Execs Be Good College Presidents in the Covid-19 Era?," *Higher Ed Dive*, October 13, 2020, https://highereddive.com/news/can -business-execs-be-good-college-presidents-in-the-covid-19-era/586867/.

20. Lauren Lumpkin, "He Transformed a Small University in Maryland. Now Freeman Hrabowski Is Ready for His Next Act," *Washington Post*, January 16, 2022, https:// washingtonpost.com/education/2022/01/16/umbc-freeman-hrabowski-retires/.

21. Rachel Leingang, "How Michael Crow Took ASU from a Party School to the Nation's 'Most Innovative' University," *Arizona Republic*, December 14, 2019, https://azcentral .com/in-depth/news/local/arizona-education/2019/02/28/michael-crow-changing -arizona-state-university-reputation-party-school-asu-innovation-global-brand /2670463002/.

22. Alice Gregory, "Picture from an Institution," *New Yorker*, September 22, 2014, https://newyorker.com/magazine/2014/09/29/pictures-institution.

23. See Brian O'Leary et al., "Public-College Boards and State Politics," *Chronicle of Higher* Education, September 25, 2020, https://chronicle.com/article/public-college -boards-and-state-politics. In four states—Colorado, Michigan, Nebraska, and Nevada—the board members are popularly elected, a process that does not appear to lead to a high level of functionality.

24. Alice Fordham, "New Mexico Has One of the Most Generous 'Free Tuition' Programs, but There Are Limits," NPR, March 21, 2022, https://npr.org/2022/03/21 /1087913840/new-mexico-has-one-of-the-most-generous-free-tuition-programs-but -there-are-limi.

25. Jack Stripling, "Too Many Trustees Can Burden a Board, More Colleges Realize," *Chronicle of Higher Education*, August 13, 2012, https://chronicle.com/article/too -many-trustees-can-burden-a-board-more-colleges-realize/.

26. "Board Fundamentals," Association of Governing Boards, accessed March 22, 2023, https://agb.org/knowledge-center/board-fundamentals/.

27. Sara Jackson, "The 3 Things Your Alumni Want to Hear," Medium, August 11, 2015, https://medium.com/@Sara_Jackson/the-3-things-your-alumni-want-to-hear -e583263b5676.

28. Chris Bodenner, "The Surprising Revolt at the Most Liberal College in the Country," *Atlantic*, November 2, 2017, https://theatlantic.com/education/archive/2017/11/the -surprising-revolt-at-reed/544682/.

29. Aftab Ali, "Yale University English Students Urge Department to 'Decolonise' White, Male Reading List," *Independent* (UK), June 2, 2016, https://independent.co .uk/student/news/yale-university-english-students-urge-department-to-decolonise -white-male-reading-list-a7062031.html.

30. Karen L. Webber, *The Working Environment Matters: Faculty Member Job Satisfaction by Institutional Type* (TIAA Institute, March 2018), https://tiaainstitute.org/sites/default /files/presentations/2018-03/Faculty%20Job%20Satisfaction_Webber_rd142_March%20 2018.pdf. There is some variation across institutional type, with faculty at baccalaureate institutions having the highest level of satisfaction: a mean score of 3.97 on a five-point scale. Those at private institutions are also more satisfied than those at public ones.

31. Joel Smith and Lauren Herckis, "Understanding and Overcoming Institutional Roadblocks to the Adoption and Use of Technology-Enhanced Learning Resources in Higher Education," Carnegie Mellon University report, June 2018, https://cmu.edu /simon/news/docs/ccny-report.pdf.

32. Quoted in Kristi DePaul, "Why Aren't Tech-Enhanced Learning Strategies More Widely Used?," *Educause Review*, April 3, 2018, https://er.educause.edu/blogs/2018 /4/why-arent-tech-enhanced-learning-strategies-more-widely-used.

33. Quoted in Becky Supiano, "'It's Not About the Evidence Anymore,'" *Chronicle of Higher Education*, June 22, 2022, https://www.chronicle.com/article/its-not-about -the-evidence-anymore.

34. Ray Schroeder, "Faculty Teaching the Way They Were Taught," *Inside Higher Education*, October 5, 2022, https://insidehighered.com/digital-learning/blogs/online -trending-now/faculty-teaching-way-they-were-taught.

35. Supiano, "'Not About the Evidence.'"

36. Derek Bok, *The Struggle to Reform Our Colleges* (Princeton, NJ: Princeton University Press, 2017), 192–93. The studies to which Bok refers include the Carnegie Foundation's *International Survey of the Academic Profession* (1992) and James L. Fairweather, "Beyond the Rhetoric: Trends in the Relative Value of Teaching and Research in Faculty Salaries," *Journal of Higher Education* 76, no. 4 (2005): 401–22.

37. Steven Mintz, "As 'Higher Ed Gamma' Approaches Its Tenth Anniversary," *Inside Higher Education*, June 21, 2022, https://insidehighered.com/blogs/higher-ed-gamma /%E2%80%98higher-ed-gamma%E2%80%99-approaches-its-10th-anniversary.

38. Joshua Kim, "'Status and Culture' and the Academic Caste System," *Inside Higher Education*, October 25, 2022, https://insidehighered.com/blogs/learning-innovation /%E2%80%98status-and-culture%E2%80%99-and-academic-caste-system.

39. "Date Snapshot: Contingent Faculty in US Higher Ed," American Association of University Professors, October 11, 2018, https://www.aaup.org/news/data-snapshot -contingent-faculty-us-higher-ed#.YqjdfdPMI1I.

40. Jon Marcus, "America's Next Union Battlefield May Be on Campus," *Washington Post*, March 25, 2022, https://washingtonpost.com/education/2022/03/25/colleges -faculty-unions-labor/.

41. Quoted in Jordan Weissman, "Master's Degrees Are the Second Biggest Scam in Higher Education," *Slate*, July 16, 2021, https://slate.com/business/2021/07/masters -degrees-debt-loans-worth-it.html.

42. Dick Startz, "How Many Humanities Ph.D.s Should Universities Produce?," Brookings, October 24, 2018, https://brookings.edu/blog/brown-center-chalkboard/2018 /10/24/how-many-humanities-ph-d-s-should-universities-produce/.

43. Jeffrey Selingo, "Colleges Are Deeply Unequal Workplaces," *Atlantic*, August 1, 2020, https://theatlantic.com/ideas/archive/2020/08/colleges-are-deeply-unequal-workplaces/614791/.

44. Paula M. Krebs, "The Faculty-Staff Divide," *Chronicle of Higher Education*, November 14, 2003, https://chronicle.com/article/the-faculty-staff-divide/.

45. Elizabeth Corey and Jeffrey Polet, "Indoctrination Sessions Have No Place in the Academy," *Chronicle of Higher Education*, October 5, 2021, https://chronicle.com/article/indoctrination-sessions-have-no-place-in-the-academy; Joshua Doležal, "Reclaiming Academe's Idealism: Lessons from Václav Havel for a Profession in Decline," *Chronicle of Higher Education*, August 1, 2022, https://chronicle.com/article/reclaiming-academes-idealism.

46. Olin relies heavily on experiential learning, and Soka has no disciplinary departments.

47. Baba Shiv, "Inspiration, Not Desperation, Drives Innovation," *Economic Times*, June 14, 2013, https://economictimes.indiatimes.com/inspiration-not-desperation-drives-innovation/articleshow/20573571.cms.

48. Jeff Lagasse, "Most Physicians Employed by a Hospital or Corporation, Report Finds," *Healthcare Finance*, June 30, 2021, https://www.healthcarefinancenews.com/news/most-physicians-employed-hospital-or-corporation-report-finds.

49. Roger McNamee and Johnny Ryan, "Amazon's Dangerous Ambition to Dominate Healthcare," *Time*, July 28, 2022, https://time.com/6201575/amazons-dangerous-ambition-to-dominate-healthcare/.

50. Justin Probyn, "Investors Excited About Africa's Private Education Opportunity," August 20, 2017, https://linkedin.com/pulse/investors-excited-africas-private-education-merit-awards/?trk=portfolio_article-card_title. Alex Lynn, "Private Equity Flocks to African Education," *Private Equity International*, July 20, 2017, https://privateequityinternational.com/pe-flocks-to-african-education/.

51. Charlie Eaton, Sabrina Howell, and Constantine Yannelis, "When Investor Incentives and Consumer Interest Diverge: Private Equity in Higher Education" (NBER Working Paper 24976, National Bureau of Economic Research, August 2018), https://nber.org/system/files/working_papers/w24976/revisions/w24976.rev0.pdf.

52. Andis Robeznieks, "Physicians Warned of the Pitfalls Behind Private Equity Promises," American Medical Association, August 1, 2022, https://ama-assn.org/practice-management/private-practices/physicians-warned-pitfalls-behind-private-equity-promises. An example of how this works: as I write, corporate giants Amazon, UnitedHealth, and CVS, none of which has a reputation for focusing on the public good, are in a bidding war for Signify Health, which is own in part by a private equity firm. The current market capitalization of Signify is about $5 billion; the bids are expected to go as high as $8 billion. There is a lot of money to be made in a health-care system that relies so heavily on the private market; health-care outcomes are another story. See Jon Hopkins, "Amazon.com, CVS Health, Option Care Health, and UnitedHealth All Understood to Be Bidding for Signify Health—Reports," Proactive, August 22, 2022, https://proactiveinvestors.com/companies/news/990653/amazon-com-cvs-health-option-care-health-and-unitedhealth-all-understood-to-be-bidding-for-signify-health-reports-990653.html.

53. Chip Paucek, "The False Narrative Around For-Profit Companies Needs to End," *Chronicle of Higher Education*, August 19, 2022, https://chronicle.com/article/the-false-narrative-around-for-profit-companies-needs-to-end.

54. Jeremy Barlow, "Board Member Responsibilities: A New and Evolving Purview," BoardEffect, May 22, 2017, https://boardeffect.com/blog/board-member-responsibilities-new-evolving-purview/.

Chapter 4

1. Earlham is a worrisome case study in the plight of even well-endowed, highly regarded liberal arts colleges located in rural areas. Its undergraduate in enrollment in 2016 was 1,102. For those counting, the decline since that time has been over 40 percent. See https://earlham.edu/about/collegiate-profile/ and https://earlham.edu/wp-content/uploads/2021/04/Common-Data-Set-2016-Fall-Enrollment.pdf.
2. Both Kerr and Hutchins are quoted in Andrew Delbanco, *College: What It Was, Is, and Should Be* (Princeton, NJ: Princeton University Press, 2012), 92.
3. David Sedaris, *Happy-Go-Lucky* (New York: Little, Brown, 2022), 239.
4. David V. Rosowsky and Bridget M. Keegan, "The Disciplinary Trench," *Inside Higher Education*, August 18, 2020, https://insidehighered.com/views/2020/08/18/what-if-there-were-no-academic-departments-opinion.
5. David Bogle, "100 Years of the PhD in the UK," paper delivered at Vitae Researcher Development International Conference, September 17, 2018, https://discovery.ucl.ac.uk/id/eprint/10068565/.
6. Delbanco, *College*, 79. Delbanco is quoting Michael Rosenthal, *Nicholas Miraculous: The Amazing Career of the Redoubtable Nicholas Murray Butler* (New York: Farrar, Straus and Giroux, 2006), 75.
7. "History of Yale Graduate School," Yale University, accessed March 23, 2023, https://gsas.yale.edu/deans-office/history-yale-graduate-school.
8. Maresi Nerad, "Introduction: The Cyclical Problems of Graduate Education and Institutional Responses in the 1990s," in *Graduate Education in the United States* (New York: Garland, 1997), iv–xi, https://www.education.uw.edu/cirge/wp-content/uploads/2008/02/grad_ed_us.pdf.
9. "Survey of Earned Doctorates," National Center for Science and Engineering Statistics, November 30, 2021, https://ncses.nsf.gov/pubs/nsf22300/data-tables.
10. James Bikales, "At Least Five GSAS Departments to Admit No Graduate Students Next Year," *Harvard Crimson*, November 24, 2020, https://thecrimson.com/article/2020/11/24/admissions-pause-faculty-student-reactions/; Meghan Zahneis, "More Doctoral Programs Suspend Admissions. That Could Have Lasting Effects on Graduate Education," *Chronicle of Higher Education*, September 28, 2020, https://chronicle.com/article/more-doctoral-programs-suspend-admissions-that-could-have-lasting-effects-on-graduate-education/.
11. Emma Pettit, "Columbia Had Little Success Placing Ph.D.s on the Tenure Track. 'Alarm' Followed, and the University Responded," *Chronicle of Higher Education*, August 21, 2019, https://chronicle.com/article/columbia-had-little-success-placing-english-ph-d-s-on-the-tenure-track-alarm-followed-and-the-university-responded/.
12. Leonard Cassuto, *The Graduate School Mess: What Caused It and How We Can Fix It* (Cambridge, MA: Harvard University Press, 2015), 2.
13. Shazia Ahmed and Lisa Rosen, "Graduate Students: Present Instructors and Future Faculty," *Faculty Focus*, September 17, 2018, https://www.facultyfocus

.com/articles/teaching-and-learning/graduate-students-present-instructors-and
-future-faculty/.

14. Eric P. Bettinger, Bridget Terry Long, and Eric S. Taylor, "When Inputs Are Outputs: The Case of Graduate Student Instructors," *Economics of Education Review*
52 (June 2016): 63.

15. Rachel Himes, "Why Graduate Students Like Me Are on Strike," *Jacobin*, November 10, 2021, https://jacobin.com/2021/11/columbia-university-graduate-workers
-strike-dental-care-higher-wages.

16. "Survey of Earned Doctorates."

17. Cassuto, *Graduate School Mess*, 57–58.

18. Cassuto, 62.

19. Derek Bok, *Higher Education in America* (Princeton, NJ: Princeton University Press,
2015), 232.

20. K. Hunter Wapman et al., "Quantifying Hierarchy and Dynamics in US Faculty Hiring and Retention," *Nature*, September 21, 2022, https://nature.com/articles/s41586
-022-05222-x.

21. Zeb Larson, "Doctoral Training Is Ossified: Can We Reinvent It?," *Chronicle of
Higher Education*, June 29, 2022, https://chronicle.com/article/doctoral-training-is
-ossified-can-we-reinvent-it.

22. Larson, "Doctoral Training."

23. Steven Mintz, "Fixing the Humanities Ph.D. Job Crisis," *Inside Higher Education*,
September 14, 2021, https://insidehighered.com/blogs/higher-ed-gamma/fixing
-humanities-phd-job-crisis.

24. Graduate Advisory Committee, "A Call for Community: A Survey of Humanities
PhD Students on Professionalization and Support," Humanists@Work, March 2,
2017, https://humwork.uchri.org/blog/2017/03/call-community-survey-humanities
-phd-students-professionalization-support/.

25. Colleen Flaherty, "The Connected Ph.D.," *Inside Higher Education*, July 8, 2022,
https://insidehighered.com/news/2022/07/08/brandeis-overhauls-phd-training
-humanities.

26. Leonard Cassuto, "Can Yale Reform Its Humanities Doctoral Programs?," *Chronicle
of Higher Education*, May 14, 2021, https://chronicle.com/article/can-yale-reform-its
-humanities-doctoral-programs.

27. See https://english.yale.edu/graduate/graduate-student-placement.

28. Meredith Young, "The Utility of Failure: A Taxonomy for Research and Scholarship,"
Perspectives in Medical Education 8, no. 6 (December 2019): 365.

29. Mark C. Taylor, "End the University as We Know It," *New York Times*, August 26,
2009, https://nytimes.com/2009/04/27/opinion/27taylor.html.

30. Jack Grove, "Academic Reputation 'Still Driven by Journal Prestige'—Survey,"
Times Higher Education, August 3, 2022, https://timeshighereducation.com/news
/academic-reputation-still-driven-journal-prestige-survey.

31. "The global rate of ROI in schooling is approximately 10 percent for primary education, five percent for secondary education and 16 percent for university education. Social ROI of education for the world is 18.9 percent for primary education,
13.1 percent for secondary education and 10.8 for higher education. Finally, private
ROI of education for the world is 26.6 percent for primary education, 17 percent for
secondary education and 19.0 for higher education." Roberto Carlos Ventura, "The

Economic Benefits of Education," Borgen Project, July 2, 2018, https://borgenproject
.org/economic-benefits-of-education/.

32. Delbanco, *College*, 90.

33. Barbara Kaufman, "Collaboration at the Heart of Successful Change Initiatives," *Academic Leader* 28, no. 9 (September 2012): 1.

34. Douglas A. Ready and Emily Truelove, "The Power of Collective Ambition," *Harvard Business Review*, December 2011, https://hbr.org/2011/12/the-power-of-collective-ambition.

35. William G. Bowen and Eugene M. Tobin, *Locus of Authority: The Evolution of Faculty Roles in the Governance of Higher Education* (Princeton, NJ: Princeton University Press, 2015), 6.

36. Adrienne Lu, "Should Colleges Make Anti-racism Part of Their Mission? Proposal at UMass-Boston Alarms Critics," *Chronicle of Higher Education*, March 11, 2022, https://chronicle.com/article/should-colleges-make-anti-racism-part-their-mission -proposal-at-umass-boston-alarms-critics.

37. Solomon Bililign et al., "A University Without Departments and Colleges—a New Structure to Strengthen Disciplinary and Interdisciplinary Education and Research," *International Journal for Innovation Education and Research* 3, no. 11 (2015): 122.

38. At Lawrence University, where I was for five years dean of the faculty, there was a sort of geographical attempt to strengthen interdepartmental ties. The offices of faculty in the Humanities Division were not clustered together by department but were sprinkled somewhat randomly throughout Main Hall, the university's oldest building. It's an interesting idea, though I did not notice that it produced any special esprit de corps among faculty within the division.

39. Matthew Reed (writing as "Dean Dad"), "The Faculty-Staff Divide," *Inside Higher Education*, October 23, 2011, https://insidehighered.com/blogs/confessions -community-college-dean/faculty-staff-divide.

40. "Harold Alfond Foundation Investing $250 Million to Bring Transformative Change to the University of Maine System," University of Maine, October 7, 2020, https:// umaine.edu/news/blog/2020/10/07/harold-alfond-foundation-investing-240m-to -bring-transformative-change-to-the-university-of-maine-system/; Peter McGuire, "UMaine's Engineering Program Underequipped to Meet Rising Demand for Grads," *Portland Press Herald*, December 18, 2016, https://pressherald.com/2016/12 /18/university-engineering-program-squeezed-as-demand-for-grads-increases/; Liam Knox, "A New College at the University of Maine Worries Faculty," *Inside Higher Education*, June 22, 2022, https://insidehighered.com/news/2022/06/22/new-maine -engineering-college-raises-questions-faculty.

41. Rosowsky and Keegan, "Disciplinary Trench."

42. Bililign et al., "Without Departments," 125.

43. Rosowsky and Keegan, "Disciplinary Trench."

44. Taylor, "End the University."

45. Rosowsky and Keegan, "Disciplinary Trench."

Chapter 5

1. Yes, there were many more than 116 members of the faculty eligible to vote—I would estimate at least twice as many. But to vote you had to show up for the meeting.

2. Several years ago, the Faculty Personnel Committee brought before the faculty a motion to eliminate voting privileges of emeritus faculty who were not teaching or otherwise employed by the college. After vigorous debate between those who wanted voting limited to faculty who were actually affected by decisions and those who didn't want to hurt anyone's feelings, the vote ended in a *tie*, meaning that the rule still stands. It was a good try.

3. "Statement on Government of Colleges and Universities," American Association of University Professors, accessed March 24, 2023, https://aaup.org/report/statement -government-colleges-and-universities.

4. Gary A. Olson, "Exactly What Is Shared Governance?," *Chronicle of Higher Education*, July 23, 2009, https://chronicle.com/article/exactly-what-is-shared-governance.

5. Susan Resnick Pierce, *Governance Reconsidered: How Boards, Presidents, Administrators, and Faculty Can Help Their Colleges Thrive* (San Francisco: Jossey-Bass, 2014), 7.

6. William G. Bowen and Eugene M. Tobin, *Locus of Authority: The Evolution of Faculty Roles in the Governance of Higher Education* (Princeton, NJ: Princeton University Press, 2015), 77.

7. John R. Thelin, *A History of American Higher Education* (Baltimore: Johns Hopkins University Press, 2004), 310.

8. Clark Kerr, *The Uses of the University*, 5th ed. (Cambridge, MA: Harvard University Press, 2001), 137.

9. "The Role of the Faculty in Budgetary and Salary Matters," American Association of University Professors, accessed March 24, 2023, https://aaup.org/report/role-faculty -budgetary-and-salary-matters.

10. Kerr, *Uses of the University*, 180.

11. Bowen and Tobin, *Locus of Authority*, 1.

12. Larry G. Gerber, "Professionalization as the Basis for Academic Freedom and Faculty Governance," *AAUP Journal of Academic Freedom* 1 (2010): 23.

13. Timothy Kaufman-Osborn, "Shared Governance Within the Autocratic Academy," *Inside Higher Education*, October 22, 2021, https://insidehighered.com/views/2021 /10/22/shared-governance-fatally-flawed-opinion. If higher education is truly an autocracy, it is surely the least effective and efficient autocracy in recorded history.

14. Lena Eisenstein, "Shared Governance Model for Higher Education Boards," Board-Effect, June 16, 2021, https://boardeffect.com/blog/shared-governance-model-higher -education-boards/.

15. Gee Ranasinha, "Why Seeking Consensus Prevents Business Innovation," Kexino, April 24, 2021, https://kexino.com/marketing/why-seeking-consensus-prevents -business-innovation/.

16. Jackie Dryden, "How Consensus Kills Innovation," *Forbes*, February 22, 2019, https:// forbes.com/sites/forbesagencycouncil/2019/02/22/how-consensus-kills-innovation/ ?sh=7f87322b597e.

17. Stephen B. Heard, "Why Are University Strategic Plans Almost Always Meaningless?," *Scientist Sees Squirrel* (blog), December 28, 2021, https://scientistseessquirrel .wordpress.com/2021/12/28/why-are-university-strategic-plans-almost-always -meaningless/.

18. "Williams College Strategic Plan," Williams College, accessed March 24, 2023, https://williams.edu/strategic-planning/strategic-plan-2021/.

19. "Williams College Strategic Plan." Though I selected Williams for this exercise, I might have chosen the plan of virtually any college or university—including the ones I oversaw at Macalester. Those plans did include one or two items that were somewhat more innovative and distinctive, and these were, naturally, the ones that generated the most resistance within the community.

20. Quoted in Lee Gardner, "The Truth About Strategic Plans, *Chronicle of Higher Education*, September 29, 2021, https://chronicle.com/article/the-truth-about-strategic-plans.

21. Andrew Delbanco, "Where Is the Faculty in the Admissions Debates?," *Inside Higher Education*, October 12, 2006, https://insidehighered.com/views/2006/10/12/where-faculty-admissions-debates.

22. Quoted from a case study of Macalester by Jack E. Rossmann, former provost and professor of psychology at Macalester, and included in Bowen and Tobin, *Locus of Authority*, 294.

23. I am of two minds about this. It is hard to argue with the logic of devoting one's time to the things that will be most important for career advancement. But often new faculty are the ones with the best ideas and the clearest picture of the world beyond the boundaries of the campus. Habits, moreover, are difficult to break: avoid committee service for seven years and you are unlikely to dive with enthusiasm into committee service in year eight or nine.

24. Kevin Gannon, "Why We Hate Our Own Meetings," *Chronicle of Higher Education*, September 20, 2017, https://chronicle.com/article/why-we-hate-our-own-meetings/; Douglas Whaley, "I Hate Meetings," blog, October 31, 2011, http://douglaswhaley.blogspot.com/2011/10/i-hate-meetings.html.

25. Cass Sunstein and Reid Hastie, *Wiser: Getting Beyond Groupthink to Make Groups Smarter* (Boston: Harvard Business School Publishing, 2015), 15.

26. Quoted in Philip Mousavizadeh, "A 'Proliferation of Administrators': Faculty Reflect on Two Decades of Rapid Expansion," *Yale Daily News*, November 10, 2021, https://yaledailynews.com/blog/2021/11/10/reluctance-on-the-part-of-its-leadership-to-lead-yales-administration-increases-by-nearly-50-percent/.

27. Matthew Reed (writing as "Dean Dad"), "The Faculty-Staff Divide," *Inside Higher Education*, October 23, 2011, https://insidehighered.com/blogs/confessions-community-college-dean/faculty-staff-divide. Jenae Cohn made the same point more recently, a year into the pandemic: "While faculty members may treasure their system of shared governance, it rarely gives voting power to the staff. Indeed, on many campuses, staff members are perceived as 'the employees' and professors as their 'bosses.'" Jenae Cohn, "Faculty and Staff Often Don't Trust One Another. How Do We Fix That?," *Chronicle of Higher Education*, March 12, 2021, https://chronicle.com/article/faculty-and-staff-often-dont-trust-one-another-how-do-we-fix-that.

28. Meredith L. Skaggs, "The Great Divide: The Perceptions and Dynamics of the Faculty and Staff Professional Relationship" (PhD diss., Western Kentucky University, 2015), x.

29. Kathy Johnson Bowles, "How Should Staff Interact with Faculty?," *Inside Higher Education*, August 9, 2022, https://insidehighered.com/blogs/just-explain-it-me/how-should-staff-interact-faculty.

30. John A. Byrne, "Columbia Business School Readies Its $600 Million New Campus for a Jan. 4 Debut," Poets and Quants, December 13, 2021, https://poetsandquants.com/2021/12/13/columbia-business-school-readies-its-600-million-new-campus-for-a-jan-4th-debut/.

31. I would like to say—as a former English professor—that English professors are disproportionately represented among higher education's internal critics because they are trained to be careful thinkers, but an equally plausible case can be made that they are merely cranky.

32. James Rushing Daniel, "Higher Ed's Cult of Growth," *Chronicle of Higher Education*, August 5, 2022, https://chronicle.com/article/higher-eds-cult-of-growth.

33. Bowen and Tobin, *Locus of Authority*, 211.

34. Joshua Doležal, "Reclaiming Academe's Idealism: Lessons from Václav Havel for a Profession in Decline," *Chronicle of Higher Education*, August 1, 2022, https://chronicle.com/article/reclaiming-academes-idealism.

35. Brian Rosenberg, "Administrators Are Not the Enemy," *Chronicle of Higher Education*, October 27, 2021, https://chronicle.com/article/administrators-are-not-the-enemy; P. Z. Myers, "Administrators Are the Enemy, You Know," Freethoughtblogs, August 4, 2021, https://freethoughtblogs.com/pharyngula/2021/08/04/administrators-are-the-enemy-you-know/; Graham Culbertson, "Administrators Are the Enemy, but Staff Members Aren't," Everyday Anarchism, November 15, 2021, https://everydayanarchism.com/administrators-are-the-enemy-but-staff-members-arent/. Administrators tend to compose posts entitled "Faculty Are the Enemy"—but only in their heads.

36. "So What Is Shared Governance? A Quick Guide," Consult QD, Cleveland Clinic, 2020, https://consultqd.clevelandclinic.org/so-what-is-shared-governance-a-quick-guide/.

37. Mary K. Anthony, "Shared Governance Models: The Theory, Practice, and Evidence," *Online Journal of Issues in Nursing* 9, no. 1 (January 31, 2004), https://ojin.nursingworld.org/table-of-contents/volume-9-2004/number-1-january-2004/shared-governance-models/.

38. Steve Andriole, "Why Companies Cannot Innovate & Why They Will Keep Failing. Unless They End-Run Themselves," *Forbes*, August 26, 2020, https://www.forbes.com/sites/steveandriole/2020/08/26/why-companies-cannot-innovate--why-they-will-keep-failing--unless-they-end-run-themselves/?sh=1049ff105a52.

39. Charles A. O'Reilly III and Michael L. Tushman, "The Ambidextrous Organization," *Harvard Business Review*, April 2004, https://hbr.org/2004/04/the-ambidextrous-organization.

40. O'Reilly and Tushman, "Ambidextrous Organization."

41. Renze Kolster, "Structural Ambidexterity in Higher Education: Excellence Education as a Testing Ground for Educational Innovations," *European Journal of Higher Education* 11, no. 1, published ahead of print, December 2020, https://tandfonline.com/doi/full/10.1080/21568235.2020.1850312.

Chapter 6

1. I am aware the most sitting college and university presidents will either support or remain silent on the question of tenure. This is to be expected, since most also want to avoid creating a firestorm and, at least for a while, to keep their jobs. I am also aware that what they say in public and what they say in private are often very different. I can assign no blame for this since it describes my own behavior.

2. Richard P. Chait, "Gleanings," in *The Questions of Tenure*, ed. Richard P. Chait (Cambridge, MA: Harvard University Press, 2005), 309. See also "Digest of

Education Statistics," National Center for Education Statistics, 2019, https://nces
.ed.gov/programs/digest/d19/tables/dt19_316.80.asp. In its "2022 AAUP Survey of
Tenure Practices," the AAUP states the number of four-year institutions that award
tenure as "over 1200." "The 2022 AAUP Survey of Tenure Practices," American
Association of University Professors, May 2022, https://aaup.org/report/2022-aaup
-survey-tenure-practices.

3. Chait, "Gleanings," 309.
4. Nicholas P. Fandos and Noah B. Pisner, "Joining the Ranks," *Harvard Crimson*,
    April 11, 2013, https://thecrimson.com/article/2013/4/11/scrutiny-tenure-harvard/.
5. Walter P. Metzger, "The 1940 Statement of Principles on Academic Freedom and
    Tenure," *Law and Contemporary Problems* 53, no. 3 (Summer 1990): 3. For anyone
    interested in the history and meaning of the 1940 statement, Metzger's long, erudite,
    and witty article is an essential read. My favorite line: "Given their way with words,
    the authors of this document, had they undertaken to rewrite the Pentateuch, would
    probably have called it the 1200 B.C. Statement on Divinized Administrative Policy
    Affecting Certain Classes of Israelite Personnel" (6).
6. "Tenure," American Association of University Professors, accessed March 28, 2023,
    https://aaup.org/issues/tenure.
7. "Survey of Tenure Practices."
8. Metzger, "1940 Statement," 6.
9. Metzger, 65.
10. "1940 Statement of Principles on Academic Freedom and Tenure," American Asso-
    ciation of University Professors, accessed March 28, 2023, https://aaup.org/report
    /1940-statement-principles-academic-freedom-and-tenure.
11. "Survey of Tenure Practices."
12. "Survey of Tenure Practices."
13. Donna R. Euben, "De Facto Tenure," American Association of University Professors,
    July 2005, https://aaup.org/issues/tenure//de-facto-tenure-2005.
14. NTT faculty at Howard University, for instance, represented by the Service Employ-
    ees International Union, argued in their most recent negotiations for the elimination
    of Howard's "seven-year limit." Though the two parties reached an agreement on a
    new contract, it appears that the seven-year limit is still in place. For other examples,
    see Ben Roth, "Harvard Does Not Care About Teaching—or Teachers," *Chronicle of
    Higher Education*, March 16, 2021, https://chronicle.com/article/harvard-does-not
    -care-about-teaching-or-teachers; and Shari Wilson, "Serving Time: The Six-Year
    Rule," *Inside Higher Education*, June 22, 2005, https://insidehighered.com/views
    /2005/06/22/serving-time-6-year-rule.
15. "National Trends for Faculty Composition over Time," Delphi Project on the Chang-
    ing Faculty and Student Success, 2013, https://pullias.usc.edu/download/national
    -trends-faculty-composition-time/.
16. American Association of University Professors, *The Annual Report on the Economic
    Status of the Profession, 2020–21* (July 2021), 14–15, https://aaup.org/file/AAUP
    _ARES_2020-21.pdf. Without meaning to belabor the point too much, I will also
    note that the Macalester tenured and tenure-track faculty deserve credit for creating
    during this period a new set of guidelines that improved the security, compensa-
    tion, review process, and promotion opportunities for NTT faculty, many of whom,

though excellent teachers, could not be candidates for tenure-track positions at the college because they lacked the terminal degree. The AAUP report observes that "at a glance, these appointments may appear to be a form of appeasement" (15). Upon more careful observation, they can be seen to be much more than that.

17. Jordan Weissmann, "Are Tenured Professors Really Worse Teachers? A Lit Review," *Atlantic*, September 25, 2013, https://theatlantic.com/business/archive/2013/09/are-tenured-professors-really-worse-teachers-a-lit-review/279940/.

18. Richard Vedder, "Tenure Is Dying," *Forbes*, April 13, 2020, https://forbes.com/sites/richardvedder/2020/04/13/academic-tenure-rip/.

19. Giulia Heyward, "Georgia's University System Takes on Tenure," *New York Times*, October 13, 2021, https://nytimes.com/2021/10/13/us/georgia-university-system-tenure.html; Colleen Flaherty, "Shoring Up Tenure, or Weakening It?," *Inside Higher Education*, October 27, 2022, https://insidehighered.com/news/2022/10/27/west-virginia-u-proposal-outlines-process-firing-faculty. Here as elsewhere, Florida seems determined to take the lead and to use New College as an experimental laboratory. Its new president—a former Republican Speaker of the House—has asked seven faculty members to "withdraw" their applications for tenure. See Arrman Kyaw, "New College of Florida Interim President Richard Corcoran Asks Seven Faculty to Withdraw Tenure Applications," *Diverse Issues in Higher Education*, April 10, 2023, https://diverseeducation.com/faculty-staff-issues/article/15382828/new-college-of-florida-interim-president-richard-corcoran-asks-seven-faculty-to-withdraw-tenure-applications.

20. Chait, "Gleanings," 318.

21. "1940 Statement of Principles."

22. Is it just me, or did the framers of the 1940 document misuse the word *which*? Perhaps none of the drafters was an English professor.

23. For a good example of "act like a jerk," see Wyatt Myskow, "This Professor Was Investigated for an 'Offensive' Land Acknowledgment. Now He's Suing," *Chronicle of Higher Education*, July 13, 2022, https://chronicle.com/article/this-professor-was-investigated-for-an-offensive-land-acknowledgment-now-hes-suing. The most thoughtful discussion of the relationship between academic freedom and extramural speech that I've read is Keith Whittington's "Academic Freedom and the Scope of Protections for Extramural Speech," *Academe*, Winter 2019, https://aaup.org/article/academic-freedom-and-scope-protections-extramural-speech#.YtAfBNPMI1I. In the end, I disagree with Whittington's central argument, which I believe places too high a priority on faculty interests and not enough priority on the interests of other parties, including students, but he raises all the right questions and examines them with great care.

24. Hudson Rogers, "The Relationship Between Tenure and Academic Freedom: Challenges for the 21st Century," *Journal of Collective Bargaining in the Academy*, no. 3 (April 2008): article 23, p. 2.

25. Rachel Levinson, "Academic Freedom and the First Amendment," American Association of University Professors, July 2007, https://aaup.org/our-work/protecting-academic-freedom/academic-freedom-and-first-amendment-2007.

26. William W. Van Alstyne, "Academic Freedom and the First Amendment in the Supreme Court of the United States: An Unhurried Historical View," *Law and*

Contemporary Problems 53, no. 3 (Summer 1990): 79, https://scholarship.law.wm.edu/cgi/viewcontent.cgi?article=1751&context=facpubs.

27. Sarah Brown, "Public-University Curricula Are 'Government Speech,' Florida Says," *Chronicle of Higher Education*, September 23, 2022, https://chronicle.com/article/public-university-curricula-are-government-speech-florida-says.

28. Jordan Smith, "University of Idaho Issues Gag Order on Abortion," *Intercept*, September 27, 2022, https://theintercept.com/2022/09/27/abortion-university-idaho/.

29. Greg Afinogenov, "Tenure Is Not Worth Fighting For," *Chronicle of Higher Education*, January 24, 2020, https://chronicle.com/article/tenure-is-not-worth-fighting-for/.

30. Rogers, "Relationship," 4.

31. *Macalester College Faculty Handbook*, accessed March 28, 2023, Section 3.1.A and B, https://docs.google.com/document/d/1jrZ3No-idNNOYiqV2pBT9HghQs_2utJRFY_eFl5mLbs/edit.

32. Emily J. Levine, "It's Time for an Overhaul of Academic Freedom," *Washington Post*, June 9, 2021, https://washingtonpost.com/outlook/2021/06/09/its-time-an-overhaul-academic-freedom/.

33. Julie A. Reuben, "Where Academic Freedom Ends," *Chronicle of Higher Education*, November 19, 2020, https://chronicle.com/article/where-academic-freedom-ends.

34. A number of recent books, including *What Is Academic Freedom? A Century of Debate, 1915–Present*, by Daniel Gordon (London: Routledge, 2022); *It's Not Free Speech: Race, Democracy and the Future of Academic Freedom*, by Michael Bérubé and Jennifer Ruth (Baltimore: Johns Hopkins University Press, 2022); and *Dirty Knowledge: Academic Freedom in the Age of Neoliberalism*, by Julia Schleck (Lincoln: University of Nebraska Press, 2022), have managed to demonstrate two things: there remains no single, clear understanding of academic freedom and there continues to exist nostalgia for a version of the university that never actually existed. In a review essay on this subject, Joan W. Scott paraphrases Schleck when writing, "Faculty members used to see themselves as part of a collective whose freedom was granted in return for the assumption of responsibility to further the public good; now they see themselves as individuals claiming rights." Joan W. Scott, "Academic Freedom Has Always Been Dirty. That's a Good Thing," *Chronicle of Higher Education*, October 4, 2022, https://chronicle.com/article/academic-freedom-has-always-been-dirty-thats-a-good-thing. Based on my own experience since at least the 1980s, the latter characterization of faculty members has always been more accurate than the former.

35. Judith Shapiro, "Free Speech Fundamentalism," *Inside Higher Education*, January 27, 2021, https://insidehighered.com/views/2021/01/27/academics-should-put-freedom-speech-context-other-values-opinion.

36. I would add Fox News, except that Tucker Carlson seems to own the white supremacist space on that network and would probably not want the competition.

37. See Scott Jaschik, "Is Penn Going to Punish Amy Wax?," *Inside Higher Education*, July 19, 2022, https://insidehighered.com/news/2022/07/19/penn-going-punish-amy-wax; and "AFA Sends Letter to Penn on Amy Wax Case," Academic Freedom Alliance, January 18, 2022, https://academicfreedom.org/afa-sends-letter-to-penn-on-amy-wax-case/. The appropriate response to the position of the Foundation for Individual Rights and Expression is stated by attorney Joe Patrice: "Fear of some

future disingenuous application isn't a reason not to do the right thing in the case at hand." "The Amy Wax Case Has Nothing to Do with Academic Freedom," Above the Law, January 21, 2022, https://abovethelaw.com/2022/01/the-amy-wax-case-has-nothing-to-do-with-academic-freedom/.

38. "Wax's behavior has nothing to do with academic freedom. That's not going to stop fellow academics from lining up to protect her out of ivory tower kinship or slippery slope panic or both." Joe Patrice, "Law School Seeking 'Major Sanction' Against Amy Wax . . . Cue the Whining About Academic Freedom," Above the Law, July 19, 2022, https://abovethelaw.com/2022/07/law-school-seeking-major-sanction-against-amy-wax-cue-the-whining-about-academic-freedom/. Fair or not, this is a widely held view.

39. Hana M. Kiros, "I Wish They Could Fire Amy Wax for Being a Literal White Supremacist," *Harvard Crimson*, April 18, 2022, https://thecrimson.com/article/2022/4/18/kiros-amy-wax/.

40. William Deresiewicz, "An Immodest Proposal," included in "The Future of Tenure," *Chronicle of Higher Education*, April 7, 2021, https://chronicle.com/article/the-future-of-tenure. Irene Mulvey, president of the AAUP, and Randi Weingarten, president of the American Federation of Teachers, similarly argue, disinterestedly, that faculty should be both tenured and unionized. See Irene Mulvey and Randi Weingarten, "Why Not Both?," *Inside Higher Education*, October 13, 2022, https://insidehighered.com/views/2022/10/13/tenure-or-unions%E2%80%94why-not-both-opinion. Aside from being incompatible with current law, "both" would provide a level of insulation against any form of actual performance review unequaled elsewhere in the American workforce.

41. Inga Vesper, "How to Protect Academic Freedom," *Horizons*, April 12, 2017, https://horizons-mag.ch/2017/12/04/how-to-protect-academic-freedom/.

42. Philip G. Altbach, "How Are Faculty Faring in Other Countries?," in Chait, *Questions of Tenure*, 166.

43. https://www.olin.edu/node/4926, accessed April 11, 2023.

44. *Bennington College Faculty Handbook 2018–2019*, p. 6, https://www.bennington.edu/sites/default/files/sources/docs/FacultyHandbook_2018-19.pdf.

45. Richard Chait and Cathy A. Trower, *Where Tenure Does Not Reign: Colleges with Contract Systems,* American Association for Higher Education working paper, 1997, p. 1.

46. Quest announced that it was ceasing regular academic operations at the end of April 2023. Innovation in higher education is hard.

47. David John Helfand, "A Radical Experiment," in "Future of Tenure."

48. American Association of University Professors, *Annual Report*. According to the same report, the average presidential salaries ranged from $603,000 at doctoral institutions, or roughly 3.7 times the full professor average, to $300,000 at associate's institutions, or roughly 3.3 times the full professor average. As I noted earlier, presidents serve on average for 6.5 years, and nearly half serve for 4.0 years or less.

49. "The Path to Becoming a Nurse Practitioner," American Association of Nurse Practitioners, November 10, 2020, https://aanp.org/news-feed/explore-the-variety-of-career-paths-for-nurse-practitioners; "Nurse Practitioner Salary Guide," Nurse.org, January 3, 2022, https://nurse.org/resources/np-salary-guide/; "How Much Money Do Public Defenders Make?," *Houston Chronicle*, August 18, 2020, https://work.chron.com/much-money-public-defenders-make-11605.html; "Clinical Psychology

Salary: What You'll Earn," All Psychology Schools, accessed March 28, 2023, https://allpsychologyschools.com/clinical-psychology/salary/.

50. Aeon J. Skoble, "Academia Would Be Worse Without Tenure," *Journal of Markets and Morality* 22, no. 1 (Spring 2019): 195.

51. A 1994 article in the *Chronicle of Higher Education* includes the claim that "tenure experts estimate that about fifty tenured professors nationwide are dismissed each year for cause," a miniscule percentage of the whole, though there is neither a definition of "cause" nor evidence for the estimate provided by the author. See Carolyn Mooney, "Dismissals 'for Cause,'" *Chronicle of Higher Education*, December 7, 1994, https://chronicle.com/article/dismissals-for-cause/.

52. Reshmi Dutt-Ballerstadt, "An Extraordinary Firing," *Inside Higher Education*, June 4, 2021, https://insidehighered.com/views/2021/06/04/universities-fire-tenured-faculty-without-due-process-are-setting-dangerous. Dutt-Ballerstadt acknowledges that she is a former colleague of Pollack-Pelzner.

53. Clifford Ando, "Princeton Betrays Its Principles," *Chronicle of Higher Education*, July 5, 2022, https://chronicle.com/article/princeton-betrays-its-principles.

54. An object lesson should be the letter that thirty-eight Harvard professors, including some of the most accomplished, submitted as an objection to the investigation of their colleague John Comaroff, who had been accused of repeated instances of sexual harassment. When the details of some of the allegations were made public the next day, nearly all of those who signed the letter issued a retraction. Not a good look. See Michael Levenson and Anemona Hartocollis, "Colleagues Who Backed Harvard Professor Retract Support Amid Harassment Claims," *New York Times*, February 11, 2022, https://nytimes.com/2022/02/09/us/harvard-sexual-harassment-letter.html.

55. Aisha S. Ahmad, "Why Is It So Hard to Fire a Tenured Sexual Predator?," *Chronicle of Higher Education*, October 14, 2020, https://chronicle.com/article/why-is-it-so-hard-to-fire-a-tenured-sexual-predator.

56. Jasper McChesney and Jacqueline Bichsel, *The Aging of Tenure-Track Faculty in Higher Education: Implications for Succession and Diversity* (College and University Professional Association for Human Resources, January 2020), https://cupahr.org/wp-content/uploads/CUPA-HR-Brief-Aging-Faculty.pdf; Daniel E. Ho, Oluchi Mbonu, and Anne McDonough, "Mandatory Retirement and the Age, Race, and Gender Diversity of University Faculties," *American Law and Economics Review* 23, no. 1 (Spring 2021): 100.

57. Richard A. Greenwald, "Protecting Tenure," *Inside Higher Education*, March 14, 2019, https://insidehighered.com/views/2019/03/14/overlooked-administrative-and-financial-benefits-tenure-opinion.

58. Afinogenov, "Not Worth Fighting For."

59. Anna Saleh, "Brain Circuit That Helps Us Adapt to Change Fades with Age, Study Says," ABC News, April 20, 2016, https://abc.net.au/news/science/2016-04-21/brain-circuit-that-helps-us-adapt-to-change-fades-with-age/7342736.

60. Steven D. Levitt, "Let's Just Get Rid of Tenure (Including Mine)," Freakonomics, March 3, 2007, https://freakonomics.com/2007/03/lets-just-get-rid-of-tenure/.

61. Adam Sitze, "The Strange, Secret History of Tenure," *Chronicle of Higher Education*, August 4, 2022, https://chronicle.com/article/the-strange-secret-history-of-tenure.

62. "Provosts' Views on Tenure, Gen Ed, Budgets, and More," *Inside Higher Education*, 16 March 2023, https://insidehighered.com/reports/2023/03/06/provosts-views-tenure-gen-ed-budgets-and-more.
63. See, for example, Nassif Ghoussoub, "Return on Investment in Faculty Rarely Captured by CFOs," *Piece of Mind* (blog), April 23, 2014, https://nghoussoub.com/2014/04/23/return-on-investment-in-faculty-rarely-captured-by-university-cfos/.

Chapter 7

1. I have been serving as an adviser to ALU for more than two years, though I can take credit for none of the more innovative aspects of the educational model, all of which are the work of Swaniker, Sunassee, and a large group of very talented people at the university. My connection has allowed me to have a front-row seat as the model has been developed.
2. Fred Swaniker, filmed at RewirED2021, YouTube video, 12:21, posted March 6, 2022, https://youtube.com/watch?v=QzgcKetU4Rc.
3. Fred Swaniker, talk given at Carnegie Foundation for the Advancement of Teaching, July 27, 2022.
4. https://algroup.org/.
5. Veda Sunassee, conversation with author, July 28, 2022.
6. Quoted in "Fred Swaniker: Opportunities in Post-COVID-19 Africa," How We Made It in Africa, December 9, 2020, https://howwemadeitinafrica.com/fred-swaniker-opportunities-in-post-covid-19-africa/76684/'
7. Jeffrey R. Immelt, Vijar Govindarajan, and Chris Trimble, "How GE Is Disrupting Itself," *Harvard Business Review*, October 2009, 3–11.
8. "Reverse Innovation to Fight COVID-19," Northeastern Center for Emerging Markets, accessed March 29, 2023, https://damore-mckim.northeastern.edu/reverse-innovation-to-fight-covid-19/.
9. Edward Paice, "By 2050, a Quarter of the World's People Will Be African—This Will Shape Our Future," *Guardian*, January 20, 2022, https://theguardian.com/global-development/2022/jan/20/by-2050-a-quarter-of-the-worlds-people-will-be-african-this-will-shape-our-future; Madison Hoff, "These Are the 15 Fastest Growing Cities in the World," World Economic Forum, February 20, 2022, https://weforum.org/agenda/2020/02/15-fastest-growing-cities-world-africa-populations-shift/.
10. Yomi Kazeem, "Only One in Four Nigerians Applying to University Will Get a Spot," Quartz Africa, February 22, 2017, https://qz.com/africa/915618/only-one-in-four-nigerians-applying-to-university-will-get-a-spot/amp/.
11. Of the more than 1.85 million Nigerian students enrolled in universities in 2019, only about one hundred thousand were enrolled in private institutions not owned by the national or state government. See "Number of Undergraduate Students at Universities in Nigeria as of 2019, by Ownership," Statista, September 16, 2022, https://statista.com/statistics/1262912/number-of-bachelor-students-at-universities-in-nigeria-by-ownership/#main-content.
12. "School Enrollment, Tertiary—Sub-Saharan Africa," World Bank, June 2022, https://data.worldbank.org/indicator/SE.TER.ENRR?locations=ZG.

13. Nineteen of the twenty countries with the lowest GDP per capita are in Africa. Tajikistan is the exception, at number eighteen.

14. "The Mobile Economy, Sub-Saharan Africa," GSMA, 2021, https://gsma.com/mobileeconomy/sub-saharan-africa; Selira Kotoua, Mustafa Ilkan, and Hasan Kilic, "The Growing of Online Education in Sub Saharan Africa: Case Study Ghana," *Procedia Social and Behavioral Sciences* 19 (2015): 2406–11.

15. See "About ALU," African Leadership University, accessed March 29, 2023, https://alueducation.com/home/about-alu/.

16. Joshua Doležal, "Reclaiming Academe's Idealism: Lessons from Václav Havel for a Profession in Decline," *Chronicle of Higher Education*, August 1, 2022, https://chronicle.com/article/reclaiming-academes-idealism.

17. Dunne is quoted in Alyssa Walker, "Africa, a Continent of Success and Challenges for PhD Students," Keystone PhD Studies, October 3, 2018, https://phdstudies.com/article/africa-a-continent-of-successes-and-challenges-for-phd-students/. See also Beth Daley, "Why PhDs Are Good—for Individuals, and for a Country," Conversation, November 6, 2019, https://theconversation.com/why-phds-are-good-for-individuals-and-for-a-country-123935.

18. The actual effect of small classes on learning is one of many areas in higher education that has been more often asserted than demonstrated. Recent research suggests that class size might not correlate as closely with learning outcomes as many academics (and *U.S. News and World Report* rankings) assume. See Ethan Ake-Little, Nathaniel von der Embse, and Dana Dawson, "Does Class Size Matter in the University Setting?," *Educational Researcher* 49, no. 8, published ahead of print, June 9, 2020, https://journals.sagepub.com/doi/10.3102/0013189X20933836.

19. In an internal study done by ALU in 2014, it was calculated that for the tertiary education attainment rate in sub-Saharan Africa to reach that of India by 2030, one would need to add about 135 Harvard-sized universities per year, every year.

20. The definitive study of this history is Jerome Karabel, *The Chosen: The Hidden History of Admission and Exclusion at Harvard, Yale, and Princeton* (Boston: Houghton Mifflin, 2005).

21. Jacques Steinberg, *The Gatekeepers: Inside the Admissions Process at a Premier College* (New York: Penguin, 2002).

22. See, for example, Helaine Olen, "College-Acceptance Fever Is Out of Control. It's Time to Spread the Admissions Wealth," *Washington Post*, April 7, 2021, https://washingtonpost.com/opinions/2021/04/07/admit-more-students-harvard-university/; and Ryan Craig, "Yale in Houston," *Inside Higher Education*, September 2, 2022, https://insidehighered.com/views/2022/09/02/houston-future-higher-ed-stuck-past-opinion.

23. Noah Millman, "Tweaking Harvard's Admissions Rules Won't Make America Less Elitist," *Week*, December 24, 2021, https://theweek.com/education/1008316/tweaking-harvards-admissions-rules-wont-make-america-less-elitist.

24. Matt Reed, "No, Yale Is Not the Answer to Economic Mobility," *Inside Higher Education*, September 6, 2022, https://insidehighered.com/blogs/confessions-community-college-dean/no-yale-not-answer-economic-mobility.

25. See Scott Jaschik, "Admissions Without Applications," *Inside Higher Education*, July 11, 2022, https://insidehighered.com/admissions/article/2022/07/11/movement

-grows-admissions-without-applications. By the fall of 2022, Concourse had already signed about 125 colleges, and even the Common Application was experimenting with a direct admissions process. See Scott Jaschik, "Direct Admissions Takes Off," *Inside Higher Education*, October 24, 2022, https://insidehighered.com/admissions /article/2022/10/24/direct-admissions-takes.

26. William G. Bowen, "At a Slight Angle to the World," in *Ever the Teacher* (Princeton, NJ: Princeton University Press, 2014), 5. The essay is a reprint of an address originally delivered in 1985, and the phrase used in the title is actually a bit of a misquote. It is based on a description by E. M. Forster of the poet C. P. Cavafy, who, he said, stood "at a slight angle to the universe." See Peter Jeffrey, ed., *The Forster-Cavafy Letters: Friends at a Slight Angle* (Cairo: American University in Cairo Press, 2009), 3.

27. Nick Burns, "Elite Universities Are Out of Touch. Blame the Campus," *New York Times*, August 2, 2022, https://nytimes.com/2022/08/02/opinion/elite-universities-campus.

28. Quoted in "African Traditional Education," *Vanguard*, December 15, 2018, https:// vanguardngr.com/2018/12/african-traditional-education/.

29. Aliya Sikandar, "John Dewey and His Philosophy of Education," *Journal of Education and Educational Development* 2, no. 2 (December 2015): 194.

30. "The 70-20-10 Rule for Leadership Development," Center for Creative Leadership, November 24, 2020, https://ccl.org/articles/leading-effectively-articles/70-20-10-rule /; Ashley Finley and Tia McNair, "Assessing Underserved Students' Engagement with High-Impact Practices," Association of American Colleges and Universities, 2013, https://files.eric.ed.gov/fulltext/ED582014.pdf.

31. "Guidelines for Assessment of Experiential Learning," McGill University, https:// mcgill.ca/tls/files/tls/guidelines_-_assessment_of_experiential_learning_1.pdf.

32. Inara Scott, "Yes, We Are in a (Chat GPT) Crisis," *Inside Higher Education*, April 18, 2023, https://insidehighered.com/opinion/views/2023/04/18/yes-we-are-chatgpt -crisis.

33. James L. Ratcliff, "The Undergraduate Major," Education Encyclopedia, accessed March 29, 2023, https://education.stateuniversity.com/pages/1726/Academic-Major .html.

34. Scott, "Crisis."

35. Diana Henderson et al., "Ideas for Designing an Affordable New Educational Institution," Abdul Latif Jameel World Education Lab, MIT, September 2022, https:// projectnei.com/_files/ugd/d859ad_d6ca8f62511b48b0a21ec6eba8e5db84.pdf. See also David Rosowsky, "Will MIT's Proposal for an 'Affordable New Educational Institution' Grab Hold or Fall Flat?," *Forbes*, October 13, 2022, https://forbes.com/sites /davidrosowsky/2022/10/13/will-mits-proposal-for-an-affordable-new-educational -institution-grab-hold-or-fall-flat/?sh=f54ad8f15f7d.

36. "Carnegie Foundation to Partner with the African Leadership University to Establish a Postsecondary Hub," Carnegie Foundation, December 1, 2021, https:// carnegiefoundation.org/newsroom/news-releases/carnegie-foundation-to-partner -with-the-african-leadership-university-to-establish-a-postsecondary-hub/; "The Carnegie Foundation Welcomes Students from the African Leadership University and College Track," Carnegie Foundation, July 29, 2022, https://carnegiefoundation .org/newsroom/news-releases/the-carnegie-foundation-welcomes-students-from-the -african-leadership-university-and-college-track/.

37. Lawrence Schall, "Pit Stop #45: The African Leadership University," New England Commission of Higher Education, November 20, 2022, https://necheontheroad.com /2022/11/20/pit-stop-45-african-leadership-university/.

38. See "More Staff Cuts on Campus . . . ," MiddFund, October 14, 2009, https://sites .middlebury.edu/middfund/2009/10/14/more-staff-cuts-on-campus/. I am reminded again of the wise philosopher Wilkins Micawber, who observed the following: "Annual income twenty pounds, annual expenditure nineteen nineteen and six, result happiness. Annual income twenty pounds, annual expenditure twenty pound ought and six, result misery."

39. Sterling College, homepage, accessed March 29, 2023, https://sterlingcollege.edu/.

40. Matthew Derr, interview with author, August 4, 2022.

41. Christina Goodwin, interview with author, August 4, 2022.

42. Andrew Van Dam, "The Most-Regretted (and Lowest-Paying) College Majors," *Washington Post*, September 2, 2022, https://washingtonpost.com/business/2022/09 /02/college-major-regrets/.

43. Cornerstone: Learning for Living, a program created at the Teagle Foundation and jointly sponsored by the National Endowment for the Humanities, is an innovative approach to precisely this issue. The goal of the program is "to revitalize the role of the Humanities in general education." "Request for Proposals: Cornerstone: Learning for Living," Teagle Foundation, accessed March 29, 2023, https://teaglefoundation .org/Call-for-Proposals/RFPs/Cornerstone-Learning-for-Living. Full disclosure: I sit on the board of the foundation.

44. "Community," Sterling College, accessed March 29, 2023, https://www.sterlingcollege .edu/life-at-sterling/community/.

45. Goodwin, interview with author, August 4, 2022.

46. See Work Colleges Consortium, homepage, accessed March 29, 2023, https:// workcolleges.org/.

47. Heidi Myers, "From Emergency to Emergence: EcoGather—a Collaborative Platform to Address Intersecting Eco-social Crises in Communities Around the World," Sterling College blog, June 3, 2021, https://www.sterlingcollege.edu/blog /from-emergency-to-emergence-ecogather-is-a-collaborative-platform-to-address -intersecting-eco-social-crises-in-communities-around-the-world/.

48. Niko Kyriakou, "Merger Between Monterey Institute of International Studies and Middlebury College Should Pay Off—Financially and Scholastically—for Both," *Monterey County Now*, August 26, 2010, https://www.montereycountyweekly .com/news/cover/merger-between-monterey-institute-of-international-studies-and -middlebury-college-should-pay-off-financially-and/article_1fef5a95-78bc-540e-aaf6 -8069c5bceb3b.html.

49. The partnership between the University of Arizona and Zovio, an online program manager with reputational and legal problems, is a good example of how these arrangements can fail. See Dan Bauman, "Two Years After Promising a 'Transformational' Partnership, the U. of Arizona and Zovio Part Ways," *Chronicle of Higher Education*, August 1, 2022, https://chronicle.com/article/two-years-after-promising -a-transformational-partnership-the-u-of-arizona-and-zovio-part-ways.

50. Barmak Nassirian, "It's Time to End Higher Ed's Gimmicky Sales Tactics," *Chronicle of Higher Education*, August 8, 2022, https://chronicle.com/article/its-time-to-end -higher-eds-gimmicky-sales-tactics.

51. Susan D'Agostino, "College in the Metaverse Is Here. Is Higher Ed Ready?," *Inside Higher Education*, August 3, 2022, https://insidehighered.com/news/2022/08/03/college-metaverse-here-higher-ed-ready.

52. At the risk of becoming yet another failed futurist, I predict that the pace of college closures will increase as the temporary life raft of federal COVID relief funding vanishes. Rachel Burns, a policy analyst at State Higher Education Executive Officers Association, is "expecting to see a 'catch-up period' of college closures that were temporarily put off" by this funding. Burns is cited in Olivia Sanchez, "With Student Pool Shrinking, Some Predict a Grim Year of College Closings," *Hechinger Report*, January 13, 2023, https://hechingerreport.org/with-student-pool-shrinking-some-predict-a-grim-year-of-college-closings/. Recent closures include a number of very recognizable institutions, including Iowa Wesleyan, founded in 1842, and Cardinal Stritch University, whose enrollment dropped from five thousand to less than fourteen hundred in a decade. See Josh Moody, "Cardinal Stritch to Close," *Inside Higher Education*, April 12, 2003, https://insidehighered.com/news/business/financial-health/2023/04/12/cardinal-stritch-close#.

53. Steven Mintz, "Where Do We Go from Here? Seven Routes to Academic Transformation," *Inside Higher Education*, August 3, 2022, https://insidehighered.com/blogs/higher-ed-gamma/where-do-we-go-here-0.

54. Jason Wingard, "Higher Education Must Change or Die," *Inside Higher Education*, August 16, 2022, https://insidehighered.com/views/2022/08/16/higher-ed-must-change-or-die-opinion. Wingard lasted less than two years at Temple. While there are many reasons for his brief tenure, most notably a mishandled response to a student workers' strike, his outspokenness about the need for change at a struggling university did not sit well with the faculty. Here is one faculty member's response to the article cited here: "All we're really left with are his published works, which are, to be honest, a little scary. . . . He [Wingard] wrote something called a 'burning platform' memo for higher ed, which was 'Higher Ed Must Change Or Die.' I mean, it's just really stark stuff." Quoted in Cory Sharber, "Temple University's Faculty Union Hopes to Send a 'Clear Message' to Leadership with No-Confidence Vote," WHHY, March 22, 2023, https://whyy.org/articles/temple-faculty-union-authorizes-vote-no-confidence-university-leadership/.

55. Derr, interview with author, August 4, 2022.

56. Mintz, "Where Do We Go?"

Acknowledgments

THIS BOOK IS the product of a decades-long career in higher education and has therefore been informed and enriched by countless people in countless ways. If I have neglected to mention anyone, please chalk it up to a faulty memory and not to a lack of appreciation.

I am indebted to all of my colleagues at Allegheny College and Lawrence University for their guidance and wisdom. Dan Sullivan and the late Andy Ford, formerly president and provost at Allegheny, could easily have lost patience with a young faculty member who thought he knew more than he did; instead they remained calm and supportive and encouraged me as I began my administrative career. Lloyd Michaels was as good a friend and counselor as anyone could hope to have. The late Rik Warch, president of Lawrence for a quarter century, was an invaluable mentor: much of what I learned about being a leader came from observing him.

I'm not sure where to begin and end thanking all those at Macalester College with whom I served for seventeen years. I was gifted with a smart and supportive board of trustees and with splendid administrative colleagues, and to all of them I offer my gratitude. Special thanks go to Mark Van der Ploeg, Dave Deno, Jeff Larson, Jerry Crawford, Kathy Murray, Karine Moe, Tommy Bonner, Andrew Brown, Lorne Robinson, Jeff Allen, Laurie Hamre, Donna Lee, Cynthia Hendricks, and David Wheaton. Without these people my time as president would have been considerably briefer.

Much of my post-presidential thinking about higher education has been shaped by my work and conversations with some very smart people.

Francesca Purcell at the Harvard Graduate School of Education reminded me what it means to be a teacher. The incomparable staff at the Teagle Foundation, led by the incomparable Andy Delbanco, remind me regularly that higher education can make a positive difference in the world and manage to keep my cynicism in check. And the remarkable educators at the African Leadership University have welcomed me into their institution and their cultures and shown me what commitment and resilience truly mean. I am indebted to Fred Swaniker, Veda Sunassee, all the members of "ExCo," and the inspiring faculty, staff, and students who are doing hard things.

Finally, as always, my largest debt is owed to my family, who mean everything: Sam, Adam and John, and Carol. "I wonder, by my troth, what thou and I did till we loved?"

About the Author

BRIAN ROSENBERG is currently visiting professor at the Harvard Graduate School of Education. From 2003 until 2020, he served as the sixteenth president of Macalester College. His articles on higher education appear regularly in the *Chronicle of Higher Education* and have also appeared in publications including the *New York Times*, the *Washington Post*, and the *Los Angeles Times*. He serves as senior adviser at the African Leadership University and as a member of the boards of the Teagle Foundation, the Haas Center for Public Service at Stanford University, and Allina Health.

Rosenberg received his BA from Cornell University and his PhD in English from Columbia University. Before arriving at Macalester, he served as dean of the faculty at Lawrence University and as professor and chair of the English Department at Allegheny College. He is the author of two books and many articles on Victorian literature.

Index